METROPOLIS
OF THE
AMERICAN
NILE

The steamboat *Robert E. Lee* begins a trip on the "American Nile," the Mississippi. From the Memphis/Shelby County Room, Memphis/Shelby County Public Library Information Center

To the Neely — Mallory — Neely House — Best wishes John E. Harkins 3/3/88

METROPOLIS
OF THE
AMERICAN NILE

An Illustrated History of Memphis and Shelby County
by John E. Harkins
edited by Charles W. Crawford
with business histories by Berkley Kalin

Sponsored by the West Tennessee Historical Society
Windsor Publications, Inc., Woodland Hills, California

By the 1850s a thriving river commerce and the beginnings of the railroad age gave Memphis a claim to being the fastest growing city in the nation. From the Memphis/Shelby County Room, Memphis/Shelby County Public Library Information Center

Travelers hail a steamboat for passage,
1871. From *Every Saturday*, Mississippi
River Museum, Mud Island

Supervisory editor: Barbara Marinacci
Copy editor: Margaret Colvin Tropp
Assistant editor: Carol V. Davis
Administrative coordinator: Katherine Howell Cooper
Business history editor: Karen Story
Business history editorial assistants: Phyllis Gray and Mary Mohr
Picture editor: Teri Greenberg
Book designer: John Fish
Layout: Cheryl Mendenhall, E. Shannon Strull, Melinda Wade
Editorial Production Coordinators: Constance Blaisdell, E. Shannon Strull
Typesetter: Barbara Neiman
Proofreaders: Karen Hartjen, Ruth Hoover, Jeff Leckrone, and Doris Malkin

Published 1982
Printed in the United States of America

First Edition

Library of Congress Cataloging in Publication Data

Harkins, John E., 1938-
   Metropolis of the American Nile.

   Bibliography: p. 218-219
   Includes index.
   1. Memphis (Tenn.)—History.   2. Shelby County
(Tenn.)—History.   3. Memphis (Tenn.)—Industries—
History.   I. Crawford, Charles Wann, 1931-
II. West Tennessee Historical Society.   III. Title.
F444.M557H37   976.8'19   81-70495
ISBN 0-89781-026-0   AACR2

INTRODUCTION

A surprising fact to students beginning the study of Memphis history, and one equally surprising to those newly arrived in the city, is that few comprehensive histories of such a large and significant municipality have been published. No other city in Tennessee approaches Memphis in population, and probably no other city in the state has a past involving more change and drama. The hold of tradition is so strong in this Southern city on the Mississippi River that an outsider who seeks to understand the town, or to make changes in it, is soon made aware of the powerful influence of the past. During the last decade, the *New York Times*, in a series of articles on Southern cities, described Memphis as "the city that wants never to change."

Surely this devotion to the perceived past is paradoxical, for Memphis has experienced limited stability during the more than a century and a half since it was founded. Always a transportation center—a crossroads—Memphis has had major shifts in its population. It has known times of slow and difficult growth and times of disturbingly rapid expansion. The city has also experienced economic booms, hard times, slavery, secession followed by civil war, emancipation, reconstruction, industrialization, and disaster. In 1878, the city, like thousands of its citizens, died from yellow fever. It surrendered its charter to become merely a taxing district of the state for more than a decade. Then, phoenix-like, it was reborn again, to grow in less than a century to a metropolis of 646,356 inhabitants.

So much has this crossroads city changed through the years that most of the evidence of its past has been replaced. For example, Memphis probably has fewer antebellum structures still standing than either LaGrange, Tennessee, with a population of 213, or Holly Springs, Mississippi, with a population of 5,729. When historic preservation became fashionable during the past decade, adherents of preservation were sometimes surprised to discover how little of the material evidence of Memphis' past was left to preserve. So powerful have been the forces for rapid change that historic landmarks are still being demolished, despite the best efforts of preservationists to save them. Few of the earliest families still exist in this large city. The Descendants of Early Settlers, an organized group of residents who trace their ancestry in the Shelby County area back to 1870 or earlier, have a membership of less than 100, even though by no means all eligible citizens are members. Memphis has thus been a city of rapid change, where the new was quickly accepted and the old was often destroyed.

This willing acceptance of the new has made the nature of the city more dynamic, and enhanced its deserved reputation for hospitality. New people have always been accepted, and generally welcomed, by the established inhabitants, most of whom were themselves relative newcomers to the city. Of the four cities in Tennessee, Memphis is the one most open to new arrivals who wish to participate in the major activities of the municipality. A recent study of the city's statues of people who achieved local prominence revealed that not a single person so honored had been born in Memphis. All had migrated there from elsewhere. Notable examples were W.C. Handy, Nathan Bedford Forrest, Jefferson Davis, E.H. Crump, and Elvis Presley.

Memphis history should be chronicled often merely to keep pace with the rapid rate of change within its boundaries. Another reason why the Bluff City's history needs to be brought up to date frequently is to make it available to new citizens who are unacquainted with it. In addition to the municipality's growth by migration into the area, there are approximately 14,000 births recorded each year in the city. There are thus many thousands of people each decade to whom the history of Memphis is a new story.

This new and comprehensive history of Memphis and Shelby County is much needed. No adequate history of the past several decades has yet been published. A considerable part of the material included in this book is therefore new, even to experienced students of Memphis' history. The "Partners in Progress" part of the book makes available for the first time the histories of many of the businesses that have played an unusually powerful role in the development of the city. New and useful material is also included in the photographic selections of the book. When the first photographic history of the city, *Yesterday's Memphis,* was published six years ago, only limited and scattered photographic material was available. Much valuable pictorial material has been assembled in archival collections since that time, and is now available for use in this history. It is a reasonable estimate that this book will be a classic one in the bibliography dealing with the history of the city built on the Fourth Chickasaw Bluff of the Mississippi River.

Charles W. Crawford
Memphis, Tennessee
February 1982

FOREWORD

This book was never intended to provide an exhaustive history of Memphis and Shelby County, although one is sorely needed. The pictorial format with its space limitations made such an ambitious endeavor impossible. Rather than providing a full-length, full-color portraiture, the text attempts to function more as a sketch or line drawing. It provides the major contours and configurations, the primary lights and shadows, of the community's history, recognizing that many other features of that story had to be barely shown or even omitted. Yet the book's many illustrations, of course, speak volumes for themselves.

Despite such reservations on the narrative itself, the book is still ambitious. It offers, I hope, a readable, concise introduction for the general reader. It should also provide enough revision and updating to make it of interest and of use to both scholars and local history enthusiasts. It tries to give greater balance than the traditional community histories, particularly in recognizing the contributions of blacks and women to Memphis and Shelby County. Lastly, the subject has been painstakingly researched; had footnotes been included in the book's format, one or more could have been included for every statement made. While no treatment of any subject will please everyone, if most of its readers think that the book meets these objectives, the writer will consider it a success.

John E. Harkins
Memphis, Tennessee
February 1982

ACKNOWLEDGMENTS

Like all writers of history, I am greatly indebted to the many persons who aided in the formulation of the ideas and the gathering of materials that have gone into this book. Unlike many writers, I am reluctant to say that there are too many of them to attempt to thank them individually. Such a statement seems to me to be a singularly ungracious way to repay the persons who have lent their time and talent to the endeavor. Not least among these are the many authors whose works appear in the bibliography.

First I would like to thank the three people whose influence led me into participation in this book. Daniel A. Yanchisin first interested me in local history and later pointed out some sources that I would have otherwise overlooked. Berkley Kalin, author of the "Partners in Progress" section of the book, suggested that I be engaged to work on the narrative and aided my work in many other ways. Charles A. Bobbitt persuaded the West Tennessee Historical Society to sponsor the book, and actually began work on it himself before a career change forced him to abandon the project before making substantial progress. However, Charles selected many of the pictures and suggested certain helpful things for inclusion. Without his early interest and efforts, the book might never have been undertaken.

Once research was under way, I received a great deal of help from persons working in the various repositories of local history. The strongest single collection for Memphis history is the History Department of the Memphis/Shelby County Public Library and Information Center. Its staff—particularly James R. Johnson, Joe Brady, Stephen M. Findlay, and Joan Cannon—gave unstintingly of their time and talent to help me. Eleanor McKay and John Terreo of Memphis State University's Mississippi Valley Collection made special efforts to aid me in finding illustrations, as did Lou Adair and Marilyn Van Eynde of the Memphis Pink Palace Museum. I received similar help in picture selection from: Jan Clement, Steve Masler, and Sheila Grannen of the Mississippi River Museum; Gerald Smith and Melissa Lehman of the Chucalissa Indian Museum; Janet C. Rowe, Deborah S. Brown, Jim Willis, and Jack Gurner of the *Memphis Press-Scimitar;* and Andy Haynes of the Shelby County Public Affairs Office. Pictures were also contributed from the private collections of Pat Mc-Carver and Brenda and Jim Connelly. Miss Roberta Church allowed pictures from her family's collection to be used.

Numerous other individuals made suggestions, helped with pictures, or discussed aspects of local history that were particularly troublesome for me. These include Rabbi James A. Wax, Robert A. Tillman, G.E. McCarver, Robert A. Sigafoos, John C. Rea, Edward F. Williams III, Lynette Wrenn, Barbara D. Flanary, Ronald Walter, Ruth W. Hunt, Joan Hassell, Guy Bates, Carole Struve, Ken Hensley, Robert A. Lanier, John B. Getz, James Gucwa, and John S. Shepherd. I wish that space permitted me to include all of the ways in which each of these people helped me.

Perhaps the persons most frequently omitted when thanks and praise are being passed out by a writer are the editors. The editors and staff of Windsor Publications who worked with me have been super throughout the whole process of getting the book together. I want to thank especially Barbara Marinacci, Margaret Tropp, Teri Greenberg, Carol Davis, and Kathy Cooper. In many ways they are coauthors of the book.

Special thanks are due to Granville D. Davis, who permitted me to read "An Uncertain Confederate Trumpet: The Erosion of Morale in Memphis and Its Region." Likewise, special thanks are due to Charles E. Pool, who helped me in many ways. Similar aid was provided by David Bowman, who wrote several sidebars as well as helped me by finding materials, captioning many pictures, and discussing ideas. The photographers who did the copying did an admirable job. Although they came from many sources, most were copied by Tom Wofford, Jim Connelly, and Bob Milnes.

Last, but far from least, thanks to Charles W. Crawford, who has been a diligent consulting editor throughout the writing of this book.

MEMPHIS & SHELBY COUNTY CHRONOLOGY

1541
De Soto "discovers" the Mississippi River, giving Spain a claim to the region.

1584
Queen Elizabeth's grant to Sir Walter Raleigh includes Bluff area in England's claims.

1663
Charles II's "sea to sea" Carolina grant gives title to group of English promoters.

1673
Marquette and Joliet descend the Mississippi and touch at the Bluffs.

1682
La Salle descends the Mississippi River, claims the Mississippi Valley for France, and visits the Fourth Chickasaw Bluff.

1729
North Carolina becomes a royal colony; claims to Bluff area revert to crown.

1739
Bienville builds Fort Assumption near the present site of the three bridges. Campaign against the Chickasaws is inconclusive, and the fort is abandoned within a few months.

1763
British victory in the French and Indian War gives England uncontested European claim to the Bluffs.

1783
Treaty of Paris, ending American Revolutionary War, greatly strengthens North Carolina's claim to the Bluff area, which is still contested by Spain. John Rice and John Ramsay enter claims for 5,000 acres each on the Fourth Chickasaw Bluff. Other North Carolina lands in West Tennessee are sold thereafter.

1790
North Carolina cedes title to present-day Tennessee to the United States, which grants territorial government.

1794
John Overton and Andrew Jackson acquire the Rice claim.

1795
(May) Spanish under Gayoso erect Fort San Fernando on Fourth Bluff in the area of Auction Square.

(October) Spain cedes its claims north of the 31st parallel, including the Bluffs, to the United States.

1796
Tennessee becomes 16th state admitted to the Union.

1797
(May) Spanish troops abandon Bluff, burning their fort.

(July) American troops occupy Bluff.

(October) Fort Adams is completed.

1798
Fort Pickering is erected near site of Memphis-Arkansas Bridge.

1802
The U.S. War Department establishes an Indian factory at Fort Pickering.

1803
Louisiana Purchase removes international boundary from Mississippi River, lessening importance of Fort Pickering. Availability of vast areas of western land reduces pressure to oust Chickasaws from West Tennessee.

1811
First steamboat, the *New Orleans*, passes Bluff en route from Pittsburgh to New Orleans on its maiden voyage.

ca. 1813-1816
Fort Pickering abandoned by the Army; only the Indian factory and squatters remain.

1818
(October) Chickasaw Cession: Indians sell land north of the 35th parallel to the United States.

(December) Jackson, Overton, and Winchester meet to plan their town.

1819
(April-May) Surveyors lay out town of Memphis and proprietors distribute first lots.

(June-July) James Winchester surveys southern boundary of West Tennessee.

(November) Tennessee legislature responds to petition of inhabitants and creates Shelby County.

1820
(May) County court organized and other county offices filled.

(December) Mail service from Reynoldsburg to Memphis and on to Arkansas begins. First post office opens. State land office opens in Memphis.

1824
Site at Sanderlin's Bluff (Raleigh) chosen over Memphis as county seat.

1826
Frances Wright establishes Nashoba near Germantown for the self-emancipation of slaves. Legislature incorporates Memphis. First newspaper, the *Memphis Advocate and Western District In-*

telligencer, begins publication.

1827
Town government is organized and first officers are elected. Marcus B. Winchester becomes the city's first mayor. County court removes to Raleigh.

1828
Charter is amended, giving Memphis the same powers as the city of Nashville. All-time high water begins formation of a sandbar fronting on the town. First yellow fever epidemic; 650 cases, 150 deaths.

1829
First volunteer fire company is organized. Stagecoach line passes through Memphis. Thespian Society is organized.

1830
Population: 663. Town is divided into three wards. First fire engine, "Little Vigor," is put to use. Town hall is built.

1833
First Bank, Farmers and Merchants, managed by Ike Rawlings, is authorized.

1834
Chickasaws cede northern Mississippi to the state of Mississippi.

1835
La Grange and Memphis Railroad is chartered.

1837
National financial panic is followed by depression. Tennessee-Mississippi boundary is corrected, extending West Tennessee, including Shelby County, four miles southward. Private company is franchised to build wharf on Memphis riverfront.

1838
First board of health is established. Two night watchmen are appointed to police the town. Inspector of weights and measures is appointed. Public cisterns are built for use in fire fighting.

1840
Population: 1,799. *Memphis Appeal* begins publishing. Town watch is increased and placed under a captain; men are given badges.

1841
Mayor Spickernagle's reforms place town on a business basis.

1842
Six miles of La Grange and Memphis Railroad are completed. Gayoso House, first luxury hotel, begins construction. Victory over flatboatmen brings rule of law. Memphis is referred to hereafter as a "city."

1843
Thirty or more brick buildings have been constructed.

1845
United States builds navy yard for oceangoing vessels at Memphis. La Grange Railroad declared bankrupt; rails reach only to White's Station. Southwestern River Convention held in Memphis urges federal aid for clearing river channels, indirectly makes Memphis choice for terminus of the Charleston-Mississippi River Railroad.

1846
U.S.-Mexican War. Town of South Memphis is incorporated. Memphis Medical College is founded.

1847
Memphis issues first bonds, chiefly for street construction.

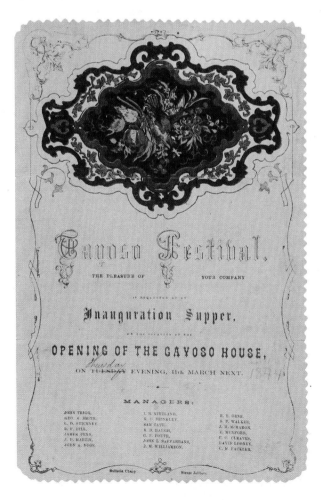

MEMPHIS & SHELBY COUNTY CHRONOLOGY

1848
Free public schools begin.

1849
Memphis and South Memphis agree to merge into one city.

1850
Population: 8,841. Building booms, roads are expanded and improved, river traffic expands.

1851
Gas company is organized.

1852
As Mississippi River port, Memphis is second only to New Orleans and St. Louis.

1854
New charter increases size. Heavy bond issues for streets and railroad subscriptions begin irresponsible city indebtedness.

1855
Second yellow fever epidemic: 1,250 cases, 220 deaths. First section of Memphis and Ohio Railroad is completed.

1857
Memphis-Charleston Railroad is completed.

1860
Population: 22,623, 31 percent of whom are foreign-born, mainly Irish and German. Improvements are made in fire and police services. Chamber of Commerce is established. Memphis votes eight to one in favor of Union.

1861
3,000 citizens stage mass meeting and vote unanimously for secession. Shelby County ratifies Tennessee secession. Confederate Army headquarters and supply depot are established. City votes funds for defense. Memphis furnishes 72 companies, between one third and one fourth of the city's population.

1862
River battle leaves Memphis in Federal hands. Memphis becomes Union headquarters, supply depot, prisoner-of-war

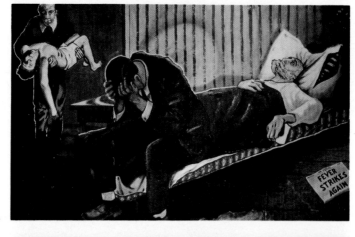

center, and center for refugee blacks.

1864
Public schools are instituted for blacks. Martial law is proclaimed. Forrest makes his raid on the city.

1865
Civil war ends. Thomas A. Edison serves as telegrapher in Memphis. Chamber of Cmmmerce is revived. Mule-drawn street railroad begins.

1866
Race riot in Memphis contributes to statewide Radical Reconstruction. Memphis is placed under state-controlled metropolitan police district.

1867
Third yellow fever epidemic: 2,500 cases, 550 deaths.

County seat returns to Memphis.

1870
Population: 40,226. Greenlaw, Chelsea, and Fort Pickering areas are annexed. Board of aldermen becomes general council.

1872
Annual Mardi Gras carnivals begin.

1873
Fourth yellow fever epidemic: 5,000 cases, 2,000 deaths. National financial panic hits. Memphis Water Company is founded.

1878
Fifth and climactic yellow fever epidemic: 17,600 cases, 5,150 deaths. City is bankrupt, its population

temporarily halved, with largely poor remaining.

1879
Bankrupt city surrenders municipal charter and becomes a "taxing district" of the state, governed by a board of fire and police commissioners and a board of public-works commissioners. Sixth yellow fever epidemic: 2,000 cases, 600 deaths.

1880
Population: 33,592. Vigorous sanitation measures are undertaken.

1887
Artesian wells are tested.

1889
Large school-building program is undertaken.

1890
Population: 64,495. Artesian water is in use.

1891
First electric streetcar is inaugurated.

1892
Frisco Bridge across the Mississippi River is completed, first bridge across the river south of St. Louis.

1893
City charter is restored. Cossitt Library opens to the public.

1895
Competing street railways emerge.

1896
Memphis cares for 6,000 flood refugees.

1897
General Hospital is built.

1899
Memphis annexes most suburbs, quadrupling its territorial limits, and extends health measures to new areas.

1900
Population: 102,320. Park commission is established; Riverside and Overton parks are authorized.

1903
City purchases water company.

MEMPHIS & SHELBY COUNTY CHRONOLOGY

Top left
As urbanization began crowding Memphians at the turn of the century, they created a fine park system. At Overton Park, shown here about 1910, people gathered for picnicking, athletic contests, and concerts by Professor Saxby's band. Courtesy, Pat McCarver

Top right
This bustling view of Memphis was made at Main Street south from Madison in the early part of the 19th century. Courtesy, Charles Bobbitt

Above
The 1934 Cotton Carnival employed an Egyptian motif in its advertising. Courtesy, Charles Bobbitt

1906
Overton Park Zoo is established.

1907
Goodwyn Institute is endowed.

1909
Commission form of government is adopted. Annexations include town of Lenox. E.H. Crump becomes mayor on reform ticket, boosted by Handy's "Memphis Blues." Shelby County Courthouse is completed.

1910
Population: 131,105.

1911
County government is restructured.

1912
West Tennessee State Normal School opens.

1916
Broods Memorial Art Gallery is built.

1917
Harahan Bridge, with vehicle roadways, opens.

1919
City celebrates its centennial. Major annexation includes town of Binghampton.

1920
Population: 162,351.

1921
City planning commission is established.

1924
City plan is designed by Harland Bartholomew.

1927
Memphis houses flood refugees.

1928
Major annexations include Highland Heights.

1929
Municipal airport is completed. City annexes 20.3 square miles of suburbs. Harbor commission is created. Municipal museum is established. Great Depression begins.

1930
Population: 253,153. City Beautiful Commission is created. Municipal employment relief is established.

1931
Airmail service begins. Cotton Carnival begins.

1934
Municipal Housing Authority is created. Citizens opt to join TVA electric system. $20-million work-relief construction program begins. Community library for blacks is established.

1938
TVA power becomes available to Memphis.

1939
City purchases Memphis Power and Light Company.

1940
Population: 292,942. Numerous defense and allied industries locate in area, boosting economy and growth. Second Army headquarters moves to Memphis.

1941
United States enters World War II, making drastic changes in way of life for Memphis.

1942
Memphis selected as site for Kennedy General Hospital, a multimillion-dollar institution that will grow to 3,000 beds. Thousands of naval personnel are stationed at Millington Base 20 miles north of city. International Harvester locates plant at Memphis. Value of Mid-South cotton crop doubles its 1940 price.

1943
War effort continues boosting economy, facilities, and population.

1944
War economy continues to boom, creating critical housing shortage.

1945

Transition to peacetime economy follows war's end. Construction of four-lane Memphis-Arkansas Bridge begins.

1946

Passage of Flood Control Bill provides for development of Tennessee Chute Project, vastly expanding Memphis harbor facilities.

1948

Construction of Tennessee Chute Project begins.

1949

New Bridge opens. Memphis Harbor Project begins.

1950

Population: 396,000.

1952

First Holiday Inn opens.

1954

E.H. Crump dies, after dominating local politics for two generations.

1955

Elvis Presley's meteoric rise focuses national attention on Memphis as music center.

1956

Election ousts many of Crump-faction political figures.

1957

Memphis State College becomes university. Frayser is annexed.

1958

Allen Generating Plant begins operation. Construction begins on expressway system.

1959

Plans for multimillion-dollar civic center and separate recreation complex are underway.

1960

Population: 497,524.

1963

Voters adopt home rule. Mammoth new metropolitan airport complex is dedicated.

1966

City replaces commission form of government with mayor-council form.

1967

Racial differences figure strongly in elections.

1968

City sanitation workers strike. Dr. Martin Luther King, Jr., is murdered in Memphis, leading to riots and curfew.

1970

Population: 624,000.

1972

Federal Express is established.

1974

County government is restructured by state legislature.

1975

Mid-America Mall is constructed.

1976

Libertyland amusement park opens. First county mayor takes over administration of county executive branch.

1977

Elvis Presley dies, home becomes unofficial shrine.

1978

Firefighters, police, and teachers strike.
County Quarterly Court is replaced by Board of Commissioners, completing the restructuring of county government.

1980

Population: 646,356.

1981

The historic Peabody Hotel is refurbished and open to the public.

Above left
Edward Hull Crump is depicted both as the young man who tamed Memphis and the older man who ruled the city until his death. In the background is the Great Bridge. Painted by James Gucwa. Historical mural in The Peabody hotel, Memphis, Tennessee

Above
Elvis Aron Presley is the name most closely associated with Memphis on a worldwide basis. His meteoric rise to fame, wealth, and cult status gave Memphis unprecedented exposure. Painted by James Gucwa. Historical mural in The Peabody hotel, Memphis, Tennessee

from
Metropolis of the
American Nile
by John E. Harkins

CHAPTER ONE

PRECURSORS TO MODERN MEMPHIS

An Ancient Namesake

Memphis! The very name evokes images of ancient Egypt, of pyramids and temples, an alabaster city riding a crest of blinding sand above a lush green river oasis. For the modern-day Memphians of West Tennessee, this name association has always exercised an irresistible exotic mystery while serving as a source of civic pride.

Memphis had few peers among the great cities of the ancient world. Situated at the apex of the Nile Delta, Memphis was founded about 3100 B.C. at the junction of the newly united kingdoms of Upper and Lower Egypt. Originally called the "White Wall" and later Hikaptah (house of the spirit of Ptah), it was known to the Hebrews in biblical times as Noph or Moph. The name Memphis, meaning "established and beautiful," came into use sometime during the Sixth Dynasty (ca. 2345-2181 B.C.).

By the time Alexander the Great entered Memphis in 332 B.C., the city had already survived nearly 500 years longer than all of history that has passed since then. It remained a provincial capital and major cosmopolitan center throughout the Hellenistic and early Roman periods. Only after the rise of Christianity did serious decay set in, as zealots defaced and destroyed its pagan monuments. The death blow came in A.D. 640 with the Arab conquest. The city was gradually abandoned and much of its remaining stone was taken downriver to be used in building Fostat, destined to become the Arab capital of Cairo.

Thus, after enduring nearly four millenia, the ancient city of Memphis disappeared, eventually even its location lost in the shifting sands of the mighty Sahara. Not until 1851 would the phantom city begin to yield some of its hidden mystery to the science of archaeology. But even before its physical unearthing, ancient Memphis would be honored by a modern namesake beside another mighty river in a far distant land.

Facing page
Nineteenth-century archaeologists
examine the ruins of the once great
Egyptian city of Memphis, after which
Memphis, Tennessee, is named. From
La Description de l'Egypte

WHAT'S IN A NAME

When the time came to lay off a city on the Fourth Chickasaw Bluff, the proprietors needed to choose a name. At that time General James Winchester—not Andrew

General James Winchester. From the Memphis/Shelby County Room, Memphis/Shelby County Public Library Information Center

Jackson, as popular myth long had it—suggested the name Memphis. His two partners, Jackson and John Overton, readily agreed.

It was hardly unusual to name a fledgling frontier settlement after one of the great cities of antiquity, as any gazetteer will show. It was such a good promotional technique that America is sprinkled with a myriad of Romes, Troys, Spartas, Carthages, and Corinths. However, except for Alexandria, ancient Egyptian names were rarely used. Why, then, did Winchester choose this particular name?

Like any educated man of his day, Winchester had some familiarity with the classics. As a soldier and a republican, moreover, he followed the events of Revolutionary France, particularly the campaigns of Napoleon. Republican France, in scrapping the cultural baggage of the ancient regime, frequently reverted to the cultural trappings of Republican Rome and classical antiquity. Americans made a similar identification in the first few decades after cutting the tie with England, and Winchester reflected this flirtation with classical antiquity in naming many of his own children—Marcus Brutus, Selina, Lucilius, Almira, Napoleon, and Valerius Publicola. Still his choices demonstrate both classical and French, but not Egyptian, influence.

The French penetration into Egypt revived an interest in things Egyptian. Winchester showed a familiarity with these developments when he came to name the Cumberland River town near his plantation, choosing the name Cairo to commemorate the French capture of the Egyptian capital

The two river cities of Memphis. From the Memphis and Shelby County Archives (M/SCPLIC)

in 1798. Winchester hoped this little river town would become the county seat. Its early residents even hoped it might one day become the state capital. Cairo, Tennessee, prospered in the early 19th century, but in less than 100 years it was a ghost town.

Winchester's second Egyptian christening was more auspicious. Regarding the Mississippi River as the American Nile, he proposed the name Memphis. Whether his choice reflected wishful thinking, as in the case of Cairo, or was designed as a promotional ploy by a seasoned and successful land speculator will probably never be known. But after a bit of initial resistance, the name stuck, and modern-day Memphians are proud of their association with ancient Memphis, onetime premier city of the ancient world.

— John Harkins

Above
Pottery is one of the archaeologist's primary tools in reconstructing past civilizations. The samples shown in these photographs are from the Chucalissa Indian Village site where many such items are displayed in its museum. Differences in the artistry and sophistication of the pieces do not necessarily indicate differences in the time of manufacture. The pieces shown are Mississippian, circa 1450-1500. Courtesy, Chucalissa Indian Village (MSU)

Right
This view not only shows two reconstructed late Mississippian Period houses, but also an Indian-type garden and the lush forest in the background. Each reconstructed house requires a huge quantity of dried grass to cover it. Every year a garden is planted in the Chucalissa Village area to show some of the typical Indian crops of the period. Such gardens are planted in the manner described by early European explorers in the Southeast. Courtesy, Chucalissa Indian Village (MSU)

The Role of Geography

The Missouri-Mississippi River (3,860 miles) is second in length only to the Nile (4,145 miles). As the Nile drains much of the world's second largest continent, so does the Mississippi drain the greatest river basin of the third largest continent. More than 40 major tributary systems between the Appalachians and the Rocky Mountains empty through the lower Mississippi into the Gulf of Mexico.

Centuries of loessial and alluvial deposits have given portions of the Mississippi Valley a fertility of soil that literally rivals that of the fabled Nile. A relatively gradual southern slope has caused the river to meander extensively, building an enormous alluvial flood plain varying between 30 and 100 miles in width from Cairo, Illinois, to the Gulf of Mexico. The Missouri River joins the Mississippi at St. Louis, as does the Ohio at Cairo. These three great river systems generally release their spring floods at different times. Periodic exceptions to this general rule bring various degrees of inundation to nearly the entire lower valley.

Ground high enough to be safely above the maximum flood stage along the river's lower course is as rare as it is desirable for human habitation. All of the river's west bank, except for a small outcropping of the Crowley's Ridge formation at Helena, Arkansas, is lower than flood stage. On the eastern shore, a slightly elevated sedimentary rock plateau fans out toward the south from its apex at the mouth of the Ohio, extending nearly to the Gulf of Mexico. Its western extremity forms a bluff line that runs roughly parallel to the Mississippi, but actually touches the river at only a few places. Between Cairo and Vicksburg the escarpment meets the river only at four sites, known collectively as the Chickasaw Bluffs, along a 60-mile strip of Tennessee's southwestern boundary. The Fourth Chickasaw Bluff, where the westward thrust of the Jackson Plain and the northernmost extension of the Tippah Highlands ridge converge to touch the Father of Waters, is the site of present-day Memphis.

Indians and Interlopers

Perhaps 40,000 years before the first Europeans entered the Mississippi Valley, the ancestors of American Indians crossed the Bering Strait into Alaska and began penetration of the Western Hemisphere. Paleolithic Indians reached West Tennessee at least 10,000 years ago. The abundance of food for hunting and gathering may actually have contributed to their cultural retardation, for the tribes in this area took about 7,000 years to reach the

Chapter One: Precursors to Modern Memphis

Archaic stage of development. Relatively rapid progress thereafter took them into the Woodland stage, manifested by pottery making, agriculture, and mound building. The last stage of cultural development, the Mississippian, began about A.D. 800 and saw the development of cities and primitive city-states.

Indians of undetermined tribal affinity occupied a string of towns running about 40 miles along the Mississippi just south of modern-day Memphis. Probably this complex of towns was the one called Quiz Quiz, encountered by the bedraggled De Soto expedition of 1541. Contrary to Memphis myth, De Soto may have first encountered the Mississippi somewhere south of the Fourth Bluff. If he did reach the site of present-day Memphis, it was very likely no farther north than the town of Chucalissa, several miles below the original town of Memphis.

Other than the unintended spreading of European diseases among peoples without immunities, De Soto's fabled expedition had little lasting impact on West Tennessee—nor, for that matter, on European civilization. Without the journals and accounts that publicized this magnificent saga of early Spanish exploration, it would have been like a tree falling in the forest with no one to hear. It is the saga itself that is important. Memphians have long believed that larger-than-life Spaniards trod the paths of their locale in a heroic, futile search for El Dorado. The epic is part of their tradition, and they have chosen to memorialize De Soto with mural and marker, and in street, park, and bridge names.

Sometime after De Soto's visit, the Chickasaws displaced the tribes they had encountered in northwestern Mississippi and West Tennessee. In the late 17th century, Marquette and Jolliet stopped at the Bluffs on their historic descent of the river. Here they came upon a tribe, which they called Mosopeleas, that had firearms and seemed to have trade contacts with the English seaboard colonies. La Salle and various other French travelers also passed or stopped briefly at the Bluffs, but again with no lasting effect. By the 1730s the Chickasaws definitely controlled the area surrounding the Fourth Bluff, but had built no town there.

By this time the French had colonized lower Louisiana. Under the leadership of Governor Bienville, they destroyed the Natchez Indians and attempted to do likewise with their allies, the Chickasaws. Bienville, who led expeditions against the Chickasaws in 1736 and again in 1739, built Fort Assumption on the Fourth Bluff. His military advantage seems to have been overwhelming, but disease, delays, and desertions caused him to settle for a weak treaty. Bienville's successor made one more futile attempt to conquer the proud and independent Chickasaws, after which the French adopted a policy of live and let live.

The treaty that ended the French and Indian War (1754-1763) transferred French claims west of the Mississippi to Spain, and those east of the river to England. Although the Chickasaws still held their hunting lands, prolonged guerilla warfare against the French and exposure to European diseases had seriously reduced their numbers.

Chickasaw neutrality in European affairs extended to the renewed hostilities of the American Revolution. Only after Americans encroached upon their territory did the Chickasaws strike, and then just at the offending fort. As soon as the Americans abandoned Fort Jefferson near the mouth of the Ohio, the Indians resumed their neutrality.

Once again a European treaty awarded "title" to the Indian interior. In a clever diplomatic ploy to drive a wedge between its former antagonists, England ceded its claims in the area to the new United States. Spain, with claims of its own, refused to recognize the cession.

In the end, the claims and counterclaims would prove irrelevant. The country that could occupy the interior and populate it with loyal inhabitants would ultimately hold it. For the time being both countries were too weak and too cautious to attempt much, and the

Metropolis of the American Nile

people with the best claim, the Chickasaws, were left in peace for a decade.

Spanish Advance and Retreat

Though many have viewed the Spanish advance up the Mississippi Valley as a genuine threat to American expansion, in reality Spain's hold on its Louisiana colony was extremely weak. Nine-tenths of the colony's inhabitants were non-Spanish, and French Creole militia made up the bulk of its puny army. Even this population of uncertain loyalty was growing at a much slower rate than that of the Americans in the Ohio Valley and in eastern Kentucky and Tennessee.

Well aware of these factors, Spain's colonial administration worked hard to counterbalance them. It imported Canary Islanders and Anglo-American Catholics to settle Louisiana. Pursuing a generous Indian policy, Spanish officials tried to buy the allegiance of the southern tribes, and in 1784 they secured treaties placing the Creeks, Alibamons, Choctaws, and Chickasaws under Spanish protection. Attempting to hedge their bets even further, Spanish officials tried to buy the loyalty of such influential frontier leaders as James Wilkinson, John Sevier, and James Robertson.

The French Revolution of 1789 delivered a major blow to Spanish ambitions in North America. Not only did Spain lose its most valued ally on the European continent, but the fidelity of Spain's Louisiana subjects, already uncertain, became even more suspect. When Spain went to war against France, Louisiana became a caldron of unrest. Rumors of Creole Jacobin plots and American filibustering expeditions abounded. In such a climate Spain moved to establish a fort on the Fourth Chickasaw Bluff.

The precise timing of this action came in response to what the Spanish perceived as four specific American threats: the proposed Genet filibustering expedition against Louisiana; John Overton's promise of arms and supplies to an anti-Spanish faction of the Chickasaw tribe; a rumor that Kentuckians planned to occupy Muscle Shoals; and the Georgia legislature's sale of large tracts of land in the Bluff area to speculators. A fort on the Bluff would enable the Spanish to secure the river route to St. Louis, increase their influence over the Chickasaws and Choctaws, strengthen their liaison with secessionists in the Miro District, provide a first line of defense in case of hostilities, and preempt American occupation of the Bluff.

Before the Spanish could occupy the Bluff, they needed permission from the Chickasaws. As often happened in such instances, tribal sentiment was divided. A majority under Wolf's Friend favored the Spanish cause, but a minority led by Piomingo were pro-American. Acting on orders from Governor Carondelet, Lieutenant Governor Manuel Gayoso treated with the pro-Spanish faction. The Indians agreed to cede a small strip of land along the Bluff front to the Spanish. In return Gayoso presented them with food, shirts, brandy, and arms. The next day, May 31, 1795, Spanish workers began clearing land for the construction of Fort San Fernando de las Barrancas. Soon Spain possessed an imposing-looking stockade with an Indian trading post on the site that would one day be Memphis.

Although the Spanish had stolen a march on the Americans, they never achieved the secure outpost that they wanted. The fort's location was poor, leaving it vulnerable to organized attack. Food shortages and recurring fevers drained the health of soldiers and civilians alike and, along with petty squabbling among Spanish officials, kept morale low. Spanish subjects at Fort San Fernando justifiably considered it a hardship post, and they were doubtlessly relieved when orders came to evacuate and withdraw across the river.

Again European conditions and a European treaty decided the immediate fate of the Bluffs. Spain, extracting itself from a war against Napoleonic France and anticipating war against England, did not want an aggrieved and hostile United States on its colonial flank. In

Chapter One: Precursors to Modern Memphis

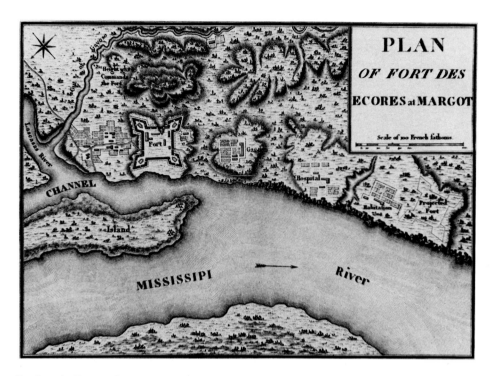

Pinckney's Treaty, Spain ceded to the United States all claims to the eastern Mississippi Valley above the 31st parallel, along with free navigation of the Mississippi River and the right of deposit at New Orleans. Thus, less than six months after beginning construction on Fort San Fernando, the Spanish had agreed to withdraw.

Doubting the wisdom and the permanence of this decision, Carondelet delayed evacuation of the fort as long as he could. Finally and reluctantly he gave the order to strip the fort of everything valuable, burn the stockade, and rebuild immediately across the river. Rumors of the impending territorial transfer alarmed and distressed the pro-Spanish Indians. At the last instant Carondelet changed his mind about evacuating the fort, but his countermanding order arrived too late. By 8:00 p.m. on March 19, 1797, the fort had been reduced to ashes.

Spanish occupation of the Fourth Chickasaw Bluff lasted just short of two years. Except for occasional place names in the area, the sojourn had no durable effect, and the site of the fort cannot even be precisely located today. Nonetheless, there is a twofold significance to the Spanish excursion. Fort San Fernando marked Spain's ultimate military advance in North America, and its evacuation began the ebb that would ultimately strip the Spanish of their New World empire. More important for local history, Fort San Fernando signified the start of permanent, non-Indian habitation of the Fourth Chickasaw Bluff.

American Frontier Forts and Posts

Although little of historical significance took place on the Fourth Bluff between the Spanish departure and the laying out of the town 22 years later, there is much about this span that is interesting in an anecdotal sense. Among the Indians and a few traders and squatters, the American army established an isolated frontier post. Some of the soldiers stationed at this outpost later achieved fame in America's pageant of history. Others simply performed their duty and furnished hospitality to the travelers whose journals have left

Metropolis of the American Nile

THE WEST TENNESSEE HISTORICAL SOCIETY, INC.

Today's West Tennessee Historical Society traces its roots back to 1857, when the Old Folks of Shelby County began holding monthly meetings and publishing a monthly journal called the *Old Folks Record*. The popular gossipy history of Memphis by James D. Davis was made up largely of material published in the *Old Folks Record*.

In 1866 the Old Folks' historical role was taken over by the Confederate Relief and Historical Association. This group was reorganized in 1869 as the Confederate Historical Association and in 1884 as Camp 28, United

Publications associated with the society include curator Eleanor McKay's *Guide to Archives and Collections,* the 1972 reprint of James D. Davis' classic *The History of the City of Memphis,* and issues of the society's regular journal, *The West Tennessee Historical Society Papers.*

Confederate Veterans. Its historian, Captain J. Harvey Mathes, produced a valuable historical volume entitled *The Old Guard in Grey,* published in 1889.

The next society in the chain of descent was the Memphis Historical Society, organized by Judge John Preston Young, who had been a leader in the Confederate Historical Association. In 1935 the Memphis Historical Society changed its name to the West Tennessee Historical Society, and in 1938 Dr.

exception of three months when Dr. J.B. Sanders, president of Memphis State College, served. Subsequent presidents of the society have been John Henry Davis, 1962-1963; Charles E. Pool, 1964; Buford C. Utley, 1965-1966; Aaron Boom, Memphis State University, 1967; James E. Roper, Southwestern at Memphis, 1968-1971; Charles A. Bobbitt, 1971-1976; Charles W. Crawford, Memphis State University, 1976-1979; and Charles A. Bobbitt again from

ton, and Weakly.

The society governs itself through the annual election of a president, a vice-president for Shelby County, a vice-president for the remainder of West Tennessee, a vice-president at large, a recording secretary, a corresponding secretary, a treasurer, and an assistant treasurer. In recent years the curator of the society has been the curator of the Mississippi Valley Collection at Memphis State University, where the West Tennessee Historical Society's archives

Dr. Marshall Wingfield (sixth from left), Governor Gordon Browning (far left), and prominent members of the West Tennessee Historical Society attend the unveiling of a monument to David Crockett in Trenton, Tennessee, October 13, 1950. Courtesy, MVC Collections.

Courtesy, West Tennessee Historical Society.

Marshall Wingfield became its president. He served in this capacity until 1961, with the

On September 28, 1950, the West Tennessee Historical Society was incorporated in Shelby County, taking over the affairs of the unincorporated society and granting charter membership to members in good standing of the predecessor organization. The society's membership, which presently exceeds 600, is drawn from the West Tennessee counties of Benton, Carroll, Chester, Crockett, Decatur, Dyer, Fayette, Gibson, Hardeman, Hardin, Haywood, Henderson, Henry, Lake, Lauderdale, Madison, McNairy, Obion, Shelby, Tip-

1979 to the present.

and collections have resided since 1974.

Meetings of the society are held every month between September and May at the Memphis Pink Palace Museum, except for spring and fall outings at historical sites elsewhere in West Tennessee. Meetings generally feature the reading of a scholarly paper or the presentation of an audiovisual program about some aspect of West Tennessee history. Members also receive *West Tennessee Historical Society Papers,* published annually in the fall.

— Berkley Kalin

sketchy portraits of life on the Bluff as it was then. The traders and squatters contributed to the economic life of the area and furnished part of the human continuum leading to the founding of the town.

Almost four months after the Spanish withdrawal, an American troop detachment en route to Natchez landed to occupy the Bluff and distribute presents to the Indians. Led by Captain Isaac Guion, the Americans hastened to build a small stockade to consolidate their position. At the insistence of the pro-American Chickasaws, Guion built Fort Adams on the precise site of the Spanish fort, rather than at a more advantageous location slightly downstream. Confident that the location could be shifted later without objection, Guion honored the Indians' wishes. By late October 1797 the fort was enclosed and the gates hung. In early November Guion proceeded south, leaving about 30 men to await reinforcements from the East.

Captain Meriwether Lewis, who later crossed the continent in America's most famous exploratory trek, was among the replacements who brought the tiny fort's strength up to about 80 officers and men. Lewis, second in seniority, soon succeeded to the position of commandant when a fever killed his superior. During the few months he commanded the post, he was visited by his friend and future colleague, William Clark. In August of 1798 Thomas Jefferson, who in five years would send the two young men on their memorable adventure, had Lewis recalled to the East to serve as his secretary.

Soon afterward the army made several changes at the Bluff that have long confused local historians. Guion had named the first American stockade Fort Adams to honor President John Adams. With the American occupation of Natchez, the army decided to reserve this name for the more important fort to be located there. The upriver fort was to be renamed for Secretary of State Timothy Pickering, but in the meantime it would also be moved as Guion had anticipated.

Captain Zebulon Pike, father of a namesake who would shortly become the third most famous man in the annals of American exploration, took command of the Bluff post and built the new fort. Acting on orders from General James Wilkinson, Pike constructed the new facility several miles downriver on a much more defensible site. Fort Adams, now supplanted in both name and function, took the name Pike's Fort for the few years of its continued existence.

The last of the Pickering commandants worthy of note was a young lieutenant named Zachary Taylor. Taylor, whose victories in the Mexican War later brought him fame and then the presidency, did nothing to distinguish himself at this first command. Even at this early date he was evidently a "by the book" soldier, and one traveler observed that his "civility" was mixed "with a small degree of the pompous stiffness of office."

Even before Taylor took command of Fort Pickering, its importance was on the decline. Following the Louisiana Purchase in 1803, the fort was no longer on the international frontier. As the fort's importance declined, so did its physical condition and the size of its garrison. As American soldiers suffered from the same fevers that had racked Spanish troops, the post soon got a reputation for being very unhealthy. At various times between 1809 and 1813 it was all but abandoned, and after 1813 there are no further references to it in military records. Travelers in 1816 and 1817 noted that there were no troops in evidence at the Bluff, though some of the buildings still stood. The Indian trading factory remained active until shortly after the founding of the town, and squatters continued to occupy the area.

The presence of squatters and traders on and near the Bluff actually antedates the Spanish occupation of the site. Their presence in fact may have been continuous from the time of the American Revolution, but this would be impossible to verify. As early as

Metropolis of the American Nile

1779-1780 Captain Richard Brashears, an officer under George Rogers Clark, had a blockhouse and trading post near the mouth of the Wolf River. Two years later General James Robertson established a trading depot on the Bluff for supplying the Chickasaws. In 1787 Brashears was still (or again) at this site as one of about 25 American traders doing business with the Indians. Shortly thereafter a Creek raiding party attacked a group of 14 Georgians who were constructing a blockhouse in the area, killing 8 of them.

The coming of the Spanish does not appear to have drastically altered the lives of traders on the Bluff. Brashears, as agent for Panton, Leslie, and Company, was trading with Indians there in 1795. Two years later, when the Spanish withdrew to Campo de Esperanza (translated later to Hopefield in Arkansas), a half-dozen white settlers, "generally allied to the Indians by marriage," stayed at the Bluff to welcome the American army. Captain Guion noted that four "white families," who had been living there for two or three years, remained after his detachment arrived. One of these families was that of Kenneth Ferguson, now Panton and Leslie agent. Another was that of John Mizell, who stayed and became one of the first citizens of Shelby County when it was created 25 years later.

During the years of military presence, whites continued to settle near the fort. By 1812 the Bluff community may have housed more than 50 persons, exclusive of military personnel. Though not all of these settlers remained, some did. Patrick ("Paddy") Meagher, later of Bell Tavern fame and myth, arrived no later than 1813 and stayed until his death in the mid-1820s. Isaac Rawlings became trading post factor in 1814 and stayed until about 1818, when the Western District was opened to settlement. After a couple of years' absence, "Ike" returned to become one of the new town's leading citizens. Although these early settlers may have gained the Chickasaws' permission to live there, they could have had no lawful title to the land until after the Chickasaw Cession.

In 1818 the Chickasaws succumbed at last, giving up the northern portion of their lands and thereby opening up all of West Tennessee to white settlement. It was the end of one era and the beginning of another. The pageant of explorer and soldier, foreigner and freebooter, trader and Indian would now give way to a tiny, struggling town, with all the blessings and ills that the coming of civilized society entails.

CHAPTER TWO

TRIUMPH OF LOCATION: 1819~1842

The name Memphis, with its ancient meaning of "established and beautiful," seems ironic indeed when portraying the Bluff City's early years. From its founding in 1819 until about 1840, Memphis was a primitive and pestilential little mudhole striving to survive as a town. It took more than two decades to become established, and during that time it was anything but beautiful.

More western than southern in its earliest orientation, Memphis required more than 20 years to outstrip rival towns, develop its hinterland, and embark on a period of dramatic expansion. Much of the area's economic growth was tied directly to the labor of enslaved Africans, whose toil converted the soils of the area into the "white gold" of cotton. This slave-based economy increasingly pulled West Tennessee into the southern cultural and political orbit, but its river contacts kept Memphis a largely atypical southern town throughout this early period.

In seeking to reconstruct the early history of the Memphis area, the modern historian encounters two basic and nearly insurmountable problems. The first lies in the prominence of the city's three founding proprietors. The second arises from the writings of a 19th-century popular "historian" who wrote an "eyewitness" account of early times in Memphis. These two phenomena have distorted the perspective and the facts of local history nearly beyond recognition.

The proprietors—General Andrew Jackson, Judge John Overton, and General James Winchester—all achieved wealth, power, and fame, and because they were men of national stature much of their correspondence has been preserved. As a result, their connection with the development of the town has been overemphasized and reported in detail disproportionate to their actual contributions. Although they were developers and promoters rather than simply speculators, none of the three ever lived in Memphis. Their interest was

This romanticized painting of Memphis in 1832 by J.H.B. Latrobe reflects the increasingly favorable accounts of the town given in traveler's journals. Almost another decade would pass before the beginning of Memphis' 19th-century building boom. From the Memphis/Shelby County Room (M/SCPLIC)

largely economic self-interest. Their ideas and efforts, although far from insignificant, would neither make nor break the town. Location alone would almost guarantee the settlement's success.

The story of the proprietors has been told, mistold, and retold at the expense of the actual settlers. The Lawrence, Carr, Bean, Bettis, Williams, and Rawlings families, plus scores of others, were the true founders and builders of Shelby County. These unsung heroes and heroines lived in the area, fought the elements, survived the epidemics and economic reverses, built the economy, shaped the spirit of the town, and gave Memphis its early direction. Unfortunately, there is little personal information available on these founding pioneers. What exists is scattered in fragments of early records or is derived from largely unreliable sources.

The second problem in reaching back to touch early Memphis is James D. Davis' *The History of the City of Memphis*. Davis, writing for popular consumption in the early 1870s, has been *the* basic source for early Memphis historiography. Chronicling a time for which there is scant newspaper coverage and little other documentary material against which to check his accounts, Davis poses monumental problems for scholars. In his accounts of the 1820s, Davis relied on memory for events that had taken place 50 years before. This would be bad enough if he were striving for accuracy, but he obviously was not. Davis was a great storyteller, not only in his style of telling, but in his sense of drama and his blatant disregard for fact. In instances where Davis can be checked against more trustworthy sources, he is very often incorrect. In the many areas where his tales cannot be checked, historians have largely accepted and repeated them.

From the standpoint of historical accuracy, it would probably be better if Davis had never written his classic tales. One could easily write an entire book simply debunking

Chapter Two: Triumph of Location: 1819-1842

JAMES DICK DAVIS, HISTORIAN

James D. Davis, born in Pennsylvania in 1810, came to Memphis in his late teens by way of Alabama. He became a professional painter, but he also worked as wharfmaster during the time of troubles with the flatboatmen; later in life he was a journalist.

Davis was among the few Memphians to remain staunch Unionists during the secessionist crisis and voted against secession in 1861. He became a Republican in the postwar era and held a federal appointive office. Surprisingly, these acts did not seem to damage his standing in the community.

During the years from 1869 to 1873, Davis' stories appeared sporadically in the *Appeal*. In the latter year they were compiled into book form and published as *The History of the City of Memphis . . . Also, The "Old Times Papers."* While his historical inaccuracies are widely recognized, Davis is considered the father of local history in Memphis. Most of his stories contain some kernel of truth, and they are very entertaining. The following sketch of "Squire" Ike Rawlings, followed by an account of his death, is given as a sampler,

James Dick Davis. From the Memphis/Shelby County Room (M/SCPLIC)

with the latter incident corrected by Professor James Roper.

A HARD STORY.

Passing Johnson's tavern once, in his very erect and rapid manner, he was stopped by Gus Young and Bob Lawrence, two pretty fast young men, but not more so than was common at that day, who asked him to settle a legal question between them. The "Squire" did not like to be stopped in the street, but legal questions had precedence over everything else, so he smacked his lips, indicating that he was ready. Gus explained that he had sold Bob a lot, with a stable on it, in the loft of which there was a quantity of corn, while outside, on the lot, there was a pile of manure. After the sale and transfer, he sent to haul away this corn and

manure, but Lawrence forbade the removal, claiming them as his property, by virtue of the purchase of the lot. Ike smacked his lips again, and decided that the corn could be removed, as it was personal property, but the manure was a part of the realty, as much so as if it was spread over or plowed into the ground. He quoted several standard authorities in support of his decision, and again smacked his lips. "Well," said Gus, with an apparently perplexed air, "can you now tell us, 'Squire, how a mule can eat personal property and discharge real estate?" Ike saw the sell at once, and after bestowing a withering look on the offenders, turned on his heel and walked off, grasping his cane in a manner that clearly said that he would like to use it on somebody, while the crowd engaged in a general and boisterous laugh.

HOW SAD THE END OF SUCH A LIFE.

The Squire became afflicted with a cancer in his spine, which terminated his life. The last time he appeared on the streets was at the Presidential election in 1840. He was carried to the polls in an easy chair, by two negro men, for he was a strong Whig, while Winchester was an equally strong Democrat. When he offered his vote with his trembling hand, he had the mortification to have it challenged, and that, too, on the ground that he was a dead man. He had been given up by his physician, and had made all

his arrangements for death sometime before. Such was the bitterness of party feeling at that time. The judges, however, paid no attention to the challenge, but took the proffered vote, and he was carried home never to leave the house again. When the illumination for the election of Harrison and Tyler came off, a number of us went to greet him. We found him in his easy chair, and rolled him to the door, as we did not want the crowd to enter, when the old man raised his palsied hands and added his dying voice to the general cheering. He said — "Now my friends I can die happy," and in a short time thereafter Isaac Rawlings was at rest forever.

The Davis version of Ike's last days is a fine story, and will no doubt survive the simple fact that it could not possibly be true as given. Several records, including Calvary Episcopal burial records and the Somerville Reporter *of September 28, 1839, attest to his death on September 19, 1839, of spinal cancer. Any poll watchers who objected to his voting in 1840 would have been on singularly good ground. The Whigs won the election of 1836 in Shelby County, but Ike was not moribund then, and the national election was lost. There seems to be no local victory which Davis misremembered in Ike's last years, and the dramatic exit has to be a pure fabrication, though of high order.*
— *John Harkins*

Davis. While such an enterprise has no place here, disproportionate space must be spent in correcting some of his more glaring falsehoods. However, such side trips will be held to a minimum, and the early story of Memphis will be told as straightforwardly as possible.

North Carolina Land Titles

The first English claim to the Chickasaw Bluffs area lay in the loose boundaries which Elizabeth I assigned to Sir Walter Raleigh's doomed Virginia colony. More than a century and a half later, Charles II's charter for the Carolina colonies granted their proprietors "title" to lands extending westward from the Atlantic Ocean to the Pacific Coast. These vague claims persisted throughout the colonial era, but had little relevance until after the American Revolution. By that time Anglo-American settlers were pouring over the Appalachians, and North Carolina's transmontane claims grew much stronger. Eventually the coastal states ceded all of their western land claims to the Union, to form territories which would eventually become new states—but not before North Carolina had granted much of these lands to its war veterans and sold off other portions to pay its war debts. Even land in the Chickasaw Nation, between the Tennessee and Mississippi rivers, was not exempt.

Exercising its dubious authority in October 1783, the speculator-controlled North Carolina government opened Chickasaw lands to purchase. Before more scrupulous legislators ended this unsavory practice seven months later, more than half of what was to become the Western District of Tennessee had been preempted by speculators. Two of the early speculators, John Rice and John Ramsey, bought title to two adjoining 5,000-acre tracts of land on the Fourth Chickasaw Bluff. Paid for in sorely depreciated currency, the approximately 16 square miles that would ultimately become the heart of downtown Memphis cost these early claimants about five cents per acre in hard money.

John Rice died in an Indian ambush in 1791, and his claim passed through his heirs and a series of purchases. During this sequence of paper transfers, ownership became divided, but the Rice grant was still held in joint tenancy. On the eve of the Chickasaw Cession, ownership of the tract was as follows: John Overton, one-half; Andrew Jackson, one-fourth; and William and James Winchester, one-fourth jointly. Immediately after the cession, Jackson sold half of his remaining interest to James Winchester for $5,000, reversing their respective proportions of ownership in the tract. With the Chickasaw agreement to relinquish their claims, the acre that had cost John Rice five cents was now worth eight dollars.

In the meantime the area which had been Washington County, North Carolina, reached a population of 77,000 and became the 16th state of the Union. Statehood was conferred on Tennessee on June 1, 1796. At the southwest corner of its boundaries lay the area later to be occupied by Shelby County and Memphis.

The Chickasaw Cession

Because of the Louisiana Purchase and the availability of other vast areas of western land at the beginning of the 19th century, Tennesseans did not immediately pressure the government to open the Chickasaw lands. In the second decade of the 19th century, however, such pressures did begin to mount. With the death of General James Robertson in 1814, the Chickasaws lost a powerful friend who had long protected their interests. A few years later the Tennessee legislature petitioned Congress "to procure a relinquishment of the Chickasaw claim." Congress responded in a surprisingly short time and appointed a special commission to treat with the Chickasaws.

Since the Chickasaw lands in question were situated within the bounds of Tennessee and Kentucky, Congress appointed General Andrew Jackson and ex-Governor Isaac Shelby to represent their respective states in dealing with the Chickasaws. Indian leaders at first refused to meet with them at all, but under the persistent blandishments of Jackson and Shelby, they joined them at last in a council at the Chickasaw Old Town site near Tuscumbia, Alabama, in the fall of 1818. Again employing tactics of intimidation and veiled threats, the commissioners secured the desired concessions.

The Chickasaw Cession, also known as the Western Purchase or the Jackson Purchase, was not necessarily the brutal rape that is usually depicted. The Indians did not live in this area but only hunted into it from their home grounds to the south. Chickasaw reluctance may in fact have been a ruse to raise the purchase price of territory they knew they would eventually lose anyway. If so, it seems to have worked.

The agreement provided that the Chickasaws would withdraw below the Tennessee-Mississippi boundary in return for $300,000, to be paid in 15 annual installments, and included various small concessions and presents for the chiefs. The area ceded encompassed approximately 6,848,000 acres at roughly 4.5 cents per acre. Although this sounds like outright theft today, viewed in its historic context it was not such a bad deal. Shelby was initially outraged that Jackson should propose such a high price; he believed the Indians would have parted with the land for one-half the agreed amount. The differences between

Metropolis of the American Nile

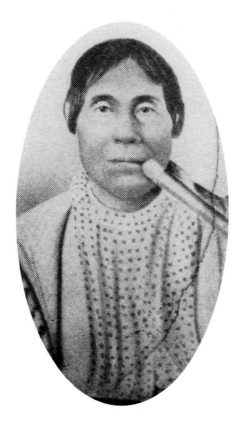

Jackson and Shelby were finally settled, and the treaty was signed on October 19, 1818. Even before it was ratified by the Senate the following January, settlers and prospectors began rushing into the ceded lands.

The conclusion of the Chickasaw treaty meant that the southern boundary of Tennessee, which had never been marked west of the Tennessee River, had to be surveyed. The results would be of particular importance to the future city of Memphis, as the Fourth Chickasaw Bluff would be very close to the line. The treaty defined the boundary in the following terms:

> Beginning on the Tennessee river, about thirty-five miles, by water, below Colonel George Colbert's ferry, where the thirty-fifth degree of north latitude strikes the same; thence due west with said degree of north latitude to where it cuts the Mississippi river at or near the Chickasaw Bluffs . . .

The treaty further required that this boundary would be established by commissioners to be appointed by the President of the United States, attended by two representatives of the Chickasaw Nation. The survey was soon begun as stipulated.

During the course of the survey, the two Indian representatives, James Colbert and Captain Seely, complained that the line was cutting too far to the south. James Winchester, head United States commissioner and proprietary partner in the Rice tract, explained that their instruments were more accurate than the path of the sun and insisted that the line was being run true. The Indians were still not satisfied and left the party shortly afterward, pre-

31

Chapter Two: Triumph of Location: 1819-1842

sumably to confer with other tribal leaders.

Colbert and Seely met with Winchester again at the Fourth Bluff, shortly after he had finished the survey. Here they declared that the recently blazed line was not the true boundary and that it must be run again. Winchester again tried to reassure them that the line was true, but they did not believe him. The Chickasaw Nation lodged a formal protest with the United States government and worked for more than a decade to get the boundary changed.

The Indian representatives had made no protest until several days into the surveying trek, when it appeared that the line might place the boundary south of the Fourth Bluff. They stayed with the commission until it became obvious that the Bluff would be outside of their recently reduced domain. Their continued protests suggest that they had not realized they were giving up the Bluff site when they signed the treaty and they wanted this piece of real estate back. Yet there is no indication of why. They had no town or known religious shrine in the vicinity, nor were there even salt springs or other natural resources close by. Why was control of this area so important to them?

If history has not answered that question, it has answered a closely related one. The Chickasaws were correct in their contention that Winchester's boundary had not been run true. But instead of cheating them by running the boundary too far to the south, Winchester actually ran the line about four miles too far north. His error gave the Chickasaws about 440 square miles more than they were entitled to under the treaty. This mistake was not corrected until 1837, after the state of Mississippi had taken title to the remaining Chickasaw lands. Winchester Road, a broad thoroughfare traversing most of the southern part of the city and county from east to west, remains a bustling memorial to Winchester's surveying error and to the unanswered question of why the Chickasaws desired so earnestly to keep the Bluff site within their domain.

The Founding of Memphis

Between the signing of the Cession treaty and the completion of the boundary survey, the Rice grant proprietors acted quickly to establish their claim, lay off a town, and begin getting a return on their investment. Indeed Marcus B. Winchester, who was to serve as on-site agent for his father and the other proprietors, left immediately from the treaty council for the Bluff to make preliminary arrangements for founding the town. Young Winchester and an even younger surveyor named William Lawrence had the immediate tasks of locating the precise boundaries of the Rice claim and quelling any opposition from squatters who might resent or resist being dispossessed.

After initial difficulty in locating the Rice entry because of the impermanence of landmarks, the surveyors laid out a little town of 362 lots, four to five blocks deep along the Bluff frontage. Contrary to popular and enduring myth, Jackson, Overton, and James Winchester *never* convened at Paddy Meagher's Bell Tavern to plan and lay out the streets of Memphis. They planned the town in absentia, based on information sent by their agents. Then, guided by the proprietors' plan, Marcus Winchester and William Lawrence laid off the town lots. By May 22, 1819, they had completed their survey, and on that date the proprietors conveyed some of the lots to several of the earliest citizens. Under Overton's direction they issued temporary titles until the state surveying district office could make formal transfers.

The proprietors, especially in the context of the times, showed a remarkable degree of enlightened self-interest in disposing of some of the town lots. Although they retained wharfage rights, ferriage rights, and most of the town lots for later sale, they made free distribution of some of the property in three ways likely to benefit the settlers. First, they gave lots to some of the squatters who had been living on the Bluff, assuring a nucleus of citizens

Metropolis of the American Nile

to attract other settlers. Second, they set aside portions of the land for permanent public use—four public squares and a large public promenade along the Bluff front. Last, they gave lots to new arrivals who were expected to make needed contributions to the economic life of the community.

An example of this third practice was the granting of two acres at the extreme northwest edge of town to Thomas Carr, in return for his pledge to build a grain mill, a blacksmith shop, and a cotton gin. His later title to the property is presumptive evidence that he fulfilled his obligations to provide early Memphis with these primitive but much needed industries. With these and other basic facilities such as stores and taverns, the town soon contained the seeds that were ultimately to grow into a commercial network servicing portions of five states.

Despite its early start, its superb location, and a vigorous advertising campaign by Overton and partners, the sale of Memphis lots did not go well. As late as December of 1820, only a very few lots had been sold and for lower than premium prices. Rival towns, the ravages of disease, and a complex of other factors kept the growth of Memphis at a snail's pace until long after all the original proprietors had departed the scene.

Creating the County

John Overton, the most closely involved of the absentee proprietors, was an experienced and shrewd land dealer. He accurately foresaw that the establishment of a county government at Memphis would significantly enhance the value of his property. Knowing that speed was essential in gaining the advantage over other towns that would soon spring up in West Tennessee, in 1819 Overton drafted a sample petition for the Bluff settlers to

Chapter Two: Triumph of Location: 1819-1842

MEMPHIS, A NEW TOWN ON THE MISSISSIPPI

MEMPHIS, a New Town on the Mississippi

A town of the above name has been laid off on the east bank of the Mississippi, at the Lower Chickasaw Bluff, in the county of Shelby, and state of Tennessee. It is also within the Western District, lately acquired by treaty, from the Chickasaw Indians.

The plan and local situation of MEMPHIS are such, as to authorize the expectation, that it is destined to become a large and populous city. It is laid off parallel with the Mississippi, the course of which, at this place, is nearly due south, with Wolf River emptying into it at the northern extremity of the town. Three hundred and sixty-two lots are designated upon its present plat; and there is any quantity of elevated, level land adjoining, suited to the purpose of enlarging it at pleasure. The streets run to the cardinal points. They are wide and spacious, and, together with a number of alleys, afford a free and abundant circulation of air. There are, besides, four public squares, in different parts of the town, and between the front lots and the river, is an ample vacant space, reserved as a promenade; all of which must contribute very much to the health and comfort of the place, as well as to its security and ornament....

The general advantages of MEMPHIS, are owing to its

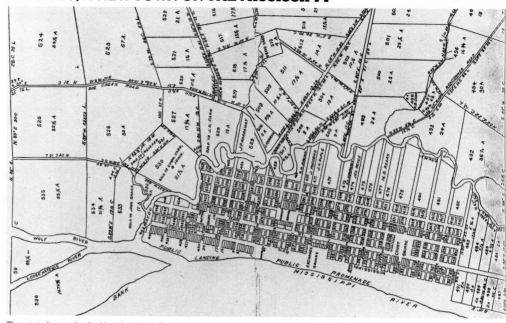

The original town plan for Memphis, 1819. From the Memphis/Shelby County Room (M/SCPLIC)

being founded on the Mississippi, one of the largest and most important rivers on the globe, and the high road for all the commerce of the vast and fertile valley through which it flows. This noble river ... may, with propriety, be denominated the *American Nile*, is about two thousand five hundred and eighty miles from its head to its mouth, and with its branches, waters two-thirds of the territory of the United States.... MEMPHIS must necessarily become a flourishing and populous town. It occupies a position which is always perfectly accessible to steam-boats, and to vessels of every size and description, which are employed in the trade of the western world. Every oppor-

tunity is also offered, at every season of the year, of traveling from this place, in steam-boats, to either of the states or territories west of the Allegheny mountains, or of going round to any state or city on the Atlantic coast. Indeed, from its favourable situation, a passage may be obtained, almost at any time, to every quarter of the globe....

The present number of inhabitants in MEMPHIS amount to about *fifty* souls; most of whom have settled there for commercial purposes, since the Indian claim was extinguished, in the year 1818. There are several families of the first respectability, who have lately become residents of the town, and the number is

gradually increasing. It is also the seat of justice for the county of Shelby, and the sessions of all the courts in that section of country, will consequently be held at that place.

From this view, MEMPHIS appears to combine most of those advantages which authorize us to pronounce it an eligible site, and which are eminently calculated to make it a populous and flourishing town. It is also believed, that there is no situation on the banks of the Upper Mississippi which is more auspicious to health, or better suited to the rapid acquisition of wealth.

— John Overton's advertisement for Memphis, published in *The Port Folio in 1820*

Judge John Overton was the most interested and the most active of the absentee proprietors of Memphis. He purchased the Rice grant and sold half of it to Jackson, who, in turn, sold portions of his half to the Winchesters. Overton did the planning and directed most of the activities of the partners' agents in Memphis. Such speculative ventures reputedly made Overton the richest man in Tennessee, but his Memphis investment was very slow in paying off. Thus, most of the benefits accrued to his descendants. From the Memphis/Shelby County Room (M/SCPLIC)

submit to the legislature. Oddly, his initial proposal suggested a triangular shape that would have excluded much of the present county above the Wolf River.

General Winchester did not like the idea of a triangular county and objected to the exclusion of rich farmlands to the northeast. Moreover, he doubted that the legislature would approve such unorthodox boundaries. Overton deferred to Winchester's judgment, and the Bluff residents submitted a petition requesting creation of a county with more conventional boundaries.

In November of 1819 the legislature created a county along lines suggested in the residents' petition, the first county to be established completely within the bounds of the Chickasaw Cession. Jackson and Overton had already been honored by having Tennessee counties named for them. Was it now Winchester's turn to be so honored? As a Memphis proprietor, an army general, a political power in the state, and head Chickasaw boundary commissioner, he should have been a likely candidate. However, this was not to be. Instead the county was named for General Isaac Shelby, military hero, first governor of Kentucky, and co-commissioner at the Chickasaw Cession—another good choice that very likely pleased the residents of the new county.

Shelby County actually began to function in May of 1820, when the quarterly court first met at Memphis, or rather "at the Bluff," as the residents continued to refer to the town for the first few years. County officers were selected, the first marriage performed, and minor legal cases adjudicated. As Overton had hoped, necessary legal business was bringing trade to his infant city.

The fly in the proprietors' ointment, however, was that the act creating the county did not permanently affix the seat at Memphis. Then, as now, there was a lot more to Shelby County than the town of Memphis, and by 1820 there were several significant settlements in the outlying areas of the county. Some of these, like the Bluff community, probably dated from before the Chickasaw Purchase.

Two such settlements existed in north central Shelby County. Big Creek, probably the older of the two, lay south of the present town of Millington. Egypt—an intriguing name to be found in Shelby County prior to the founding of Memphis—lay a few miles south of Big Creek. Settlers with strong ties to the Baptist faith were apparently living in both areas at the sufferance of the Chickasaws before the Cession, but the precise date of origin of these settlements is now lost in legend.

Big Creek and Egypt were sprawling farm communities of the familiar frontier pattern, rather than towns. However, they were fairly densely populated and prosperous, and residents of the two areas naturally wanted the county seat located nearer than the southwestern corner of the county at Memphis. Theirs and other voices outside of Memphis would be heard.

Overton may have foreseen this potential problem as early as 1819 when he advanced his original odd shape for the county. Viewing retention of the county seat as absolutely vital to the success of his town, Overton was determined to keep county government in Memphis, and in 1822 he lobbied successfully for state legislation favorable to that end. The act provided for a popular election to determine local preference and a four-member commission to make the actual selection. Exerting his great influence, Overton also persuaded the legislature to delete the customary clause requiring that the seat be located within three miles of the geographical center of the county and to staff the selection commission with members whom he considered friendly to his interests. Finally, to ensure that the voters would choose correctly, he planned to distribute free whiskey liberally at election time.

All of Overton's efforts and scheming went for naught. The referendum was never held,

and Overton was outmaneuvered in the legislature in 1824. A new act of that year empowered the commissioners to fix the seat of Shelby County wherever they pleased, with no popular election being held. To Overton's surprise and dismay, the commission chose the virtually uninhabited site of Sanderlin's Bluff on the Wolf River, 10 miles east of Memphis.

The commission reported its decision in February of 1825. In August of that year the state appointed another commission to lay out the town of Raleigh at Sanderlin's Bluff. When this commission failed to report back, the state appointed still a third commission, which finally completed the task. Within two years Raleigh was laid out, a substantial courthouse had been erected there, and the county court moved out of Memphis.

The elevation of Raleigh to county seat gave Memphis a very serious political and commercial rival for more than a decade. Despite the fact that Raleigh's central location was more equitable for the county at large, it is still surprising that Memphis should have lost the seat at this time. Although Jackson had divested himself of his Memphis holdings prior to the transfer, he was still closely allied politically and economically with Overton, Winchester, and their new partner, John C. McLemore. Moreover, the Jackson faction, of whom these men were stalwarts, was the most powerful political force in Tennessee in the mid-1820s. Even if some group had been powerful enough to thwart the Jackson combination, who would have been foolish enough to risk the consequences? No even remotely satisfactory explanation to this question has yet been offered.

How seriously did the loss of county government hurt Memphis? For this question too there is no satisfactory answer. Although some historians argue there was little or no long-range harm, initially the change must have damaged Memphis quite considerably. During its first decade Raleigh grew rapidly, and by 1836 the new city had equaled or passed Memphis in population. Before long, however, some of the court functions were again being shared by Memphis. In the 1840s Memphis began a growth spurt that exploded into a boom era lasting through the Civil War, and Overton's axiom that commerce would follow the courts was turned on its head. By the 1860s the primacy of Memphis was such that the political seat followed the path of commerce back to the Bluff City of the American Nile. This second coronation, however, came only after many years of frustration and failure.

Challenges to Development

Considering its numerous intrinsic advantages, Memphis made a shockingly slow start toward achieving the regional preeminence that it eventually attained. Various factors retarded the growth of the infant town, some of which have been misinterpreted in general histories until now. In the frontier context, the first two decades were not as bad as they have sometimes been presented.

The initial development of all of West Tennessee was stunted by the financial panic of 1819 and its ensuing depression, which took a particularly heavy toll on the endemically credit-ridden West. By the time the economy began to recover and the migration of settlers resumed its normal rate, the initial advantages enjoyed by Memphis had diminished considerably. Consequently, the town developed less rapidly than might otherwise have been the case.

After their early efforts on behalf of their investment, the three original proprietors did not give sufficient attention to the town to guarantee its progress. By 1824 Andrew Jackson had left the partnership and was making his first bid for the presidency. Overton, credited with being the richest man in the state, had numerous other enterprises to attend to. In his mid-50s, moreover, he embraced the responsibilities of marriage and family life for the first time. He added to these demands on his time and attention by managing Jackson's political campaign. As for James Winchester, he was involved in diverse interests away from

Metropolis of the American Nile

Memphis and had only a short time to live.

Ironically, Jackson, the partner who had put the least into the Memphis project, was the only one of the three to profit significantly from the venture. Winchester died in 1826 without realizing a profit, and by 1833, when Overton died, Memphis was still struggling for its existence. Although Overton and Winchester heirs would eventually gain from the Memphis holdings, leadership of the town passed into other hands.

Probably more important than neglect by the proprietors as a factor in Memphis' slow start was the competition from another river town 42 miles upriver on the Second Chickasaw Bluff. Founded in 1823 and named for the great rebel republican, John Randolph of Roanoke, Randolph, Tennessee, was Memphis' most serious commercial rival. For most of the 1820s and 1830s, Randolph's challenge was even greater than that of Raleigh.

Unlike the First and Third Chickasaw Bluff sites, Memphis and Randolph both had deep-water channels that were unlikely to meander and leave them stranded away from the vital river artery. Although Randolph was perched atop a somewhat smaller bluff, it enjoyed one important advantage over Memphis. While the major Memphis tributary, the Wolf River, was not always navigable 10 miles inland to Raleigh, the Hatchie River was usually navigable about 70 miles inland from Randolph to Bolivar, Tennessee. Situated near the confluence of the Hatchie River with the Mississippi, Randolph was thus at a natural trade junction for the interior of West Tennessee.

Besides its tributary advantage, Randolph had a justifiable reputation for being healthier than Memphis. As under Spanish and American military rule, early Memphis suffered a spate of devastating diseases. Between 1826 and 1832 Memphis had two outbreaks of cholera, one of dengue or "break bone fever," a bout with smallpox, and its first major yellow fever epidemic. The yellow fever siege, occurring in 1828, recorded 650 cases and 150 deaths. Such catastrophic illness not only took a severe direct toll on the population, but caused some of the residents to emigrate and scared other potential settlers away. Steamboats and flatboats naturally preferred another port of call, and the misery suffered by Memphians contributed to the rise of Randolph.

In 1836 the ascendancy of Randolph seemed almost assured. A year earlier the *Randolph Recorder* had referred sneeringly to its rival as "the great, grand fungus of the West," calling it "a depot for mud and strumpets." Both towns now had populations of about 1,500, but Randolph had more steamboat traffic and was shipping more cotton. The state had commissioned a study for a Hatchie-Tennessee canal project and seemed ready to help underwrite its construction costs. Had the canal actually been cut, the trade advantages to Randolph might indeed have strangled Memphis economically.

But Memphis contained some nearly undetected features that would unfold as West Tennessee developed. Most important, the Fourth Bluff was a natural east-west crossroads. Prior to European incursions, Indian trails converged at the mouth of the Wolf River as a favorable crossing point into Arkansas. This factor and the urging of the proprietors secured for Memphis the promise of early mail service. Mail routes meant road building, and roads meant development of trade. By late 1820 Memphis was astride two postal routes. Afterward, as the jumping-off place for points west, Memphis enjoyed more mail runs than Randolph.

As long as riverboats remained virtually unchallenged as a mode of transport, Randolph's river advantage might hold sway. However, the same Hatchie River that gave Randolph its river advantage would later impede the development of a road network. More important, it would make Randolph a less practical terminus for railroads. By the mid-1830s these factors were beginning to come into focus.

Like the Indians, white men of perception and vision recognized that the Fourth Bluff

Chapter Two: Triumph of Location: 1819-1842

was a nearly ideal point for crossing the Mississippi River. This circumstance had two important consequences for Memphis. First, it made Hopefield, immediately adjacent to Memphis, the eastern terminus for the Arkansas Military Road to Little Rock, Fort Smith, and points west. Second, it made the Fourth Bluff the front-runner as the western terminus of the rails that would eventually join the lower Mississippi to the Atlantic Ocean.

Speculation and investment in Memphis as a potential rail center began prior to 1831, at which point the legislature granted the first state railway charter to the Memphis Railroad Company. In 1835 the La Grange and Memphis Railroad Company was incorporated and capitalized at $375,000, with the state purchasing one-third of the stock. Construction began eastward from Memphis but made only limited progress before the panic and depression of 1837 brought the company to the verge of bankruptcy. Only massive investment and reorganization by John C. McLemore kept the enterprise solvent into the 1840s, and the rails ran only 12 miles east to White's Station when the company failed. Although his faith in the future of the Fourth Bluff cost McLemore the bulk of his great fortune, his sacrifice was not completely in vain. His efforts began the rail age in Memphis, built a climate of expectancy that Memphis would be the railhead, and furnished 12 miles of rails and a longer right-of-way for a river-to-coast railroad in the 1850s.

The depression of 1837 severely hurt all of West Tennessee, including Memphis. Randolph's businesses, however, until then riding a crest of prosperity and expansion, were hurt the most. The first panic ruined several of the city's most important merchants. The next year an unusually low river level diverted much of Randolph's trade to Memphis, ruining more of its commercial houses, and by 1840 many of the survivors had moved their operations to Memphis. Randolph soon stagnated, never again to challenge Memphis as a midway metropolis of the American Nile.

Growth of the Hinterland

The development of Memphis into an urban trade center ultimately depended on the development of its hinterland. Once the slow tasks of taming the land and cutting the roads were seriously under way, the effects were dramatic. The hinterland blossomed and broadened, rivals withered, and the growth of Memphis accelerated at a dizzying pace.

The commercial development of West Tennessee's farmland was initially hampered by

Metropolis of the American Nile

the fact that speculators had grabbed most of the good land before Tennessee became a separate state. A combination of economic depression, speculators' holding the lands for higher prices, and the availability of other rich western lands inhibited early settlement. When these factors changed, Carolinian and other migrants streamed into the area. In 1820 the population of West Tennessee was only about 2,500. Ten years later it had grown to 100,000, and within another decade it was double that. The vast majority of these people belonged to farm families. As soon as they were able to grow enough food for themselves, they began raising cash crops and seeking the best market for their products.

During the first 15 years after its founding, Memphis was cut off from nearly half of its potential hinterland. Just below the town lay the Mississippi boundary, where the whole northern portion of the state remained a Chickasaw reservation. Memphis enjoyed only "small" trade with this area, exchanging cloth, trinkets, and whiskey for pelts. Then, in 1834, the Chickasaws were forced to sell their last large preserve and either move west or acclimate to the white man's ways and laws. With this cession the potential hinterland for Memphis effectively doubled, but it still took several years for northern Mississippi's agricultural production to develop.

The filling up of the rich virgin lands of West Tennessee and northern Mississippi coincided with the explosion of the cotton culture in the Old Southwest. Interacting with and enlarging upon its hinterland, Memphis grew into the commercial agrarian entrepot for the region. Expansion for both entrepot and hinterland was tied directly to the construction of roads, necessary for getting crops to market and distributing manufactured goods to the rural areas. Post and stage routes initially connected Memphis with more distant places, forming the skeleton upon which a network of roads soon developed. Prior to 1836 these roads had only dirt surfaces and there were very few bridges across the area's many streams. By 1850 settlers and slaves had cut many more roads, constructed some plank roads, bridged some of the streams, and stationed ferries on broader water courses.

The growth of trade, wealth, and population in Memphis stemmed directly from these steady, even mundane, developments. As late as 1830 the city's hinterland did not even include the whole of Shelby County. By 1840 improved transit had expanded the Memphis market perimeter to include six counties in West Tennessee, the northernmost

Chapter Two: Triumph of Location: 1819-1842

The economic development of the Old Southwest, including West Tennessee and Memphis, was tied directly to cotton production. Eli Whitney's 1793 invention of the cotton gin made short-staple cotton extremely profitable and gave the declining institution of African slavery a new lease on life. The design was so simple that manufacturers could evade patent restrictions. Memphis was a producer and distributor of this necessary tool in the land where cotton became "king." Located opposite Beadle, Payne and Company's cotton gin stand factory was Watt C. Bradford's Union Foundry and Machine Shop, which manufactured, among other things, steam engines. From the Memphis/Shelby County Room (M/SCPLIC)

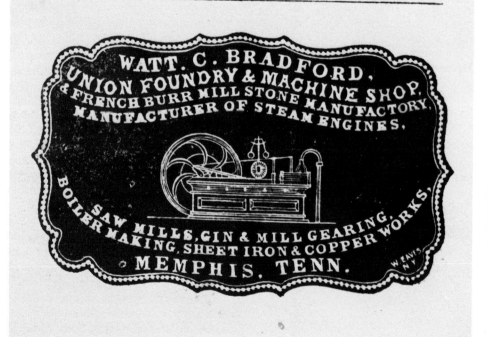

Mississippi counties, and a few areas in eastern Arkansas. By 1860 the trade area had grown to about the size it is today, including all of West Tennessee, the eastern third of Arkansas, most of northern Mississippi, and small portions of northwestern Alabama and southeastern

Most of the phenomenal growth of Memphis and its hinterland can be attributed to the cultivation and marketing of cotton. Beginning with a scant 300 bales of the white fiber in 1825, the cotton trade passed 35,000 bales in 1840, when Memphis replaced Randolph as the principal steamboat landing on the mid-Mississippi. By 1850 Memphis was the largest inland cotton market in the world. The year before the Civil War, Memphis shipped 400,000 bales of cotton, the mainstay of the $53 million worth of trade goods that passed through the city that year.

Cotton would indeed become "king" in the Memphis area. It would dominate the local economy, both as benefactor and as tyrant. The arrival of the "white gold" staple also brought the black men and women whose enforced labor would be so vital in the creation of the region's wealth.

The Fellaheen of the Cotton Kingdom

The earliest known contacts between blacks and whites took place in Egypt's Nile Valley, where the river first pierces the great Sahara barrier. Ultimately the Nubians or Kushites entered ancient Egypt in the 8th century B.C. as conquerors. As a dramatic contrast, disparate groups of black Africans came into the valley of the American Nile most

41   Chapter Two: Triumph of Location: 1819-1842

FRANCES WRIGHT

Frances Wright, founder of the utopian colony Nashoba, was one of the best known—and certainly one of the most avant-garde—women of her day. Although her early experiment in interracial communal living failed, she was for many years a prominent figure in American political life.

An intense, outspoken Scotswoman, Frances Wright was born in Dundee in 1795, the daughter of a merchant who had once daringly circulated the works of Thomas Paine. Orphaned at an early age, she went to live first with wealthy relatives in England and then with a professor uncle in Glasgow. Independently wealthy, intellectually precocious, and rebellious by nature, Fanny was soon off on her own.

In 1818 Fanny and her younger sister, Camilla, set sail for America, where they spent the next two years traveling through the mid-Atlantic states. Fanny's enthusiastic impressions, *Views of Society and Manners in America,* were published after her return to England in 1821. The young author received numerous letters of praise, among them one from the Marquis de Lafayette, aging hero of America's War of Independence. Correspondence led to friendship, and when Lafayette made his triumphant tour of the United States in 1824, Frances Wright accompanied him.

In the course of this second

Frances Wright. From Cirker, *Dictionary of American Portraits*

trip, she frequently pondered and discussed the problem of slavery—that jarringly discordant institution in a liberty-proclaiming land. Learning of socialist Robert Owen's plan for New Harmony in Indiana, Fanny conceived a different kind of idealistic community, to be located in the South, where slaves could learn to live in freedom while working to achieve it. Eager to begin, she bought acreage near Memphis on which to try out her scheme, then published a pamphlet which she sent to a number of the country's leading statesmen in the hope that her program might eventually be adopted on a large scale as the means of gradually eradicating slavery.

Early in 1826 a dozen slaves and a handful of white colonists, including Fanny and Camilla, began clearing the land and planting crops of corn and cotton. Fanny pushed herself too hard, riding

out in all kinds of weather, zealously surveying the work, sometimes even sleeping out of doors. After suffering a near-fatal attack of dengue fever, she returned to the healthier climate of Europe, where she tried to recruit new settlers for Nashoba.

One of those impressed by her idealism was Frances Trollope, who arrived with several of her children in 1827. The reality was far from the ideal, however, as she later recalled in *Domestic Manners of the Americans.* "One glance sufficed to convince me that every idea I had formed of the place was as far as possible from the truth. Desolation was the only feeling, the only word, that presented itself." Other visitors agreed, and in 1829 the experiment was finally abandoned. Fanny Wright retained ownership of the property, leasing it out to tenant farmers.

In 1828 Frances Wright began editing the New Harmony *Gazette* in partnership with Robert Dale Owen, son of the community's founder. The following year they moved to New York City and founded the radical *Free Enquirer.* Among those influenced by Fanny's revolutionary ideas in politics, economics, education, morality, and religion was young Walt Whitman, who later recalled her as "a woman of the noblest make-up . . . one of the best in history." She opened a Hall of Science, offering free courses

to working people, and helped form the Workingmen's party—popularly known as the Fanny Wright party.

Long opposed to marriage, in her mid-30s she married a Frenchman, Phiquepal D'Arusmont, and soon after gave birth to a daughter. The family eventually moved to Cincinnati, and from there Fanny continued to pursue a busy schedule of writing, politics, and lecture tours on both sides of the Atlantic. On occasion her travels took her back to Memphis, and she considered reviving the Nashoba experiment.

In order to "protect" her from squandering her money on such foolish schemes, Fanny's husband sought and obtained legal control of her property. Fanny filed for divorce in Shelby County, and in 1850 the court at Raleigh granted the decree—a remarkable event in its day. Frances Wright continued her independent career until an accident in Cincinnati two years later resulted in her death at the age of 57.

Frances Wright's Nashoba survives today only in some traces of building foundations in suburban Germantown east of Memphis. Though her scheme for ending slavery endured but briefly, Frances Wright has earned her place in history as a woman of vision, courage, and independence far ahead of her time.

— Carol V. Davis
and Barbara Marinacci

often as enslaved laborers. Present along the lower Mississippi for more than a century, a few blacks probably lived at the Bluffs before the Chickasaw Cession. In the 1820 census slaves comprised about 20 percent of Shelby County's population, and this percentage increased gradually through most of the 19th century.

The importance of the Afro-American contribution to the economic growth of Memphis, Shelby County, and the whole South Central region can scarcely be exaggerated. Because of the nature of the South's "peculiar institution," however, it is extremely difficult to document the details and the extent of blacks' contributions as a group. It is even harder to dig out the individual stories needed to personalize and enliven this history. But a few contours at least can be sketched in for this early period, in the hope that they may encourage future historians to discover and reveal still more of the local Afro-American story.

Memphis has always had an atypical history of race relations. Perhaps the most astonishing factor in the city's early racial history is James Davis' enduring report that the first mayor married a woman who was one-quarter black. According to this tale, Marcus B. Winchester wed the former quadroon mistress of Thomas Hart Benton and thereby committed social and political suicide. Davis is the sole source for this story, and sufficient details of his rendering are so palpably false that they cast doubt on the whole. However, there evidently was something unusual about Winchester's marriage and there may be some truth to the notion that he and his family had troubles arising out of it. Historians have apparently repeated Davis' version of this mystery because none of his contemporaries challenged its validity at the time he published it. If Davis lied, what could have been his motive and why would it have gone unchallenged?

On the other hand, if the Davis story should be true, having the city's first "first family" racially mixed could provide a rallying point for a city badly divided along racial lines at present. Even should the story eventually prove false, there are other instances of racial harmony, affection, and trust in the Memphis heritage. For example, Memphis' second mayor, Isaac Rawlings, undoubtedly lived in a common-law marriage with his slave (Indian or black) housekeeper. Before he died, Ike acknowledged his son William by her and left the bulk of his estate to this young man. Ike's considerable estate included several slaves, and his will expressed the hope that William would free all of them.

Whatever the truth of Winchester's first marriage, there is no doubt where his heart lay regarding the institution of slavery. He encouraged his slaves to work for wages and kept careful account of their savings toward the purchase of their freedom. Perhaps more important, he advised and encouraged Frances Wright in her communal effort to free slaves.

Miss Wright, a protege of General Lafayette and a new follower of fellow Scottish utopian socialist Robert Owen, was a wealthy, strong-minded young woman with radical ideas. In 1825, on the advice of Andrew Jackson, Fanny, as intimates called her, launched an emancipation experiment in Shelby County by purchasing a 2,000-acre tract of land. It was named Nashoba—wolf in Chickasaw—for the nearby Wolf River. She also acquired some slaves, planning to educate them for living free while the profits from their labors mounted toward the purchase of that freedom, to be undertaken away from the U.S. The surplus funds of the community would then buy more slaves who would in turn work their way to freedom. As these cycles were repeated, the number of black participants would expand. Success would encourage more such communities, so that eventually the system would free all black Americans.

Had the Nashoba plan worked, it might have saved the nation the bloodbath of the Civil War. Unfortunately, it never really had a fair test. Within two years of its inception, Fanny became seriously ill and left the area to recover her health. During her absence her associates transformed her community into "an experiment in free love, racial equality, and

amalgamation.'' Although such ideas were acceptable to Fanny, who defended them in letters and articles published in the nation's newspapers, they were hardly so to most white Shelby Countians. Locals, many of whom had initially encouraged the Nashoba project, were outraged by the now-national notoriety of the place. Meanwhile, mismanagement, disease, and death were wrecking the little community's finances and morale. Discouraged, Fanny abandoned the project, but only after she had freed the several dozen remaining blacks and settled them safely in the Republic of Haiti.

One other exception of the dearth of information on blacks in early Memphis and Shelby County is in the sphere of religion, ever the major forum of black cultural expression in American history. Memphis' first resident preacher was a black Methodist named Harry Lawrence. The Reverend Lawrence preached to members of both races in the earliest years before there was a resident white preacher, and he continued to do so even after local worship became largely segregated. Other black preachers also ministered to both races. Even segregated congregations shared the same buildings and services while the early churches were developing. These practices must have encouraged racial accommodation and mutual tolerance.

Even though it is impossible to recount the contributions and achievements of individual blacks in the Memphis area during the antebellum years, it is possible to draw some general conclusions about their collective lives at that time. Most blacks lived on farms or budding plantations where life was rigorous in the extreme. They shared the back-breaking work and primitive living conditions which early white settlers endured, but blacks were at the bottom of the ladder of material well-being, with no hope that their lot would be im-

Metropolis of the American Nile

proved by the success of their labors. Most of the few blacks who lived in town were domestic servants, riverfront roustabouts, or skilled artisans working for the profit of others. Unless free, blacks had no economic or legal rights. Although Shelby County had more free blacks than other areas of West Tennessee, this group was still a minute fraction of the black population.

During the very early years after settlement, race does not appear to have been a very important consideration. When whites thought on the matter at all, their views were mild by later standards. Besides the initial encouragement for the Nashoba experiment, most white voters of Shelby County favored the gradual emancipation of slaves. Early Memphis even boasted an emancipation society. Most such emancipation advocates were racist to the extent that they wanted blacks freed and then colonized elsewhere. Even though such attitudes were hardly egalitarian or just, a climate of toleration and hope seems to have prevailed. Free blacks were also allowed to vote.

Beginning in the 1830s, events and circumstances combined to destroy this tradition. As Memphis became less a free-wheeling frontier town, eastern conventions and social stratification began to manifest themselves. More important was the fact that, with the rise of the cotton culture, area planters imported ever larger numbers of blacks to work the fields. It is a bitter irony that as the black economic and social contributions increased in proportion to their numbers, their political hopes and general well-being declined accordingly.

By 1830 approximately one-third of southwest Tennessee's population was composed of slaves. Ten years later blacks comprised more than 40 percent of the total. Although the black population of Memphis remained less than half of this percentage, the proximity of so many unfamiliar and potentially hostile blacks inspired a deep fear of servile rebellion. The 1831 Nat Turner massacre in Virginia sent shock waves through the South and lent substance to a growing and malignant paranoia. Closer to home, rumors of a general slave insurrection, stemming from the trial of West Tennessee "Land Pirate" John A. Murrell, added to the whites' fears and suspicions. As plans for general emancipation became obviously less practicable, such fears gave vent to increased repression of blacks, a growing acceptance of the permanence of slavery, and increased alienation between the races.

In this new climate of fear and repression, Tennessee revised its constitution. The 1834 revisions stripped away the very limited rights of slaves, made manumissions nearly impossible, stripped free blacks of their rights of citizenship, and denied them protection under state law. Sadly, most white Shelby Countians probably approved of these so-called "reforms."

Tone of the Town, Tenor of the Times

Descriptions of Memphis and the early Bluff community are derived mainly from the journals of visitors. Almost invariably their first sighting of the locale was from the river. From here the steep, amazingly broad bluff escarpment rose 60 to 80 feet above the water level. The red clay soils of the banks were multitoned, with strata of purple and violet painting irregular horizontal stripes upon its surface, which was punctuated by small tufts of vegetation. Uneven, erosive gullies, cut by near-monsoon rains, gave this panoramic tapestry a variegated vertical texture, which light and shadow played upon, enriched, and gave depth. This fantastic, ever-changing scenic canvas was framed by the river at its base, the town with its clearing on top, and virgin broadleaf forests tapering off on either side. In spring and summer lush verdant foliage and a choking network of huge vines created an almost tropical, primordial atmosphere. This was the vista, slowly to be spoiled by the works of men, that greeted the earliest visitors to the Bluff.

Ascending the Bluff to the tiny town, the newcomer was treated to a much less Rousseau-like picture. As in most developing settlements, people's puny efforts to circumvent nature were unimpressive. The crest of the Bluff, probably partially cleared since Indian days, boasted small clusters of ramshackle buildings and a great deal of mud.

When Fanny Wright first entered Memphis in 1825, she referred to "this dozen of log cabins baptized by the sonorous name of Memphis," and speculated that the American town was "as wretched as Memphis, the Ancient." Reuben Davis, who rejected Memphis and settled in Mississippi, rendered an even harsher retrospective judgment. Of the 1820s Bluff settlement Davis later wrote:

> Memphis was then a small town, ugly, dirty and sickly; with miserable streets.
> . . . Everything pointed to the certainty that in a short time this squalid village
> must grow to be a great and wealthy city, but I had no confidence in my destiny
> as one of the builders of it. For many years the population would be rough and
> lawless, and the locality and sanitary conditions of the town promised that dis-
> ease and death would hold high carnival there.

Davis' prophecy would be uncanny for its accuracy, except for the fact that he was speaking from hindsight.

Not all observers were so harsh on early Memphis, and there was a general tendency for their judgments to improve. In 1826 Jeremiah Evarts wrote:

> It is not yet so rich or so populous, as the ancient capital of Egypt. There are
> four or five stores, and perhaps ten loghouses, with two or three poor frame
> houses. . . . The land of the back country is rich, but very sparsely settled, and
> the people are poor.

Even the condescendingly critical Frances Trollope found Memphis a picturesque little town, occupying "the most beautiful point on the Mississippi." Her 1828 account also points to a growth in the number of tradesmen and artisans, noting that between 50 and 100 "shopkeepers" of the town wolfed down their daily meals at her hotel. In 1831 Mrs. Trollope's fellow Briton, Captain J.E. Alexander, proclaimed himself—

> . . . much pleased with the site and appearance of Memphis. . . . The town now
> contains about a thousand inhabitants. The framehouses had a clean look about
> them; and the hotel where I put up was a respectable establishment [and] the
> charges were extremely reasonable.

Such differences in perceptions of Memphis may have been largely in the eyes of respective beholders, dependent on the season, or influenced by the depth of mud in the streets. But doubtless the town was improving too, and organization helped.

When Raleigh preempted the county seat in 1826-27, the state legislature issued a charter of incorporation for Memphis. James Davis depicted this move as a power play sprung by the proprietors on the unsuspecting residents. Actually the bill was introduced by a petition from Memphis citizens. The proprietors were the ones surprised, for they would assume a tax burden on their property yet unsold while the residents would reap benefits from municipal services financed by local taxation.

Another part of the Davis story of this time that calls for further investigation is his

Metropolis of the American Nile

Above
During his trip down the Mississippi River, Charles-Alexandre Lesueur took advantage of the opportunity to draw a number of Choctaw Indians in their native costumes. The drawing reproduced here, like most of the Lesueur Indian sketches, was made at Memphis. This is rather curious since the Choctaws lived much further south. From the Museum d'Histoire Naturelle, Le Havre, France

Right
Although the legendary Davy Crockett did not live in Memphis, he was the congressional representative for the Western District of Tennessee, including Shelby County. Crockett campaigned and visited in the area, and left through Memphis on his way west to Texas. There are numerous stories about the man in local lore, including several in James D. Davis' *History of the City of Memphis*. His picture here exemplifies the essentially Western nature of the Memphis area in its early years. Courtesy, Shelby County Public Affairs Office

contention that the first two mayors, Marcus B. Winchester and Isaac Rawlings, were bitter personal, political, and business rivals. Davis paints Rawlings as a rough-cut, shrewd old curmudgeon of the cracker-barrel philosopher type, of a poor family background, and nearly illiterate. Davis' Winchester, by contrast, emerges as a polished and dashing young aristocrat. While both men were merchants and leaders in local civic, political, and economic affairs, there is no evidence outside of Davis that any of the rest of this scenario is true. As for the crude old curmudgeon versus the educated young fop, there was only eight years' difference in their ages. Rawlings was quite literate and from a good family background. His abilities as factor, or merchant, at various government-operated trading posts had been highly valued. As for Winchester's being a suave gentleman, his family background was hardly as exalted as Davis implies. His father was a frontier surveyor and military leader who married his mother only after the birth of their fifth child. Marcus' upbringing was in bucolic surroundings, which limited his formal education.

Davis' claim of an antagonistic relationship is also suspect. These two early leaders could hardly have been intense rivals for the *vox populi,* since the first mayors were not popularly elected. They were chosen by the city's aldermen from within their own ranks. Moreover, Winchester and Rawlings worked together on many enterprises. Besides serving on the city council together, they were co-directors of incorporated business enterprises. Such association hardly supports Davis' contention that they cordially detested each other. Yet uncritical acceptance of Davisian mythology persists. Even Gerald Capers in his seminal *Biography of a River Town* (1939) writes that Rawlings' enmity to Winchester was "the foremost obstacle to the progress of the town."

Winchester served as mayor for the first two years of the town's corporate existence. Rechartering in 1829 gave Memphis the status of a city, and the new charter, reflecting that of Nashville, prohibited federal employees from serving as mayor. Forced to choose between his two offices, mayor and postmaster, Winchester chose to retain the latter which, unlike the mayoralty, was compensated. Rawlings then served as mayor for five of the next seven annual terms, while Winchester served as alderman during two of those terms.

Although the charter of 1829 made Memphis legally a city, it was scarcely that in fact.

Metropolis of the American Nile

Its appearance was much like that of the raw western towns of a later era. Memphis in the early 1830s was still surrounded by wilderness teeming with game and marauders, and the town itself was rife with gamblers and swindlers. Indians often came up from the Chickasaw Nation to trade. Investing some of their pelts in whiskey, they would drink outside the stores and give out fierce-sounding yells, which frightened loitering children and sent them scurrying for home. The cowboy role was adopted by the flatboatmen. These freshwater teamsters, like other drovers and sailors, really let themselves go when they hit town. "Lickered up," they were more fierce and more feared than the Indians. Their lawlessness was legendary.

As in the later western towns, this lawless element was the economic lifeblood of Memphis. Conversely, dependent on the river for commerce, transportation, and communication, Memphis was an integral part of the greater river community. Unlike the more seaboard-oriented older sections of the state, Memphis was part of a newer West, with a closer economic and cultural affinity for New Orleans, New Madrid, and Natchez than for Nashville and Knoxville. In fact Memphis often resented the artificially drawn boundaries that made West Tennessee the abused stepchild of the other two divisions of the state. Such feelings were so strong that until 1841 there was a genuine separatist movement. Spearheaded by Memphis, the movement sought to create a new state out of the Jackson Purchase areas of Tennessee and Kentucky and the newly opened Chickasaw lands of northern Mississippi. Support for the idea was serious enough to get a measure introduced and voted on in the Tennessee legislature. The resolution failed mainly because of partisan politics and would likely have been rejected by Kentucky and Mississippi anyhow. Although the separate-state movement never had more than the proverbial "snowball's chance," it is significant nonetheless, clearly demonstrating the weakness of Memphis' attachment to the older areas of Tennessee and emphasizing the city's westward-facing, river-subculture orientation.

As long as Randolph remained a viable commercial rival, Memphis could not afford to lose the flatboatmen's trade. Despite their crude behavior, their bullying and brawling antics, and their refusal to pay wharfage fees, the boatmen played a vital role in the town's

economy. But by about 1840, with the dramatic increases in steamboat traffic and the decline of Randolph, economic motives for kowtowing to the boatmen had diminished considerably. By now their lawlessness was probably damaging the town as much as their trade was helping it, and the time had come when they had to be tamed. It was a rite of passage that Memphis would have to face before coming of age.

In 1841 Mayor William Spickernagle, the city's first salaried chief executive, put the town on a more businesslike basis. Offering a 25-percent commission on fees collected, he hired a wharfmaster who would stand up to the boatmen. Simultaneously the city formed two volunteer militia companies that offered their services to help enforce local laws. Faced with this united front, the unorganized boatmen gave way.

The following spring a flatboat bully named Trester determined to reimpose the old order. If this cock-of-the-walk succeeded in defying the town, his fellows would also resist paying the wharfage charge. In the ensuing confrontation a few citizens were injured and Trester was killed, but a combination of the militia and armed citizens cowed the 2,000

boatmen into submission.

Most historians date this 1842 "Flatboatmen's War" as *the* turning point for the town. Of it Capers says:

> Here the flatboat days end. Like the vigilantes of a later day in the Far West, by this spontaneous and unanimous action citizens announced to the valley that the reign of law had come to Memphis. The conquest of the flatboatmen is significant because it indicated a new attitude and the beginning of a new era. . . . To achieve it [Memphians] had been willing to risk their economic security and even their lives.

Of course flatboats continued to come to Memphis for many years and were still relatively important in the economy, but the boatmen never again ran roughshod over the town. Other rudiments of civilization appeared at about the same time, and these may have helped the citizens find the courage to unite and throw off the tyranny of the boatmen.

Beginning in 1832 a number of churches sprang up, and a short time later private schooling was available. A permanent newspaper, the *Appeal,* began publication in 1840. A volunteer fire department had been functioning for a decade, with primitive but effective hand pumps that pulled water from public cisterns. The Farmers and Merchants Bank, nearly a decade old, had survived the crisis of 1837 and now competed with two newer banking houses. The city also boasted a marine insurance company. The La Grange and Memphis Railroad, with six miles of its track laid eastward, was bringing the beginnings of the rail age to the town. A board of health had been formed to fight disease, and two regular night-watch policemen patrolled the streets. A local thespian society brought drama to the citizens, and construction had begun on the Bluff community's first luxury-class hotel. A growing complex of economic and social institutions was subtly changing the character of life on the Bluff. Memphis was indeed becoming the *city* that she had long aimed—and now claimed—to be.

Chapter Two: Triumph of Location: 1819-1842

CHAPTER THREE

THE BOOM ERA: 1843~1860

If Memphis made laggardly progress over the first two decades of its existence, the city seemed determined to make up for lost time during its second score of years. The advantages of location manifested themselves at last, and the city grew with bewildering speed. Changes in technology and federal government policies redounded to Memphis' favor as river traffic and freight multiplied, the iron horse conquered overland spaces, and the national government built a shipyard on the city's doorstep. Population growth and construction were phenomenal, with significant numbers of immigrants lending their numbers, their energies, and their experience to creating the boom.

Behind the silver lining, however, lay very dark clouds. Memphis' enthusiasm for the Mexican War rested in large measure upon its citizens' support for the extension of slavery into Texas. The plight of local blacks worsened detectably as the domestic slave trade became a thriving local enterprise and municipal legislation continued to curtail the activities of black Memphians. Unthinkable as secession was during this era, it and a brutal conflict lay just beyond the horizon. Bustling Memphis rushed through the decades of the 1840s and '50s in blissful ignorance of what lay in store.

Steamboat Decades

Although the Mississippi River's steamboat era technically began with the descent of the *New Orleans* in 1811, steamboats did not become the dominant form of river transport until some years thereafter. The *New Orleans* drew far too much water for the western rivers and could make only about three miles per hour against the current. In addition, steamboats were extremely expensive to build, and the ever-present dangers of running permanently aground or ripping open the hull on a submerged tree made early steamboating hazardous both physically and financially. But engineering skill would ameliorate these drawbacks and dangers, and then the steamboat would do more for Memphis than the flatboat had ever done.

Henry Miller Shreve, almost unknown in modern Memphis, deserves the lion's share of credit for solving the major problems of early steamboat navigation. Recognizing and solv-

Facing page
Among the immigrant families who settled in Memphis in the mid-19th century, the German Jews were particularly notable for their contributions to the business and commerce of the city, especially in the dry-goods and clothing businesses. Many of their enterprises carried over into the 20th century as the city's major department stores. B. Lowenstein and Brothers is an example of this tradition. Founded in the 1860s, the store grew until the mid-20th-century when it was bought by a national chain. Only in 1981 did the venerable institution close its doors. Memphis/Shelby County Room (M/SCPLIC)

Chapter Three: The Boom Era: 1843-1860

Henry Lewis' depiction of the Memphis waterfront in the late 1840s shows both the serene beauty of the city and commerce on the river. From the Memphis/Shelby County Room (M/SCPLIC)

ing the problems of the *New Orleans* and other early steamcraft, Shreve designed and built shallow-draft boats with more powerful engines above decks. Challenged in the courts by New York's powerful Livingston family, Shreve took until 1819 to clear his design of legal entanglements so as to begin to run his steamboats unhindered on western waters.

In 1819—coincidentally the year of Memphis' founding and Shreve's settling his legal problems—the United States Congress saw the need to aid in keeping river channels cleared of snags. Authorizing the Army Corps of Engineers to make a study of the Mississippi and its tributaries, Congress made a modest appropriation to meet the study's expenses. Five years later Congress enacted a River and Harbor Act permitting the President to spend $75,000 for removal of trees in the Ohio and Mississippi navigation channels. The Corps of Engineers had responsibility for the work, but it did not have the technology to get the job done. Once more Captain Shreve provided the answer.

Shreve designed a shallow-draft, double-hulled snag boat, the *Heliopolis*, that straddled tree trunks and, using an A-frame winch-pulley system, raised the snag so it could be sawed into harmless bits and discarded. Shreve's boat was a fantastic success. Its most dramatic achievement was the clearing of a 160-mile logjam on the Red River in Louisiana, in return for which the grateful residents named the town of Shreveport after him. In 1824 Shreve made his design available to the United States government and supervised construction of its snag boats. As a result of Shreve's genius, the Army Corps of Engineers "opened western waters as never before, establishing river highways into the interior." Only then did the romantic steamboat era truly begin, bringing with it an economic floodtide of river commerce.

Memphis, of course, benefited greatly from these developments. By the mid-1840s there was more traffic on western waters, albeit with smaller cargos, than on the Atlantic Coast and the Great Lakes combined. By 1852 Memphis had clearly emerged as the third most important port on the Mississippi, bowing only to St. Louis and New Orleans in volume of commerce. With the great growth of commerce came additional economic opportunities and a corresponding growth in the Bluff City's population.

Metropolis of the American Nile

Ironically, at the same time that water-transport technology was dealing generously with the Mississippi Valley with one hand, it was taking away with the other. New York Governor De Witt Clinton's grand "ditch," the Erie Canal, reached completion in 1825. During its first decade this man-made waterway was used mainly by upstate New Yorkers, but after 1835 it was enlarged and began to handle the great bulk of northwestern freight by connecting the Great Lakes with the Atlantic. By the 1850s the New York route was diverting an ever-increasing portion of the interior's import-export trade from the Mississippi Valley and its port cities. Memphians, delighted with their city's growth and dazzled by the ever-growing number of docking steamboats, took scant notice of these developments.

Westerners were very much aware of the benefits of federal snagging operations, as well as the extent of federal expenditures on harbor improvements for the coastal cities. This awareness manifested itself in a plethora of commercial "River Conventions," several of which were held in Memphis. These meetings drummed up support and issued demands for greater federal participation in navigation projects, such as snagging and dredging operations, and in flood control. Perhaps the most notable of these was the 1845 Memphis convention at which John C. Calhoun presided. Calhoun—in an apparently sophistic inconsistency, since he had traditionally opposed federal internal improvements—christened the Mississippi River system the "great inland sea" and demanded that it be given as much federal attention as coastal waterways.

Such conventions, however, had only marginal political effect. Except for snag removal and the Swamp Lands Act (1850), which aided state levee construction and maintenance, the federal government did little until after the Civil War. Only in the postwar era would the Army Corps of Engineers at last undertake a mighty, ongoing, and eventually successful effort to "tame the giant."

Even with such improvements to navigation as were made, steamboat journeys remained extremely dangerous. Perhaps the very danger and uncertainty of traveling on the river contributed to its drama and romance. Glamorous steamboats with colorful names, dashing pilots such as Mark Twain, legendary gamblers like George Devol and heroic cap-

Chapter Three: The Boom Era: 1843-1860

Steamboats were so profitable in the mid-19th century that one could pay for itself in a very short time. Despite the storied romance of the era, the boats were "fancy firetraps" that killed or injured more than 4,000 persons prior to 1850. A boat could be ripped open and sink, could explode, or might simply run hard aground and have to be abandoned. More were built to replace those lost, however, and steamboats transformed the commerce of the port of Memphis, making it the leading city of the mid-Mississippi Valley. Courtesy, Memphis District of the Army Corps of Engineers

tains like C.B. Church, visions of mysterious beauties taking meals in their cabins, all laid claim to the popular imagination. In reality the steamboats were "fancy firetraps" that killed or injured more than 4,000 persons before 1850, but each one projected a distinct personality and commanded a loyal cadre of voyagers and shippers.

Although the passengers and ships' companies provided the personalities that gave the steamboats their storied romance, it was freight that provided the high profits and created the multiplication of steamcraft on western waters. Despite a high disaster rate, steamboats were profitable. One could pay for itself in less than six months, and shipowners were willing to risk losses to garner such profits.

These profit-making time bombs transformed the commerce of the port of Memphis. Cotton, brought in first by ox team and later by train, was *the* export. Products entering Memphis by steamboat included apples, potatoes, cider, cheese, bacon, pork, cabbages, and peach brandy, as well as manufactured goods. Increasingly, grain products were also imported as local farmers and planters turned more of their acreage to cotton. Early in the period Memphis was served mainly by independent steamboats, but increasingly the city became a scheduled stop for the bigger packet lines.

Metropolis of the American Nile

The Memphis Navy Yard

With such a high rate of profit, combined with plenty of hardwood and an ideal location, one might well expect Memphis to have been in the forefront of the early steamboat-building industry. Yet few boats, even small ones, were built in West Tennessee. Memphis entrepreneurs shied away from this enterprise, and the only local shipyard of note was the federal navy yard of the 1840s.

The Memphis Navy Yard was the brainchild of Lieutenant Matthew Fontain Maury, a distinguished United States and later Confederate naval officer and a naval scientist of deservedly worldwide repute. In the context of its inception, building a naval depot and dock almost 1,000 miles inland by river was not nearly as idiotic as it seems. Maury argued persuasively that in view of threatening wars with Great Britain and Mexico, where the theater of action was likely to be in the Gulf of Mexico, a facility on the Mississippi River for oceangoing warships had numerous advantages. It would not be as far from the probable fighting as New York or Boston; it would be much safer from seaborne attack; the river below Memphis was navigable year round; supplies would be readily at hand in the

Mississippi Valley; and the Memphis location would make for fairer distribution from the Congressional pork barrel. After a Navy Department study of the project's feasibility, Congress adopted the program and purchased the waterfront riverbank between Auction and Market streets in 1844.

Memphians were jubilant and waxed eloquent over the prospects of the yard, as well as the federal arsenal for which they were also lobbying. The arsenal never materialized, and the navy yard had severe problems from its beginning. Even as the buildings and facilities were being constructed, between 1844 and 1846, military and civilian personnel could not get along. Constant bickering, misunderstandings, and low morale made for costly errors. During its 10-year life span, the Memphis Navy Yard outfitted only one ship, the *Allegheny*. The ship had only limited success in the long run, but it was never the laughingstock portrayed by James Davis.

The *Allegheny*, the nation's second iron warship, was an experimental vessel of radical and uncertain design. The hull was constructed in Pittsburgh, then towed down two rivers to Memphis for outfitting. The ship made its trial run on the river on May 17, 1847. In sharp contrast to Davis' derogatory account of this test, the *Daily Enquirer* waxed positively pur-

Probably the foremost proponent of a federal navy yard at Memphis was Lieutenant Matthew Fontaine Maury. Although the navy yard did not work out, this was neither the fault of Maury's planning nor of any fault in the Memphis location. Maury had a distinguished career in both the Union and Confederate navies and was an oceanographer of deservedly worldwide repute. From Cirker, *Dictionary of American Portraits*

ple in praise of the ship's abilities. Other knowledgeable, if less hyperbolical, observers also considered the tests successful.

Two weeks later the *Allegheny* weighed anchor for New Orleans, Key West, and Norfolk. After alteration to its paddles to increase the ship's efficiency, the *Allegheny* served in the Brazil and Mediterranean squadrons during 1848 and 1849. This tour is omitted by Davis, who claims the ship was a failure upon first reaching Norfolk.

The ship did return to Norfolk in 1849, when a naval board determined that its propulsion design was too inefficient for use and ordered the ship's boilers, engines, and internal paddle wheels replaced. After two years' work the ship's machinery was in worse shape than ever, and the *Allegheny* failed its trial run. After a second full investigation a traditionalist naval board determined that the ship was a poor design badly executed, and rather than waste any more money on it, the Navy Department decided to make the *Allegheny* a receiving ship. It served in this capacity in Baltimore harbor until 1869.

The *Allegheny*'s failure represented a waste of $500,000, a prodigious sum at the time. Even though the failure was not the fault of the Memphis Navy Yard, and the continuing problems at the yard were not the fault of its location or the Memphis community, the taint remained. The yard received decreasing federal appropriations until 1855, when the government at last abandoned it and returned the property to the city. More than $1.5 million had been spent, but Memphis was not destined to be a federal dockyard or an arsenal.

During the Civil War the Confederates made a tardy beginning at building ships at Memphis. One of these actually threatened the Union Navy's superiority in the lower Mississippi. Had the Memphis Navy Yard been a going concern at the outbreak of hostilities, it might well have altered the whole course of the war.

In another ironic footnote to history, during World War II a local iron company built 192 warships the size of the *Allegheny* at Memphis. Perhaps Maury's ideas were not wrong after all, but simply 100 years ahead of their time.

The Mexican War

The anticipated war with England never materialized; the anticipated war with Mexico did. At issue lay the long-postponed U.S. annexation of the former Mexican province of Texas. There could be little doubt where Shelby Countians stood on this issue. The affinity between Tennesseans and Texans began with the founding of Austin's colony and continues to the present.

Tennesseans were numerous among the early immigrants to Texas. Sam Houston, a former governor of Tennessee, made his way west through Memphis before he led Texans in their war for independence. Others such as Davy Crockett, a former Congressional representative from Shelby County and West Tennessee, jumped off to join the Texas war from Memphis. Some of these, again like Crockett, found martyrdom at the Alamo or at Goliad.

Mexico, beset by severe internal problems and never able to launch a serious attempt to reconquer Texas, refused to recognize the new country's independence. The United States, sorely divided over the issue of western extension of slavery, was long unable to accommodate Texas with annexation. During the late 1830s and early 1840s an armed truce existed. Each spring rumors of a major Mexican invasion of Texas reached Memphis. Usually the rumors proved false, but in 1842 the Mexicans actually launched an invasion.

When the "war" news from New Orleans received confirmation, Memphians reacted in the "volunteer" tradition. They rallied to a mass meeting, then armed and equipped the 80-member Wolf Hunter Company. This group set out immediately for Galveston to help defend Texas.

The Mexican invasion was genuine but much overrated, and the Memphis company saw little action. Having endured privations caused by bungling on the part of Texas officials, with little prospect of actual fighting, about three-fourths of the Memphians went home in disgust. The remaining one-fourth did take part in the indecisive battle of Lipantitlan, but were mustered out soon thereafter. These men also returned home disgusted with their treatment at the hands of the Texans.

Despite the experience of the Wolf Hunter Volunteers, when the real war with Mexico came in 1846, Memphis quickly raised six militia companies. Anxiously awaiting the call to arms, these militiamen were angry and embarrassed as they watched other soldiers pass through their city while Governor Neill S. Brown delayed in getting Tennessee's units mobilized. Finally three of the Memphis companies were called up and sent to fight in Mexico. Other Memphians and Shelby Countians served in the regular army, the state militia, and other volunteer units.

Probably the most notable Memphian in service was General Gideon J. Pillow. Because of his close personal and political relationship with President Polk, Pillow was given command of Tennessee's volunteers. Under Pillow's questionable leadership at the major battle of Cerro Gordo, many of the Memphis volunteers were killed or wounded, perhaps needlessly. American forces went on to capture Mexico City and win the war, but Pillow had soured the victory for fighting Memphians.

Virtually all surviving Memphis officers blamed General Pillow for the debacle at Cerro Gordo, and upon their return to Memphis they demanded his immediate court-martial. A court-martial was held in which Pillow was cleared of all charges, but his reputation severely damaged recruiting efforts in West Tennessee for the rest of the war.

Major General Edmund Pendleton Gaines, commander of the U.S. Western Army, was a prime mover in making Memphis an early railroad center. He desired good interior roads and railroads for troop mobility and pushed unceasingly for their construction. He made detailed plans for three railroads to converge on Memphis and helped promote their construction among entrepreneurs in the private sector. One of these railroads became the Memphis and Charleston, which he had ordered surveyed by Stephen H. Long. From Cirker, *Dictionary of American Portraits*

Memphis' first major train station was built in 1857 for the Memphis and Charleston Railroad. In this photograph a dozen horse-drawn hackney cabs and private carriages are waiting for the arrival of a train. The long vehicle at the right belonged to Patterson Transfer Company, which performed shuttle service from one depot to another. From the Memphis/Shelby County Room (M/SCPLIC)

For most Memphians the Mexican War was more of a patriotic frenzy than a real war. They carried flags, cheered recruitment and departures, staged parades, delivered and listened to speeches, raised funds for celebrations, and attended barbecues and banquets. They also nursed returning sick and wounded and buried those who died, but the reality of it all was largely missed as the carnival atmosphere prevailed on the home front.

The Mexican War added vast territories to the country and greatly increased the sectional controversies over the slave question. Northerners saw the war as an imperialist plot by the "slave power" to extend slavery farther west—something they were determined to stop at all costs. Southerners saw Northern attitudes as inimical to their constitutional rights. If they could not secure these rights within the Union, they would withdraw. Thus the spoils of the Mexican War hardened attitudes and set them on a collision course. The war resulting from this ideological confrontation would pale the genuine horrors of the Mexican War into insignificance.

Beginnings of the Railroad Age

Although the United States had been woefully unprepared for the Mexican War, which had been a decade in coming and should have surprised no one, the issue of military preparedness was to become a paramount factor in making Memphis a major railroad center.

Major General Edmund Pendleton Gaines, commanding general of the U.S. Western Army, was an ardent advocate of federal internal improvements to facilitate troop mobility. He surveyed the Natchez Trace, moved Western Army headquarters to Memphis, and gave unstinting support to the push for the Memphis Navy Yard and a federal arsenal in Memphis. Gaines was probably the most important single factor in bringing railroading to Memphis.

An excellent military strategist, Gaines saw the ability to move troops quickly and effectively as absolutely vital to national defense. He first promoted military roads; after trains had proved themselves, he promoted railroads. By 1838 Gaines had detailed plans for five interior western railroads, three of them converging on Memphis, and he pushed unceasingly for their construction. Under his command Stephen H. Long surveyed the route that was to become the Memphis and Charleston roadbed.

Metropolis of the American Nile

General Gaines was hardly alone in his advocacy of railroads for Memphis. Joining him in promotion, and also active in speculation, investment, and management, was a unique group of citizens who together formed a marvelous pool of entrepreneurial talent. Headliners of this group included Robertson Topp, ex-Governor James C. Jones, Robert C. Brinkley, Colonel Sam Tate, Colonel John T. Trezevant, and W.B. Greenlaw. These men invested heavily of their own fortunes in local railroads, and most of them also invested their energies and talents in raising millions of dollars and managing construction.

The Memphis and Charleston became the first and most successful of the Memphis railroads. Chartered in 1846 following the Memphis River Convention, the railroad raised money and was constructed with dispatch under the aggressive presidency of James C. Jones. Completion of the railroad in 1857 was the occasion of wild celebration among Memphians, who had risked more than $500,000 in the venture. The celebration, which lasted several days, included a symbolic "marriage of the waters," with Memphis Mayor A.H. Douglas pumping Charleston seawater into the Mississippi. Such ceremonies were hardly excessive, for the rails symbolized a new age of prosperity for Memphis. According to leading local historian Paul Coppock, "Hardly anything in Memphis history can be compared with this railroad in building up the city and its business."

Nearly as important and profitable for Memphis as the M & C was the Memphis and Ohio, connecting the Mid-South with Louisville and the Northeast. Started somewhat later, under the direction of Colonel Trezevant, this road became profitable long before its completion in April of 1861, the same month that the Civil War erupted. A third line, the Little Rock and Memphis, began construction later than the other two and encountered severe engineering problems in the lowlands of eastern Arkansas. With construction interrupted by the war, this line was not completed until the 1870s.

With the acquisition of California and Oregon in the 1840s, most thinking Americans realized that rail and telegraph lines would be essential in tying the sprawling young country together. Each of the Mississippi Valley cities, from Chicago to New Orleans, entered the competition to become the eastern terminus of the anticipated transcontinental railway from the West.

Among the cities pushing their claims, Memphis enjoyed a number of real advantages to commend its selection. In the early 1850s it was the fastest growing city in the nation. A southern route from Memphis through Arkansas and Texas would avoid snow and ice in winter and would pass south of the obstacle of the Rockies. The 1853 Gadsden Purchase of a patch of territory from Mexico suggests that these were indeed serious considerations. In 1858 Memphis was already the eastern terminus for the Butterfield overland mail route to California. Through its existing and in-progress rail lines, Memphis could connect the transcontinental to the Midwest, the Northeast, the Atlantic Coast, and the Gulf.

In spite of all these advantages, it is doubtful whether Memphis ever had the political and financial clout to get the plum. Sectional agitation delayed selection of a route until after the Civil War began, and then the choice fell on Omaha. Although Memphis achieved transcontinental linkups in the decades after the war, it lost the advantage and prestige of being first. Nonetheless, the more than $1 million that Memphis invested in railroads greatly aided the city's growth and guaranteed its position as "queen city" of the Mid-South.

Growth and Ethnic Diversity

During the 1850s Memphis grew at a faster rate than any other city in the nation. From fewer than 1,800 people in 1840, it exploded to more than 22,000 in 1858.

One reason for the rapid growth of Memphis during this era was the annexation of its neighbors on the Bluff. Settlement on the Bluff to the south had begun in an unorganized way before the city's founding. In 1840 streets were laid out, and development became more orderly. By 1846 this community was about as populous as Memphis, and it incorporated under a separate charter, taking the name South Memphis. South of the new city lay an unincorporated area that went by the old name of Fort Pickering.

Only three years after the incorporation of South Memphis, the citizens of the two cities staged a mass meeting and agreed to merge under the name Memphis. Some of the original support for incorporation of the southern city, in fact, may have been aimed at forcing the issue of merger, which became official on January 1, 1850. A portion of the Fort Pickering area was excluded from the newly combined city. It incorporated in 1861 under the name Chickasaw City, but after the war it too was annexed by Memphis.

Right
Much of the atmosphere of Memphis was still that of a raw western town in the 1850s. This view of Front Street looking north from Jefferson depicts a scene that could provide a set for a western movie. The Commercial Hotel (right) housed the offices of the Butterfield Overland Stage lines in the 1850s. From the Memphis/Shelby County Room (M/SCPLIC)

Far right
The Ramsey grant immediately south of the Rice grant was the site of the separate town of South Memphis and several other settlements. As the document shows, the proprietors of Memphis were significant owners in the southerly bluff tract as well. Overton, McLemore, and the Winchester heirs owned most of the northern portions. In 1849 when the two cities agreed to merge under the name of Memphis a considerable boost resulted in the community's population figures. From the Memphis/Shelby County Room (M/SCPLIC)

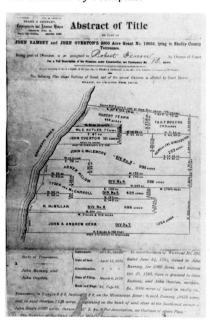

Metropolis of the American Nile

THE GAYOSO HOUSE

One of Memphis' most daring acts of entrepreneurship was the building of the Gayoso House. Barely 20 years old at the time, the city had no buildings of any size or architectural significance, and neither the population nor the wealth to finance such an undertaking.

But a wealthy young aristocratic planter named Robertson Topp had visions of how Memphis would achieve greatness. One was to get a railroad, and Topp was at the center of that undertaking. Another was to create a new development known as South Memphis, a group of finely constructed houses, commercial buildings, warehouses, and a hotel.

The centerpiece of this development was to be the Gayoso House, and Topp commissioned James Dakin, one of the 12 founders of the American Institution of Architects in 1837, to create the design and the plans. Among Dakin's other notable buildings were the New Orleans Custom House, the Bank of Louisville, and the original campus of New York University.

The hotel was built in 1842 at the then-extravagant cost of $144,000. Topp's group of investors —George McCall, William Vance, and others— have been memorialized in the street names around the hotel. Topp's own name, unfortunately, has been forgotten.

In 1858 Topp decided to double the hotel's size, adding 100 rooms to its original 150. Once again he chose a top architect, Isaiah Rogers, designer of America's first modern hotel, the Tremont House in Boston, in 1829, and a host of other hotels including the Burnet House in Cincinnati and the Maxwell House in Nashville.

Rogers, another AIA founder, had moved his architectural practice to Cincinnati while working on the Burnet House, and there he had attracted several bright young men to work for him. The brightest, a young British-born engineer named James B. Cook, handled all the details for the new and complicated systems of plumbing and heating that were essential to the Rogers hotels. Sent to Memphis to supervise work on the Gayoso House, Cook remained and went on to design many of the city's greatest buildings.

The hotel had its own waterworks, gasworks for gaslighting, bakeries, wine cellar, sewer and drain system, and of course indoor plumbing. In an era when nearly all Memphians still had privies and washtubs, the Gayoso House had hot showers, marble tubs with silver faucets, and flush toilets. It was sheer luxury and a must stop for travelers coming through Memphis by steamboat, train, or stagecoach. It did considerable business as a "convention hotel" as well, hosting the Commercial Convention of 1845 at which John C. Calhoun urged the importance of developing America's inland waterway system.

After the Civil War the hotel underwent a series of temporary closings, changes of management, and renovations. The biggest renovation was in 1883, financed by a private bond issue of $60,000. Among the improvements was a remarkably modern-looking second-floor galleria, "225 feet long and 15 feet wide, affording a magnificent promenade, commanding a view of the various parlors, elevators, stairways, lobby, and intersecting halls."

On the night of July 4, 1899, the great Gayoso House burned to the ground.

— David Bowman

Gayoso Hotel stock coupons. Courtesy, West Tennessee Historical Society

Contrary to popular mythology, there is no real evidence that Memphis and South Memphis citizens maintained a bitter mutual animosity. The oft-cited "Pinch-Sodom" quarrel in fact had nothing to do with South Memphis. The north end of the city was called Pinch because of the pinch-gut appearance of its paupers living near Catfish Bay on the Wolf River. The reason why the Pinchites called the area of southern Memphis, between Winchester and Union, Sodom is both more obscure and intriguing. Presumably they thought its citizens pretentious and pleasure-seeking. Whatever the reason, it was the southern part of the original city, and not the separate town of South Memphis, that was so denigrated.

Though parochial rivalries existed, some of which persist to this day, there was never any serious doubt that with continued growth the Bluff settlements would one day abut each other and merge. When this happened in 1849-50, Memphis grew territorially from one-half a square mile to three square miles and doubled in population. Again contrary to popular myth, Union Avenue was not named for the union of the two towns. Coincidentally it. was the dividing line on the southern boundary of Memphis, but the name Union appears on Overton's original city plans, thus antedating the merger by some 31 years.

Very little is known about South Memphis and Fort Pickering prior to the 1849-50 annexation. Serious development was begun by John C. McLemore and taken over by Robertson Topp. Under Topp's guidance the town sprouted a high-fashion residential neighborhood with mansions along Beale, Vance, and Linden streets. Perhaps those with means were attracted to South Memphis to avoid Memphis city taxes and to put some distance between themselves and the Pinch slum area.

Topp also built the deluxe Gayoso House hotel in South Memphis. After it opened in 1846 it enjoyed the cities' carriage trade, hosting men of the stature of Sam Houston, Zachary Taylor, James K. Polk, and Andrew Johnson. Although never much of a commercial success, the first Gayoso remained a landmark of the united cities for many years.

South Memphis enjoyed only three years of independent legal existence, and whatever corporate records were maintained have been long since lost. We do know that the city's three mayors were Sylvester Bailey, John T. Trezevant, and A.B. Taylor, all men of prominence, energy, honesty, and ability. Taylor also served as mayor of the newly united Memphis in 1851, 1853, and 1854.

The merger of the two towns, besides doubling the city's population and sextupling its geographic area, ended any possible doubts of the Bluff community's ultimate unity. Memphis population figures for 1830 and 1840 thus do not accurately reflect the growth of the Bluff community as a whole, but after the 1850 episode Memphis strove to annex its suburbs and show maximum growth on the census rolls.

Apart from the "artificial" boost given population figures by the merger, Memphis was indeed growing rapidly during this period. Increased economic opportunities, created by improvements in transportation, brought a vast influx of people. Although most of the newcomers were Anglo-Southerners, a very significant portion came from outside the United States. These immigrants, largely Irish and German, contributed notably to both population and economic growth. At the same time, their ethnic diversity gave the city a more cosmopolitan flair and made it a culturally richer place to live.

The Irish were the first immigrant group to come in large numbers. Although there had been Irishmen such as Paddy Meagher at the Bluff since before the city's founding, the major influx began after 1840. Leaving their homeland because of periodic famine and political and religious oppression, most Irishmen arriving in Memphis were displaced small farmers, largely unskilled and often unlettered. The bulk of these people competed with blacks in the manual labor market, and like the blacks, they made significant economic contributions.

Metropolis of the American Nile

They worked on the steamboats and the docks, handling the goods that built the area's economy. They made up the crews that constructed roadbeds and laid tracks, bringing the railroad age to the Southwest. They built the levees that protected crops and lives from inundation. They put up the buildings and cut the streets of Memphis. By performing these back-breaking tasks, they helped change the economic fabric of the new country. Clustered in the Pinch area and victims of prejudice, the Irish poor occupied a social slot somewhere between the blacks and the Anglo-Southerners.

While the bulk of the Irish may have been undereducated, they were by no means stupid. They filled jobs in the local fire and police departments and were politically astute. United, they had a political impact vastly disproportionate to their numbers. Regrettably, their effectiveness probably contributed to creating the "machinism" that would plague city politics for the next 100 years.

Among the early Irish success stories were those of the Magevney brothers and Henry A. Montgomery. Eugene Magevney began as one of Memphis' earliest private school teachers, then made a fortune in real-estate speculation and development. As a civic and community leader, he served on the board of aldermen and was the driving force in establishing the city's free public school system. As a leader in his religious community, he helped

to found the city's first Catholic school. His brother Michael, also successful in real estate, created the Hibernian Mutual Relief Society in 1848. Henry Montgomery's prewar contributions lay mainly in the field of telegraphic communications. His companies connected Memphis with the North, South, and West. When the war cost him his telegraph holdings, Montgomery built a second successful career in the cotton business.

Never as numerous locally as the Irish, and coming in slightly later, German immigrants also made numerous contributions to the community. Like the Irish, the Germans fled their homeland because of famine and political oppression. If one includes the German Jews among them, then religious persecution can be added to the list of motives.

Coming to Memphis largely after the failed liberal Revolution of 1848, the Germans gave a new economic dimension to the community. Thrifty and industrious German Protestants, Catholics, and Jews did not share the typical Southern anti-urban, anti-tradesman, and anti-industry attitudes that crippled many aspects of economic development. In the 1850s the Germans, and some Jews who were not German, became vitally involved in the business and commerce of the city. Their multitudinous business activities included cotton brokerages, wholesale and retail groceries, bakeries, commission sales, dry-goods, crockery and glassware, and jewelry. German Jews were especially successful in the dry-goods and

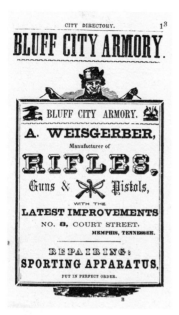

clothing business. In the 1850s and 1860s they owned more than half the clothier firms in town, and their successes in this area carried many of their names into the 20th century as major department stores. Pre-Civil War immigrants also achieved success in the hotel and restaurant business.

The Germans, even more than the Irish, kept their special cultural traditions. Although they lived in various parts of the city, they maintained their own clubs, newspapers, and religious congregations. Despite this clannishness, the immigrants were also community-minded. They actively participated in the political process and formed militia companies which volunteered to serve in the Mexican War. When the state failed to call up these local contingents, many of their members served in other units.

The Germans are credited with being Memphis' leading patrons of the arts, especially music. They furnished musicians, teachers, and the appreciation to support them. Their *Mai Feste* continued until 1909, and its spirit has been resurrected in the current "Memphis in May" and *Oktoberfest* festivals.

The German population of Memphis was especially active in the creation of small industries. These local industries were tied primarily to lumber products, cotton production, and the local construction industry. Although the Mid-South trade area could have sup-

ported them, major industries such as textile mills were never seriously attempted. A plan to run a canal from the Wolf River through Memphis to furnish waterpower for mills was never acted on. Instead, pre-Civil War industries were limited to low-capital, small-scale enterprises such as boot making, hat making, and cabinetry.

One reason for the region's failure to diversify economically—although the *Appeal* began calling for such efforts as early as 1846—was its fanatical addiction to cotton culture and the plantation ideal. Not only did cotton production distort the Southern economy, it also remained *the* predominant item in American commerce until the eve of the Civil War. What local capital was not tied up in slaves, cotton, railroad building, and riverboats went mainly into the construction boom of a town bursting at its seams.

Memphis business leaders proved bold and aggressive city builders. The first rank of entrepreneurs included Robertson Topp, William Bickford, Frederick H. Cossitt, Eugene Magevney, J. Oliver Greenlaw, William B. Greenlaw, John T. Trezevant, John C. McLemore, Sam Tate, Robert C. Brinkley, Henry Montgomery, and James C. Neeley. The city's building boom started in 1843 with the construction of some 30 brick buildings. Not all of these structures were for business purposes. A few, like the slightly earlier Topp mansion, were truly elegant and spacious. Physical growth mushroomed thereafter, despite a

Above
One of the mainstays of the early Memphis economy was the distribution of manufactured goods, especially hardware. Guns were an important element in this trade and, as this ad shows, local gunsmiths also enjoyed a thriving business. Small-scale gun manufacturers such as the Bluff City Armory would be part of the source of arms when the Civil War erupted less than a decade later. From the Memphis/Shelby County Room (M/SCPLIC)

Above Right
The Western Foundry is representative of the small-scale industry of antebellum Memphis. As this 1855 advertisement shows, shops such as this provided gin and mill gear, steam engines, sheet metal work, plows, and various other kinds of machinery. After the outbreak of hostilities, such foundries would be absolutely essential to the Confederate war effort. Before its fall, Memphis would be one of the South's major producers of war materials. From the Memphis/Shelby County Room (M/SCPLIC)

Above, far right
The stately residence of Robertson Topp, one of the finer homes in Memphis, stood at Beale and Lauderdale. Topp, who was one of the prime movers in the development of early Memphis, was particularly active in developing South Memphis into a high fashion residential town and also in building the Gayoso House. He was also a first-rate railroad promoter. From the Memphis/Shelby County Room (M/SCPLIC)

serious yellow fever epidemic in 1855 and the ravages of a national financial panic in 1857, climaxing in a building frenzy just before the Civil War. Approximately 1,400 structures were completed in 1859, and even more than that in 1860.

During the 1850s the number of banks grew to 20, and the number of newspapers to five. Municipal fire and police services were kept adequate to the city's needs, and a good deal of money was spent on public works. The major failure of city government was the condition of the streets, which remained miserable into the 20th century.

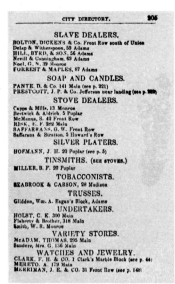

Top
It is sometimes easy to forget how mundane slavery seemed to Southerners before the Civil War. The 1855 city directory exemplifies this by listing slave dealers on the same page with soap and candle dealers. Even more remarkable is the fact that the Adams Street addresses of most of the dealers were right in the midst of the city's church district. What thoughts may have gone through the minds of churchgoers as they passed such establishments on the way to services? From the Memphis/Shelby County Room (M/SCPLIC)

The city's efforts to improve the streets led to heavy bond issues in the 1850s, the beginning of the city's disastrous indebtedness. During the same period—perhaps partly because of rampant growth and partly because there was finally money in the city's coffers to steal—city government became "notoriously corrupt and inefficient." Decent, capable citizens often refused to run for office or to serve.

"Let My People Go!"

Memphis and Shelby County blacks, contributing heavily to the economic prosperity of the boom decades, remained largely outside the social and economic mainstream. Forced to continue living at a primitive, subsistence level, blacks did not share in the new prosperity they were helping to create. If anything, most blacks found their scope for development and enjoyment of life shrinking. Increasingly the South, including Memphis, would deny their very right to human dignity.

Prior to the mid-1840s there was no commercial slave trade in Memphis. Although blacks were bought and sold in private transactions, they were not forced to submit to the indignity of the slave market, whose repellent atmosphere was increasingly described with such telling effect by abolitionists. Tennessee law forbade the domestic slave trade, and this law was evidently observed in letter, if not in spirit, until the middle of the decade. In the early 1840s slaves were "shown" in Memphis or Fort Pickering and then moved across the river to the Ferry Landing in Arkansas Territory for sale. Beginning about 1845, however, some slave dealers began operating openly in Memphis. Eventually the state repealed the prohibition on slave dealing, and the odious business became legal as well as lucrative.

With slaves selling for an average of almost $1,000 apiece in the 1850s, slave traders made huge fortunes. Most slave dealers maintained their "marts" along Adams Street, where their black prisoners were kept locked in rooms behind the showrooms which fronted on the street. The dealers evidently had about the same sort of reputations currently ascribed to pimps and some used-car dealers.

The leading Memphis slave dealers included Byrd Hill, Nathan Bedford Forrest, Ike Bolton, Tom Dickens, Wade Bolton, and Wash Bolton. These men bought slaves mainly in Kentucky and Virginia and resold them in the cities of the lower Mississippi Valley, where they frequently had branch establishments. Byrd Hill and "Bed" Forrest began as partners and later split up. Wade Bolton started as an independent dealer but later joined his brother Ike's firm, Bolton-Dickens Company.

The intermarried Bolton-Dickens partners finally fell out over money, thereby igniting one of the bloodiest and most bizarre feuds in the annals of American history. By the time it ended in 1871, at least eight persons had been murdered, and all of the known parties to the feud were dead. Wade Bolton's will was even stranger than the feud. Part of the legacy included a school endowment which, ironically, later benefited some of the descendants of the slaves he had trafficked in.

In contrast to the perhaps fitting end of the Bolton-Dickens partners, Bedford Forrest became a Confederate war hero and a leading Memphis citizen after the conflict. This tough and tough-minded man led a life that rivals the wildest fiction for danger, adventure, and achievement. Even so, legends and myths have grown up about his name. Some writers have claimed that he was such a fair and kindly slave dealer that blacks greatly preferred being sold through his mart. Although there is no direct evidence to controvert this story, it is surely suspect. During the Civil War Memphis blacks, reacting to a rumor that the Federals had captured Forrest, turned out en masse hoping to see him humiliated or hanged.

Though during the Civil War Memphians resisted surrendering their city, it eventually fell into Union hands. Here, the "Stars and Stripes" are being raised over the post office. From *Harper's Weekly*, 1862, Memphis/Shelby County Room (M/SCPLIC)

important than preserving the Union, but most Memphians believed they could have both. To them Stephen A. Douglas seemed the likely Democratic nominee for President, and the probable winner. If the Democratic party could stay united and pick up the support of the Southern Whigs, another compromise would surely be achieved.

As the four-way 1860 presidential election approached, Memphians saw both Douglas and John Bell of Tennessee as pro-Union candidates. The "extremist" candidates, Abraham Lincoln and John C. Breckinridge, seemed unthinkable choices. Memphians voted their convictions in November, giving almost 90 percent of their support to either Douglas or Bell. Early post-election jubilation turned to dismay as Northern returns indicated a solid electoral-college victory for Lincoln and the "Black Republicans."

With Lincoln's election the unthinkable had happened, and Memphians were faced with the question of what to do next. The *Appeal* at first favored giving Lincoln a chance. If he violated Southern rights, then would be the time for revolt. While hoping for a workable compromise, Memphians became increasingly aware that, if war should come, Tennessee would cast its lot with the South. As the Crittenden Compromise was being discussed, Memphians embraced the attitude toward perceived Northern intransigence that "they must recede or we will secede." With the failure to compromise and the pell-mell secession of the deep Southern states, the *Appeal* and many Memphians abandoned moderation and solidly advocated secession. Despite this swing, as late as February 1861 nearly 60 percent of Memphians still opposed secession and favored finding some way to preserve the Union.

But the tide of public sentiment was clearly turning in Memphis. Local secessionists

Chapter Four: Defiance and Defeat,
Disease and Disaster: 1861-1879

FOR GOVERNOR:

I. G. HARRIS,

For the Confederate Congress.

FOR SENATOR:

FOR REPRESENTATIVE:

FOR FLOATER:

For the Permanent Constitution.

became increasingly vocal, and by March war fever was growing in the city. The April 12 firing on Fort Sumter and Lincoln's call to arms against the Charleston rebels killed the last public expressions of pro-Union sentiment in Memphis. At a public meeting the local citizenry "resolved itself out of the Union," offered allegiance and aid to Jefferson Davis, and began making preparations for war. The machinery of state government proved more cumbersome, and Tennessee's referendum on secession did not take place until June 8. In that election Shelby County voted more than 7,000 to 5 in favor of secession, although the statewide margin was only about two to one.

In less than six months Memphis had made a quantum leap in attitude. In November's election Memphians had voted eight to one for pro-Union candidates. By May they were even more overwhelmingly secessionist. The explanation for this seemingly total reversal is that the choices had changed. By May of 1861 it was no longer possible to save the Union; the question now was, "Which side?" On this question Memphians seemed almost unanimous, and the intensity of their newfound ardor earned their city the nickname "the Charleston of the West."

As soon as Memphis opted for secession, the city government began preparations for defense. Raising $50,000 in funds borrowed from local banks, the city fathers set about converting a warehouse into an armory and planning fortifications for the city. The second step did not get past the planning stage, for in July the defense effort was taken over by the state and the Confederacy. Former Episcopal bishop, now Confederate general, Leonidas Polk established his headquarters at the Gayoso House, and the city's young and not-so-young men began answering the Confederacy's call to arms.

Memphians were justifiably proud of their city's enlistment record. About 3,800 men volunteered at the initial call. From a community of just over 22,000 people, of whom about 17 percent were blacks, this impressive figure represented a bigger percentage than in any other major city, North or South. Memphis volunteer companies took colorful and fanciful names, including the Bluff City Grays, Harris Zouaves, Crockett Rangers, Steuben Artillery, Emerald Guards, Jeff Davis Invincibles, Garibaldi Guards, and Shelby Reds. As in the Mexican War, there were parades and a carnival-like atmosphere prevailed. West Tennessee was becoming an armed camp, and Memphis readied itself for conflict with dash and defiance.

With its excellent transportation network, Memphis quickly became a military depot and ordnance center. Manufacturing, though still limited, turned largely to war production.

The city's small factories produced uniforms, knapsacks, and leather equipment for men and horses. The Memphis Arsenal employed more than 200 women and produced 75,000 rounds of handgun ammunition a day. Most important, the city's three foundry and machinery works made cannon, critically short items in the South. The most famous of these, Quinby and Robinson, established a production schedule of two fieldpieces a day. Later the navy yard converted steamships to military purposes.

Memphis' war production, though modest by Northern standards, was critically important to the industrially retarded South. Yet the Confederacy did almost nothing to build up the city's defenses, instead concentrating nearly all of its efforts upriver and at the state's border defenses on the Cumberland and Tennessee rivers. If these defenses held, all would go well for the defiant Bluff City. If not, Memphis had scant means of protecting itself.

Before the Fall

Memphians were unrealistically confident, even complacent, before the shooting war started. The rout of the Federals at First Manassas (Bull Run) seemed to justify Southern optimism, and Memphis celebrated by naming a street in honor of the battle. Misgauging Union resilience and tenacity, some Mid-Southerners speculated that the war would not last until the next spring.

But last the war did, and the reality of it was rammed home to Memphians before spring. Their first taste of this grim reality came with the Battle of Belmont, Missouri, across the river from Columbus, Kentucky. Although the South won the battle, Confederate casualties were high, and most Memphians had a dear one among the 3,000 local troops serving upriver. As the casualty lists were received by telegraph, the city converted the Overton Hotel into a hospital and waited in gloom to receive the dead and wounded.

In February 1862 Tennessee's perimeter of defenses began falling into Federal hands. Forts Henry and Donelson surrendered, opening the road into central and western Tennessee. Memphis served briefly as state capital after Nashville was abandoned to the Union Army, but this was slight comfort to Memphians who saw the noose closing about them. The fall of these two forts caused the South to abandon its strong Mississippi River position at Columbus, Kentucky. The war had suddenly drawn much closer.

Chapter Four: Defiance and Defeat,
Disease and Disaster: 1861-1879

FORT PICKERING

Shortly after Memphis fell into Federal hands in June 1862, General Halleck ordered construction of a fort large enough to accommodate a garrison of 10,000 men. The result was Fort Pickering, a system of fortifications more elaborate than that of any Federal-controlled city except Washington itself.

General William T. Sherman arrived in July to superintend the occupation forces and construction of the fort. Blacks were pressed into service, both slaves and refugees, and by the time the fort was completed in November 1862 the work force had swelled to about 6,000. In return for their labor the men received clothing, food, shelter, and one pound of chewing tobacco per month. Compensation was promised to Union-loyal slavemasters "at the end of the war."

The fort stretched two miles along the southern riverbluffs below Beale to the Indian mounds in what is now De Soto Park. The bluffs formed a natural defense along the western edge. The northern, eastern, and southern lines of the fort were zigzag earthworks consisting of ditches 7 feet deep and 12 feet wide, with ramparts created from the dirt thrown up on the fort's inner sides. In those pick-and-shovel days it was a massive undertaking, possibly the biggest "public works" project in the city's history.

The earthworks perimeter was guarded by heavy ordnance, including 32-pounders, 8-inch seacoast howitzers, 20-pounder Parrotts, and 8-inch Columbiads, positioned at the salient angles where they could sweep the ground in all directions. Inside the fort most of the existing buildings were demolished, except those needed for officers' quarters and other purposes. An inner citadel, or keep, with its own set of earthworks, was constructed in the area of what is now Martyrs' Park, as a second line of defense in the event enemy forces were able to penetrate the perimeter.

Except for its use as a depot for military supplies, Fort Pickering played no prominent role in the war. But its formidable defenses, well known to the Rebels, meant that it was never to be attacked, not even during Forrest's famous raid on Memphis in 1864. Its presence may have ensured that the city suffered no damage during the war.

— David Bowman

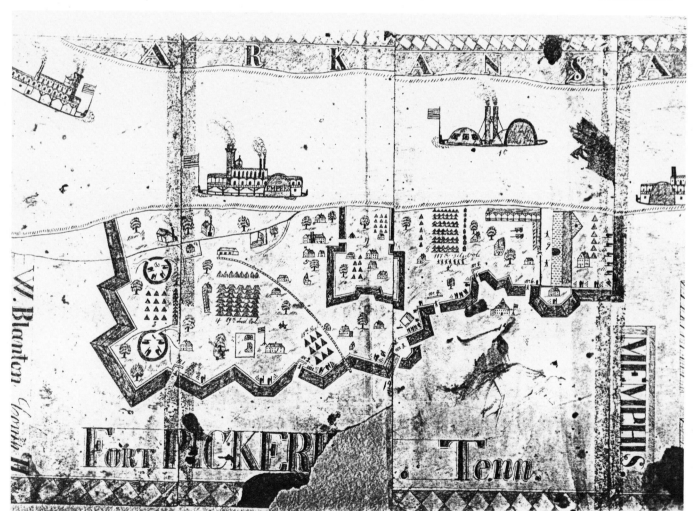

Map of Fort Pickering. From the Memphis/Shelby County Room (M/SCPLIC)

In March General Bragg, apprehensive about the civilian administration in Memphis, placed the city under martial law. In April the Confederacy surrendered a strong fortification at Island Number 10 above Memphis and lost the critical battle at Shiloh Church. With the loss of Island Number 10, only Fort Pillow, 60 miles above Memphis, stood as a formidable obstacle to the invading forces. The defeat at Shiloh exposed the Confederate rail junction at Corinth and left Memphis extremely vulnerable to attack from the east. The noose was drawn tighter.

While hyperbolic Confederate war propaganda continued unabated and orators swore that Memphis would not fall, it became increasingly apparent that the army would make no serious attempt to defend the city. By the end of April Union forces had occupied New Orleans and Federal gunboats were bombarding Fort Pillow. Rumor abounded that fanatics would burn the city rather than see it fall into Union hands, and Mayor John Park proclaimed that he would personally hang any arsonist caught in the act. Secret Unionists printed handbills declaring, "Our deliverance is at hand. Let us prepare to welcome it." But most Memphians continued to talk tough and hope for a miracle.

No miracle came. The Confederate Army evacuated Forts Pillow, Randolph, and Harris, and the river route to Memphis was open. Many Memphians fled south. The departing army commandeered what supplies it could carry, poured thousands of barrels of molasses down the riverbank, and set fire to an estimated 300,000 bales of cotton on the waterfront. The total value of goods destroyed has been estimated at $129 million.

The ironclad rams under construction in the Memphis harbor would not be allowed to fall into Union hands. The *Arkansas*, sufficiently finished to be towed south, was later completed and briefly terrorized the Union's river fleet. The *Tennessee* was not far enough along to save, and its hull was burned in the harbor.

By this time only the certifiably insane or the moronically gullible might still believe that the city would be spared. General Jeff Thompson, whose small force had been left in the city, was neither, but he grossly underestimated the Union's naval power. With the Confederate river fleet, he had been extremely lucky in disabling two Union ironclads near Fort Pillow. Now claiming that he could hold the city for a month, he tried to rouse the citizens to their own defense. Memphians ignored his call to arms and waited, hoping against hope that the little makeshift war fleet in the harbor could keep the inevitable blow from falling. Thompson waited too, still claiming that victory was within reach.

The River Defense Fleet was the last Confederate hope for keeping control of the Mississippi River and saving Memphis. Commanded by Commodore J.E. Montgomery, it was composed of eight converted river steamboats, each protected by compressed cotton and railroad iron. Fitted with rams and two open-deck cannon (the *Jeff Thompson* had four), these ragtag ships were faster than the Union ironclads but inferior on all other counts.

The Union fleet now contained five ironclads, 19 rams, and various auxiliary ships including troop transports. The ironclads, known as "Pook's Turtles," were slow, heavily armored steamers with 13 heavy cannon each. The rams, products of the genius of Charles Ellet, were wooden, unarmored, well constructed, without cannon, and very fast. Their job was simply to ram and sink enemy ships, but their effectiveness was untested and untrusted until the Battle of Memphis.

Memphians knew that the Federal fleet was near, and there was some doubt as to whether the Confederate ships would even stay and fight. But when the Union ironclads rounded the bend in the river above Memphis shortly after dawn on June 6, Montgomery's fleet was drawn up in a double line to do battle. An estimated 10,000 Shelby Countians had assembled on the bluffs to watch the battle that would determine their futures.

Captain Charles Davis, the cautious Union commander, disliked fighting downstream

75

Chapter Four: Defiance and Defeat,
Disease and Disaster: 1861-1879

with his ungainly craft. He knew that any disabled ship would be carried into enemy hands by the current, and to minimize this danger he brought his five ironclads downriver stern first. Montgomery, ignoring his own ships' capacity for ramming, began firing at Davis' vulnerable targets. The exchange of cannon fire did no damage to either side, but it did alert Colonel Ellet that the battle was on.

Captain Davis had had so little confidence in the rams that he did not even let Ellet know he was attacking. In his excited rush to join the battle, Ellet was able to bring only two of his rams into action, moving them through the Union battle line to attack the Southern ships. The two rams were enough. In the melee that followed, they were responsible for sinking or disabling three Confederate ships, while the ironclads sank or disabled all the rest but one. Only the *Van Dorn* escaped south to the protection of Vicksburg. On the Federal side only one ship, Ellet's *Queen of the West*, was disabled, but Ellet himself received a wound that later proved mortal. The Union fleet with its superior ships had won a decidedly lopsided victory, and now Memphis was truly defenseless.

Why had Montgomery, so obviously outclassed, chosen to stay and fight? Lee N. Newcomer offers the following explanation:

Perhaps he felt that it was better to fight to the bitter end rather than scuttle. There had been much criticism heard that spring about the Yankees walking into New Orleans virtually unopposed. And to fight, though risky, was not necessarily desperate. The Federal rams had been taken as some sort of transport; there were only the five ironclads against him. He had knocked out two others at Plum Point Bend. It was better to fight now before these returned. His last sortie had been successful; perhaps he could catch the Federals off guard again and strike home with his rams. If not, he could always break off the fight and escape from the slow ironclads. A haven at Vicksburg was waiting.

There were other considerations. Montgomery was too chivalrous to abandon the Charleston of the West without a struggle. He reassured excited Memphians, "I have no intention of retreating any farther. I have come here, that you may see Lincoln's gunboats sent to the bottom by the fleet which you built and manned." Here was gallantry and the grand gesture.

Whatever the reasons, however gallant the gestures, the fleet was now gone. A demoralized Memphis was open to invasion.

Metropolis of the American Nile

Invasion, as such, never came. Under a white flag four Union emissaries brought a formal demand for the surrender of the city. Mayor Park responded that he did not have the authority to surrender. Neither did he have the means to resist, however, and he admitted that the city was in Union hands. As the Stars and Stripes were raised over the post office, only a noisy demonstration, a few thrown stones, and a single shot fired (no one knows by which side) marked the capitulation of the "Charleston of the West."

Military Occupation

The naval battle that had sealed the city's fate had lasted less than 90 minutes. The bitter fruits of defiance and defeat would last through nearly three more years of war and at least five years of Reconstruction. For some, these years would bring privation and hardship unknown since frontier days. For others, they would mean a new freedom and new economic opportunities. For almost all, the world that they had known was gone. The new world was topsy-turvy, and they were strangers in it.

Immediately after its fall Memphis presented a miserable picture. Smoke and soot from the still-smoldering cotton hung over the city like a pall. Molasses ran down the riverbank like lava. Bereft of its fighting-age men and suffering from wartime shortages and a depression of business activities, the city was suddenly unkempt and shabby. Although the municipal government would continue to function for most of the war's duration, the city was obviously under Yankee control. The blue-uniformed soldiers and unsubmissive blacks that filled the streets served to remind the defeated of their helplessness and humiliation. Although physically intact, Memphis looked bleak, and its future looked bleaker.

The initial Federal policy for Memphis was to try to restore the loyalty of its citizens. Those who had fled the city were urged to return, and merchants were requested to resume normal business activities. Rumors of strong pockets of pro-Union sentiment, and the knowledge that some Memphians felt the Confederacy had beggared and then abandoned them, led Federal officials to extend a liberal trade policy in the hope of further stimulating renewed allegiance to the Union. A swarm of Northern opportunists descended upon the city in the wake of the Union war fleet, and business activity was soon humming again.

In less than a month Federal officials were disabused concerning the sympathies of most Memphians. Among the immigrant population a significant proportion fought for and remained loyal to the Confederacy, while others embraced the Union. For the occupation forces neither the stiff-necked diehards nor the fair-weather friends posed a significant problem. But the mass of Anglo-Southerners presented a united front that could be a serious threat to the Union war effort. They felt encouraged too by the brilliant guerilla-tactic successes of cavalry officer Nathan Bedford Forrest, who operated just south of the Tennessee border, in northern Mississippi.

Chapter Four: Defiance and Defeat, Disease and Disaster: 1861-1879

A combination of loyalty to the Confederate cause, crass profiteering, and corruption turned Memphis into a contraband center that supplied the rebels with an estimated $12 million worth of supplies during the first eight months of occupation, and perhaps $30 million worth before July of 1864. This smuggling was absolutely vital to the Confederate war effort, and it had to be stopped. A succession of Union commanders, including Generals U.S. Grant, W.T. Sherman, S.A. Hurlbut, and C.C. Washburn, all imposed regulations and restrictions intended to minimize such trade, but the effects were mixed. When they clamped down too hard, Memphis business ground nearly to a halt, working a severe hardship on the civilian population of Memphis and its trade area. It also stopped the northward flow of cotton, needed for Union war materials including clothing and tents. When rules were relaxed, the flow of money, food, medicine, cloth, lead, and gunpowder to the insurgents resumed. As a result, Sherman complained, Memphis was "better to our enemy than before it was taken." Less than a year before the war's end, General Washburn declared, "Memphis has been of more value to the Southern confederacy since it fell into Federal hands than Nassau [the Confederate blockade runners' trade center in the Bahamas]."

Although mild by modern wartime standards, the restrictions placed upon them were onerous to Memphians. They resented the repeated taking of loyalty oaths, hated the military pass systems, and were confused and frustrated by the frequent changes of regulations. Those who belonged to the former power elite were particularly rankled that their former status worked against them and that their large homes were requisitioned for military purposes. Even the churches became embroiled in the loyalty-pride shoving match, and in one case an appeal to President Lincoln was required to settle the issue. Newspapers came under Union control or outright censorship—all except one. The scrappy *Appeal* escaped south as the city fell and continued to function from various locations as a Confederate propaganda organ until the close of the war.

Although loyalty was never as important to Union officials as the issue of contraband smuggling, Federal generals did attempt to eliminate open displays of disloyalty. Guards were ordered to shoot anyone attempting to remove or desecrate the United States flag. Those suspected of rebel sentiments might be ordered from the city, as happened in the case of Mrs. Elizabeth A. Meriwether, who was pregnant and had two small children at the time. Others were simply thrown into Irving Block prison, the dreaded "Bastille of the South." The presumed disloyalty of Mayor John Park was responsible for General Washburn's imprisoning him and dissolving the municipal government in 1864, even though the city council had voted a resolution of appreciation praising General Grant after he starved Vicksburg into surrender in 1863. Park holds the unusual distinction of having had both Confederate and Union generals replace his administration with martial law because of his nonconformist attitudes.

Despite all the illicit movement of goods during occupation, there was simply not enough to go around. Supplying the nonproductive military of both sides, the scorched-earth policies used by both armies, a severe drought in 1863, desertion of farm and field by newly freed blacks, providing for the largely unproductive black refugees, hoarding by fearful whites, and wartime disruptions of regular commerce all took their toll. There was famine in much of the countryside, and soaring inflation in the city put many everyday items, even if available, out of the reach of most people. In some areas whites were reduced to eating and wearing things that even slaves would not have touched before the war.

Blacks, of course, were freed from bondage. Even before the Emancipation Proclamation, slaves owned by rebels were considered "contraband" and given protection if they reached Federal lines. Those whose owners claimed to be loyal Unionists were not forcibly

Metropolis of the American Nile

returned, although the now-doubtful owners were permitted to try to talk them into return-ing. Memphis, as an island of Yankee control in a basically rebel countryside, attracted large numbers of black refugees. More than 15,000 poured into the area, many of them concen-trated in refugee camps south of the city and one large camp on Presidents Island. These refugees may have done as much to help the Union war effort as white Memphians did to impede it.

The first work that the Union officials set their new charges to perform was establishing adequate fortifications. Buying up the high bluff land in the vicinity of the present Mississip-pi River bridges, the Army had blacks build a two-mile long earthwork fort, with a com-modious interior for barracks and a drill field, and with powerful cannon commanding both the city and the river.

Union policy at first did not permit blacks to join the Army, and once it did, there was no confidence that they would make good fighting men. During 1864 more than 7,000 blacks enlisted and were trained in the Memphis area. Across the state the number of black enlistments exceeded 20,000. Union officials planned first for blacks to be laborers and later for them to perform routine patrols and garrison duty.

But the black soldiers, most of them newly freed from slavery, were eager to prove their fighting mettle. As early as December of 1863, black units fought well at the battle of Moscow, Tennessee. Expected to break and run at the Confederate onslaught, they held their ground, delivering their artillery fire accurately into the Confederate ranks. Colonel Frank Kendrick wrote to Sherman of this engagement, "The affair at Moscow the other day was more spirited than I believed. The Negro regiment behaved splendidly."

Black troops were also part of the garrison at Fort Pillow when Nathan Bedford Forrest attacked it in April of 1864. Significantly outnumbered and open to Confederate sniper fire, the Federal position was hopeless. Recognizing this, Forrest asked for its surrender in order to avoid useless bloodshed. The Union command stalled in the hope that reinforcements would arrive by river to save the fort. The Confederate forces drove off incoming Union sup-port and gained better ground while a truce was still in effect. When the garrison still refused to surrender, Forrest's troops took the fort by storm. This resulted in the bloodbath that Forrest had tried to avoid.

Chapter Four: Defiance and Defeat,
Disease and Disaster: 1861-1879

The Battle of Fort Pillow was bloody, but it was not the "massacre" that the Union press claimed in an effort to arouse faltering Northern war spirit. This extremely distorted account claimed that Forrest had violated the rules of war and ordered the slaughter of the garrison, especially its black soldiers. Later investigation proved that no such action even occurred and that the rebel troops committed no war crimes. However, the propaganda mills did their work well. The "Fort Pillow Massacre" became a rallying cry for black soldiers who vowed that they would never again surrender to rebels.

It was because of the unpredictable threat posed by Forrest that blacks initially became more than armed laborers, serving with distinction as part of the forces that hunted him in North Mississippi. At Brice's Crossroads and Tupelo, black troops performed better than some of their white Northern counterparts, and though they were given dirty and dangerous work, such as rearguard assignments, their valor did not go unrecognized. General William Jay Smith reported, "The colored Brigade under Colonel Bouton fought exceedingly well; and I am free to confess that their action has removed from my mind a prejudice of twenty years standing." These black soldiers played a significant role in containing Forrest's guerilla warfare.

Forrest's Raid and War's End

More than two years after the city's fall, the possibility of the Confederacy's recapturing Memphis was fading rapidly. Sherman was beginning his Georgia campaign, and he ordered the Memphis command to hold Forrest in the West. It could prove disastrous if "that devil Forrest" broke through into eastern Tennessee or northern Georgia and destroyed Sherman's supply lines.

Forrest, with about 5,000 effectives in northern Mississippi, had been raiding into West Tennessee almost at will. The Union command at Memphis, unable to stop his raids or trap him in Tennessee, determined to track him to ground in Mississippi. On each of the first three attempts, Forrest succeeded in turning back superior Union numbers. On the fourth attempt, more than 18,000 Union troops closed in on his position at Oxford. Outnumbered more than three to one and in a nearly hopeless position, Forrest pulled one of those daring moves for which he is ranked among the greatest cavalry commanders in history. He decided to attack the Union stronghold at Memphis.

Leaving 3,000 men to keep the advancing Federals occupied, Forrest and the other 2,000 men rode hell-bent for Memphis. Forrest had no realistic chance of capturing the city, which still had a garrison of 6,000 men plus the strong walls and dominating cannon of Fort Pickering, but he knew what he was doing. He had three major objectives: to capture the three Union generals posted in the town; to release Confederate prisoners from Irving Block; and to draw the strong Federal force out of northern Mississippi. The essential element was surprise.

Metropolis of the American Nile

Losing about one-fourth of his troops on the way because of exhausted horses, Forrest and the remaining 1,500 men reached the outskirts of Memphis at dawn on Sunday, August 21, 1864. Taking advantage of a thick fog and claiming to be a Union patrol with Confederate prisoners, Forrest's men were on top of the Federal pickets before their suspicions were aroused. Galloping through the Memphis streets, the attackers split off to pursue their separate missions.

One of the generals was not at home, and the other two got sufficient warning to escape. General Washburn's case was close, though. He ran down an alley in his nightshirt and escaped to the fort, leaving his wife and his dress uniform to fend for themselves. The try for Irving Block also failed, as Forrest and the main body of this force bogged down battling Union troops at the State Female College on McLemore. By noon the raiders had withdrawn and headed back to Oxford, but their most important objective had been achieved. The Union army in Mississippi returned to safeguard Memphis.

During the raid on Memphis, Forrest and the main body of his troops became occupied fighting Union troops at the State Female College (shown here) on McLemore near Hernando Road. Although Forrest failed to capture any of the Union generals or to free the prisoners in Irving Block, he did capture hundreds of fresh horses, and the stroke drew the 18,000 Union troops which had been hunting him out of North Mississippi. Forrest was still fighting when the war ended. From the Memphis/Shelby County Room (M/SCPLIC)

Forrest's raid has given rise to some marvelous bits of folklore. In a gesture indicating that the Civil War still had some 19th-century touches of class, Forrest sent Washburn's uniform back to him under a flag of truce. Washburn, not to be outdone, had Forrest's Memphis tailor make a dress gray uniform and sent it to the Confederate general. Contrary to popular legend, the Forrest who rode into the lobby of the Gayoso in search of General Hurlbut was not Bedford but his brother, Captain William Forrest. Other aspects of the raid also became confused in folk memory, but Washburn's Escape Alley is accurately named to this day.

The audacity of the raid thrilled Confederate sympathizers in Memphis. Their attitude probably had an adverse effect on military-civilian relations, but a little bravado cheered an exhausted and bewildered people as they watched their cause crumble and collapse.

And collapse it did. Never beaten in the conventional sense of the word, the Confederacy simply ran out of men and materials to continue the struggle. Sherman was the first to understand that this was a war of attrition. Without malice he fought it that way, earning generations of Southern hatred. Grant fought it that way, too, slamming his troops without finesse into Confederate defenses in a terrible carnage. He knew that he could replace his losses of men and equipment, and that Lee could not.

The South lost the war because it was living in the past, a past not wholly real. When the tenets of Southerners' almost mystical beliefs failed them, when their soldiers only killed two Yankees for each one they lost, rather than the 10 or 20 predicted in early hyperbolic speeches, many Southerners embraced their "cause" even more desperately. With growing rather than diminished fervor, they declared the South would rise again.

Chapter Four: Defiance and Defeat, Disease and Disaster: 1861-1879

But the South was beaten, inevitably and irretrievably. Most of the harsher measures enacted by the Radical Republican-controlled Congress were unnecessary, only adding to the burdens of a devastated land and weighing heavily on the emotions of a vanquished people. The vicissitudes and readjustments of Reconstruction would leave their imprint more deeply on Southern consciousness than the agonies of the war itself. A feeling of violation and injustice would give birth to the myth of the Old South.

Memphis emerged from the war relatively unscathed physically. This view of the city from further south on the bluff should be from a vantage point near Fort Pickering. The scene shows the shanties and some of the newly freed blacks that were part of the war's legacy. The influx of freedmen created a situation that Memphis was unequipped to deal with. Little more than a year after the war's end, Memphis would have a bloody race riot. From *Harper's Weekly*, 1866, Memphis/Shelby County Room (M/SCPLIC)

Reconstruction

Contrary to a popular history of Memphis, Reconstruction in the Bluff City was *not* a "Return to Normality." True, business activity, growth, and people's workaday lives resumed, but what had been "normal" before the Civil War was gone forever. The huge influx of newly freed blacks, soon to have constitutionally guaranteed rights under the protection of the military and Republican government, changed the very fiber of life in Memphis.

Racial pluralism was now the salient fact in the city's makeup, and the need to build a framework for dialogue and harmony became the city's greatest challenge. But Memphis failed, as did other communities across the nation. Memphians, black and white, were victims of a shared past and destined to become victims of a joint future. Radical rule attempted too much, too soon, and for the wrong reasons. White backlash, manifested in the Klan, paternalistic accommodation, subordination of black rights, and Jim Crow laws, all failed to solve the problems of living together in true harmony.

This view of the Memphis levee in 1871 shows the return to business as usual and prosperity, as captured by *Every Saturday*'s Alfred R. Waud. In examining the cultural patterns of modern Memphis, Waud speculated about the connection with ancient Egypt. Noting "archaeological" finds, he stated: "There are unmistakable evidences of . . . Egyptian occupation of the country about Memphis in pre-historic times." Was he just having fun with his readers? Or had some Memphians been having fun with the artist? From *Every Saturday*, 1871. Courtesy, Mississippi River Museum, Mud Island

Metropolis of the American Nile

This is not to say that Memphis did not have a better record of race relations than most Southern cities. Despite some notable and highly publicized failures, it did. But over the long run Memphis, nostalgic for its past rather than planning for the future, simply buried its race problems. Almost a century later these problems would surface again, bearing bitter fruit and still defying solution. But the seeds of the problems are to be found in the Reconstruction era.

The Reconstruction era in Memphis really began with the military occupation of the city, and manifestations of it continued until at least the mid-1870s. Official Reconstruction—the political reorganization of state and local government and the struggle for political control—was of much shorter duration.

Tennessee reentered the Union quickly. State government was reorganized under Lincoln's mild 10-percent plan, and a presidential proclamation of 1864 declared that the state was readmitted. Congress, wanting more control over ex-rebels and more repentance from them, did not seat the state's delegation until July 20, 1866. Because of the disfranchisement of former rebels, Tennessee returned to the Union under the political control of the Republican Party dominant in the eastern part of the state. Under this government the state repealed secession, abolished slavery within the state, and ratified the 13th, 14th, and 15th Amendments to the Constitution. Because of its rapid reentry to the Union, Tennessee was spared the harsh measures of Radical Congressional Reconstruction.

Within the state, however, the lot of ex-rebels was not much different from that in other parts of the South. State government came under the control of East Tennessee's Radical Republicans, led by Governor William G. Brownlow. Brownlow bitterly detested the former power elite who had taken the state out of the Union. Backed by Federal troops, he imposed a Radical regime on Tennessee that rivaled that of Congress in its punitive nature. By his high-handed and extralegal tactics, Brownlow eventually alienated his bases of support, and the Tennessee Conservative Party gained control of the state in 1869-1870.

Among the principal factors allowing Brownlow to consolidate his power within the state was the Memphis Race Riot of 1866. Contrary to common assumption, this most disgraceful episode in the city's history was not a manifestation of animosity between the former slave and master classes. Rather it was the climax of long-smoldering resentment between the blacks and the Irish.

The huge influx of freedmen created a situation that Memphis was poorly equipped to handle. Thousands of blacks, living in dreadful conditions on the outskirts of town and subsisting largely on government rations, doubtlessly depressed the wages for Irish and other day laborers resident before refugees came. In addition these blacks were believed to be responsible for a great deal of Memphis' nighttime thefts and violence. Given their extreme poverty and different standards of conduct fostered by the plantation system, the charge was probably accurate. No native Memphians, including blacks, wanted or welcomed this horde.

Below right
Alfred R. Waud's 1871 sketch of black ship's hands shows the unfortunate tendency of 19th-century artists to caricature blacks for their Northern readers. However, as before the Civil War, blacks and their labor were a mainstay of the transportation system that brought commerce and wealth to Memphis. Working on the river was hard, but apparently many preferred it to staying on a farm or plantation. From *Every Saturday,* 1871. Courtesy, Mississippi River Museum, Mud Island

Far right
River work was not regulated by the sun. As this 1871 drawing shows, boats were frequently refueled long after dark by torchlight. In the days before liquid fuels and conveyor belts, simple tasks like refueling required a monumental amount of manual labor. The contributions of blacks to this necessary work have only recently begun to be appreciated by historians. From *Every Saturday,* 1871. Courtesy, Mississippi River Museum, Mud Island

83

Chapter Four: Defiance and Defeat,
Disease and Disaster: 1861-1879

Without realizing it, black Memphians were sitting on a powder keg. The fuse was ignited when some of the 4,000 black soldiers awaiting discharge at Fort Pickering were abusive toward some of the Irish whites in that area. On May 1, 1866, a riot broke out between the blacks and the Irish, including some policemen and other minor officials. The violence lasted for three days. When the smoke cleared, 46 persons had been killed, 44 of them blacks, and 75 persons had been wounded. Of black buildings, four churches, 12 schools, and 91 homes had been burned. Order was restored only after white troops sent in from Nashville placed the city under martial law.

The consequences of the riot were many and mixed, with repercussions at the municipal, state, and national levels. Both the Freedmen's Bureau and the Army launched immediate investigations into the causes of the rioting. When these probes seemed unlikely to place the guilt squarely on ex-rebels, Congressional Radicals began their own investigation. Military authorities concluded that some intoxicated black soldiers had started the trouble, but that whites were responsible for aggravating and prolonging it. The Congressional Radicals' investigation had only one purpose: to prove that white Southerners should lose the right to vote. Although their report did little to help or protect blacks, it successfully obscured the issue with sensationalism.

At the local level the consequences for blacks were the most disheartening. Perhaps most significant was the psychological impact, for the rioting destroyed the illusion of safety that blacks had enjoyed under Federal protection. To defuse the situation the Army either transferred or mustered out all the remaining black soldiers. Many vagrant blacks left the city to take up farm labor rather than face the risk of another riot. At the same time 17 of the 21 white teachers educating blacks were intimidated into leaving the city, crippling the freedmen's educational opportunities.

White Memphians displayed a mixed reaction to the riot. Local newspapers and former leading citizens condemned the killing and arson for the heinous crimes they were. Prior to the arrival of troops from Nashville, ex-Confederate soldiers offered their services to quell the violence (an offer that was declined). Yet local whites were unquestionably pleased with some of the consequences: the departure of the black soldiers and the white teachers, both

The Civil War and Reconstruction meant terrible dislocations for blacks as well as whites. Among those most harshly affected were the children. In the immediate postwar era blacks had the aid of the Freedman's Bureau. This group portrait from *Harper's* shows life in a black orphanage in Memphis. Note the young man to the left enjoying the new found right to read, a right which would have been forbidden him just a few years earlier. From *Harper's Weekly*, 1866, Memphis/Shelby County Room (M/SCPLIC)

THE SHELBY COUNTY JAIL

Shelby County Jail and yard. From the Memphis/Shelby County Room (M/SCPLIC)

The Shelby County Jail was completed in March 1868 at a total cost of $281,209.88. Considering that in those days an elegant brick townhouse could be built for about $2,000, and the sum total of Memphis' other public buildings (market houses, firehouses, and the city hall portion of the Exchange Building) could not have exceeded $40,000 in value, the price of the jail was a staggering sum.

The kind of graft that was prevalent all across the United States in those turbulent postwar days may have accounted for the astronomical total. Local newspapers, including the *Argus* and the *Public*

of whom had been considered rabble-rousers, and the drifting of black vagrants back to the countryside.

Memphis taxpayers rebuilt the buildings that had been destroyed, generally replacing them with bigger and better structures than the originals. But lives could not be replaced, and justice was not done. There were no indictments for the many killings—a result not so much of white racial solidarity as of circumstance. Ex-Confederates and blacks could not serve on grand juries. Most whites who could, belonged to the class of poor whites and immigrants who had participated in the rioting and would not serve.

The repercussions at the state and national levels were chiefly political. Governor Brownlow, seizing upon the fact that some policemen were party to the rioting and the rest of the force was unable to restore order, dismissed the entire police force and replaced it with one responsible to him—an enormous political advantage to the Radicals at election time. At the national level the Memphis race riot, along with an even more vicious one in New Orleans and lesser riots in Norfolk, Nashville, and Vicksburg, helped persuade Northern voters that the South needed chastising. Convinced that President Johnson's Reconstruction policies were inadequate, they elected a veto-proof Republican Congress in 1866, and Radical Reconstruction of the South began in earnest.

Ledger, alleged that the city's aldermen were growing rich off the taxpayers by requiring, among other things, fat commissions on every contract awarded. But then, as the *Memphis Daily Appeal* editorialized in 1867, the citizens may simply have wanted a "grand public building."

The architect of the jail, James B. Cook, created a design to foil even the most determined prisoners. Between two brick walls was a space filled with dry sand. At the top of the sand was a weight connected by a cable and pulleys to an alarm system. If a prisoner removed any bricks, the sand would pour out into his cell, lower the weight, and set off the automatic alarm bell.

Doors, windows, and cell ceilings were of cast iron, of a special design created by Cook and J.W. Heath, head of the Chickasaw Iron Works, the city's largest foundry. Once the patterns were constructed (out of maple), the Chickasaw Iron Works could manufacture jail components to be shipped all over the United States. In 1876 Cook and Heath took their patented designs to the Centennial Exposition in Philadelphia, where they excited considerable national attention and admiration.

In some ways, however, the new jail resembled a rather exotic-looking hotel. Its handsome castellated Gothic design, 80 feet wide and 120 feet long, stood at the northwest corner of Front and Auction. The 80 cells were each five by seven feet, and eight feet in height. Arranged in four levels, with 20 cells per level, they could hold up to 350 prisoners. Amenities included steam heating, ample ventilation, an exercise yard, bathhouses (four for men and two for women), a washroom, and a bakehouse with an oven "capable of baking enough bread to supply the largest hotel in the country." The 50-

foot-high brick tower in the corner of the yard was not a guard tower but a water tower, holding 5,000 gallons of water for bathing, washing, and cooking. All in all, prisoners were afforded creature comforts denied at least half of the local citizenry in those decidedly unhygienic days.

This remarkable edifice was demolished in 1935 to make way for a dog pound, a jail for animals instead of people, but most of the magnificent 12-foot-high cast-iron fence can still be seen at the site where the Coast Guard is today.

— David Bowman

Jefferson Davis was the most conspicuous of the many former Confederate officials who took up residence in Memphis in the late 1860s and early 1870s. Memphis threw off the restrictions of Reconstruction so quickly that it became something of a mecca for such men and their families. Davis lived and worked in Memphis as the head of an insurance firm. From the Memphis/Shelby County Room (M/SCPLIC)

It is worth noting that none of the investigations of the Memphis riot suggested any possible involvement of the Ku Klux Klan. The story of the Klan in West Tennessee is a twice-told tale. The traditional Southern-white rendering depicts it as a vigilante group rectifying the great wrongs of corrupt and capricious Reconstruction. Revisionist historians have painted quite a different picture of the "Invisible Empire." Because of the secret and outlaw nature of the first Klan, the true story will probably never be told. However, it is known that the KKK was active in West Tennessee between 1867 and 1869, and Nathan Bedford Forrest was reputed to be its Grand Wizard. According to several of the group's former members, every ex-Confederate Memphian was a Klansman.

Black and White Politics

Despite all the difficulties and injustices in Reconstruction Memphis, the lot of blacks was vastly improved over their prewar status. Among their most prized new freedoms were those of assembly and worship, which came immediately upon Union occupation of the city. Local ministers such as H.N. Ranklin, Africa Bailey, and Morris Henderson built their congregations and their churches virtually without white aid. Henderson's Beale Street Baptist Church was the most successful of these, and Henderson became the most influential black Memphian of his time, respected and esteemed by both races. One reason for his almost universal approval by whites was that, unlike some others, he stayed completely out of politics.

In the immediate postwar period black fraternal and benevolent societies rivaled the churches for importance and influence in community life. Besides their very significant charitable work, these fraternal orders became the focus of black political involvement in Memphis. Interestingly, for as long as their leaders remained militant, blacks were represented by officeholders of their own race. Once their leaders moved toward a policy of accommodation with conservative whites, black officials failed to achieve reelection.

Memphis' first black militant may have been Ed Shaw. A free black man before the war, Shaw moved to Memphis during the 1850s. After the war he ran a saloon and made his articulate and forceful voice heard on the political scene. Feeling betrayed by white Republicans who did not want to share the spoils of office with their black allies, Shaw deliberately sabotaged former Union General W.J. Smith's 1870 congressional bid. His defeat showed white Republicans that they could not win unless they treated blacks fairly and with respect. From then on, black Memphians screened white Republican candidates carefully to be certain of their attitudes and to obtain commitments on the issues.

A strong voice for integration and social equality, Ed Shaw led local blacks to political victory in the early 1870s. With the unified support of the fraternal orders, blacks claimed two city council seats in 1872 and four seats the next year. Finally, in the 1874 election an Afro-Irish-Italian coalition swept all the Anglo-Southerners from city hall. Shaw was elected wharfmaster, the highest-paying office in local government.

On the heels of achieving local political control, the black fraternal orders abandoned their militant political stance. Motivated by the implied threat of white violence, a crisis of confidence, and a loss of faith in the Republican party, conservative fraternal leaders deserted Shaw, opting instead for an alliance with white Democrats and the politics of accommodation.

Under the leadership of Hezekiah Henley, blacks took the initiative in promoting reconciliation with the former ruling caste. In 1875 they sponsored a biracial Fourth of July celebration at the fairgrounds. The featured speaker was none other than former slave trader, ex-Confederate general, and rumored leader of the KKK, Nathan Bedford Forrest! Stressing the theme of common background and mutual understanding, Forrest advocated

Metropolis of the American Nile

closer friendship, cooperation, and mutual economic advancement. He said nothing about equality.

In the next municipal election about half the black electorate voted for white Democrats, breaking Ed Shaw's claim to political leadership in the black community. Although blacks continued to vote and hold some offices until the mid-1880s, their political power was gradually eroded. Enforcement of the state's poll-tax law beginning in 1891 virtually ended effective black participation in the local political process. During this time of decline the black community transferred its allegiance from the fraternal orders to the black clergy.

Despite full black participation in the postwar political process, white Radical Republican control did not hold up very long in Memphis. The local Radical leadership was viciously split, nearly from the war's end. Motivated mainly by the desire for spoils of office, the local Radicals consumed their energies in infighting. Vitriolic campaigning and dirty tricks during the 1867 and 1868 campaigns gave victories to the conservative element, and only Governor Brownlow's unethical vote counting kept a Radical in office as West Tennessee's Congressman until 1870. In fact, Memphis freed itself of Radical control so early that starting in 1869 the city became a refuge for ex-Confederate leaders, including Jefferson Davis. Many of these former officials lived and worked in Memphis until 1876, when the contested election and ensuing Compromise of 1877 ended Radical Reconstruction in the South.

Oddly enough, it was a Memphian who helped give the presidential victory to Rutherford B. Hayes, the Republican candidate. A former Whig, Douglas Democrat, Confederate colonel, and newspaper publisher, Andrew J. Kellar embraced conservative Republican fiscal ideology during the early 1870s. When Hayes Republicans promised a policy of reconciliation and concessions to the South, it became apparent that a friendly Republican ad-

JOHN GASTON, CITIZEN

John Gaston. From the Memphis/Shelby County Room (M/SCPLIC)

Jean Gaston was born on a small farm in the southerly Department of Aveyran, France, on January 4, 1828. At the age of 12 he went to Paris, where he worked for an uncle in a small restaurant. Tiring of this impoverished life, he became a ship's steward on a liner plying the Le Harve-New York run.

While on shore leave in New York after one of his crossings, he passed a French restaurant and decided to apply for employment. Hired on at the world-famous Delmonico's, he learned the finer points of cooking and restaurant management under the master's tutelage.

After a variety of jobs, experiences, and adventures, Gaston settled in the South. When war came he served with the Confederate forces. At the war's end, a penniless John Gaston came to Memphis, where he finally made a permanent home. Now in his late 30s, Gaston saved enough money to open his own cafe and his life turned upward. He created one of the finest hotel-restaurant combinations in the South, serving

the best meals at the lowest prices of any quality establishment in town. His business expanded to become a 100-room hotel with gracious amenities and a staff of 40 persons.

From the start of his success, Gaston shared his time, talents, and good fortune with others. Long known for his quiet kindnesses, his love of children, and secret philanthropies this French immigrant of humble origins became one of the city's leading citizens. In 1900 he donated five acres of his south Memphis estate to the city for use as a park and playground. Such a gift could not be kept a secret and was named Gaston Park.

Gaston died in 1912 at the age of 84, leaving his fortune

to his second wife, Theresa. When she died nearly 20 years later, she left the bulk of the estate to the city for the establishment of a municipal charity hospital. Supplementing this donation with federal depression relief funds, the city built a six-story, modern hospital which was dedicated to Gaston's memory in 1936. On his home site adjoining Gaston Park, the city erected a commodious community center.

Thus, although Gaston's fine hotel is only a memory, his name lives on in public institutions that are fitting tributes to a citizen whose name was so closely associated with generosity and hospitality in late 19th and early 20th century Memphis.

— John Harkins

ministration could do more for the South than the Democrats. Although contested state election returns were decided by a bipartisan commission, Southern congressmen's acceptance of its decision was vital if the compromise was to work. Andrew Kellar, who had a vested interest in a railroad venture supported by Hayes, was the key person through whom the Hayes organization reached enough Southern Democrats to make the deal. Ironically, Kellar's venture—a Memphis, Pine Bluff, and Shreveport connection to the Texas and Pacific Railroad—failed despite Hayes' support.

The Compromise of 1877 symbolized Northern abandonment of the freedmen and the beginning of Southern subordination of their rights. These developments had little effect on Memphis, however, where race relations remained relatively good until the 1890s. Long before then, locals of both races had their attention absorbed by a threat far more serious than any that had come before.

Aedes Aegyptus and the Saffron Plague

There is a terrible irony in the fact that Memphis had its population halved and its very existence jeopardized by a species of mosquito named for Egypt. This tiny insect, the *Aedes aegyptus*, vector of the yellow fever virus, had spread misery and death in the Caribbean and the Mississippi Valley from earliest colonial times. Between 1803 and 1900 New Orleans alone had 37 outbreaks of the disease, including the Great Epidemic of 1853 that saw 30,000 cases and 11,000 deaths. Memphis had likewise been buffeted by the saffron plague over its much shorter history.

In addition to outbreaks thought to be yellow fever at the Bluff's military outposts and in the city's early history, Memphis had clearly diagnosed episodes in 1855 and 1867. These epidemics, claiming 220 and 595 lives respectively, were terrible but not uncommonly so for the times. They were also far enough apart in time not to have cumulative effects. Memphis in the 1870s was less fortunate.

In 1873, following an unusually severe winter, the city experienced running epidemics of cholera, smallpox, and yellow fever. Of these the yellow fever was easily the worst, with approximately 5,000 cases and 2,000 deaths. Three years later the city had not yet fully recovered. A special census showed that the population of 1876 had increased by only four persons over that of 1870.

Despite periodic attempts at cleaning up the town, Memphis was frequently a sty whose filth rivaled that of a medieval village. Although science would not discover the cause of yellow fever until the early 20th century, Memphians were observant enough to realize that filth and standing water were disease related, and they assumed because of the stench that it had something to do with noxious gases. In response to repeated calls for better sanitation, especially after the horror of 1873, some cleanup efforts were made, but the city was in dire financial straits and there was little follow-through.

Above

Though virtually all local organizations aided in the relief work, the Howard Association, the Citizens Relief Committee, and the Catholic and Episcopal priests and nuns carried the greatest share of the burden and the risks. Many of these suffered the supreme penalty for their abiding charity. Thirteen Catholic priests and 30 sisters died while ministering to the stricken during the epidemic of 1878. From the Memphis/Shelby County Room (M/SCPLIC)

Above right

When yellow fever was declared to be present in the city, people fled in all directions to escape contagion. Those with neither the means to go far nor friends or relatives to turn to went to the countryside where the risks were considerably reduced. The plague of 1878 caused over half of the city's people to flee, some only to be arrested by the safety patrol. From *Harper's Weekly*, 1878, Memphis/Shelby County Room (M/SCPLIC)

Above, far right

When the fever hit, every town and village within a 200-mile radius imposed a quarantine against people fleeing from Memphis. This drawing shows that such quarantines were deadly serious as "grim-faced men, armed and ready to shoot, turned the refugees back." Times of terror let us know how thin the veneer of civilization really is. From the Memphis/Shelby County Room (M/SCPLIC)

With luck, and by enforcing a quarantine, it might have been a dozen years before yellow fever struck again. But the city's luck held only until 1878. Knowing that New Orleans was in the grip of the fever, Memphis imposed a quarantine and took the standard precautionary measures. Sprinkling the ground with lime and firing cannon to dispel "miasma" in the air, Memphians hoped that like biblical Hebrews they would be passed over.

The fever struck probably in late July, apparently brought in by travelers on the river. As usual the board of health delayed making a precise diagnosis for fear of starting a panic, unwittingly helping to spread the disease by suppressing their suspicions. Rumors abounded that the fever was present in the city, and hundreds of Memphians had already fled by August 13 when the board announced the first definite death from yellow fever. Then followed the immediate panic that authorities had sought to avoid.

Within four days an estimated 25,000 people fled the city by every imaginable conveyance and in all possible directions. Many of these were already carriers, spreading the disease to other locations. Perhaps even more would have fled, but virtually every town and village within a 200-mile radius imposed a quarantine against Memphis. Many of the smaller outlying communities enforced their edicts at gunpoint. About 5,000 Memphians who had no place else to go congregated in various refugee camps a few miles outside the city.

The uninfected who fled were wise to do so, for there was no prevention and no cure once the fever struck. When the *Aedes aegyptus* bit an infected person it became a vector, carrying the fever virus to all whom it would later bite. At its onset the disease manifested itself with chills, fever, and aching pains. At its climax the virus attacked the body's internal organs, especially the liver, whose malfunctioning gave the skin a yellowish cast. If a patient survived the attack, he enjoyed some degree of immunity afterward. The mortality rate varied greatly.

If the disease did not kill the patient, the treatment might. The average mid-19th-century physician had less accurate medical knowledge than a good present-day practical nurse. Some practitioners bled their patients and prescribed huge doses of purgatives and quinine. Others advocated ice-water baths, hot foot baths, or hot plasters. These and other useless remedies and preventatives would be humorous if the situation had not been so ghastly.

In spite of the pitiful state of medical knowledge, the efforts of the 111 physicians fighting the disease were truly heroic. The plague struck 54 of these doctors, killing 33. Other citizens and outside volunteers matched the heroic sacrifice of these healers.

Virtually all local organizations aided in the relief work, but the Howard Association, the Citizens Relief Committee, and the Catholic and Episcopal priests and nuns carried the greatest share of the burden. Many of these suffered the supreme penalty for their abiding charity. Others outside of the associations and religious orders also made the greatest

Chapter Four: Defiance and Defeat, Disease and Disaster: 1861-1879

sacrifice. Annie Cook, madam of one of the city's most fashionable bordellos, dismissed all of her girls and turned her house into a hospital until death claimed her three weeks later. The stories of selflessness and heroism are far too numerous to catalog here. However, the contributions of one group have too often been ignored or underrated.

Black Memphians rose to the challenge of 1878. In terms of selflessness this was perhaps their finest hour. They furnished a large proportion of the 3,000 nurses serving under the supervision of the Howards. They distributed supplies, comfort, and care for any and all of the stricken. Nor was this work without considerable risk. Although blacks had earlier been practically immune to yellow fever, the strain that struck in 1878 was so virulent that it smote blacks as well as whites who had survived earlier bouts and were presumed immune.

Blacks numbered about 70 percent of the population that remained in the city, and they provided virtually the entire work force for the stricken community. They distributed

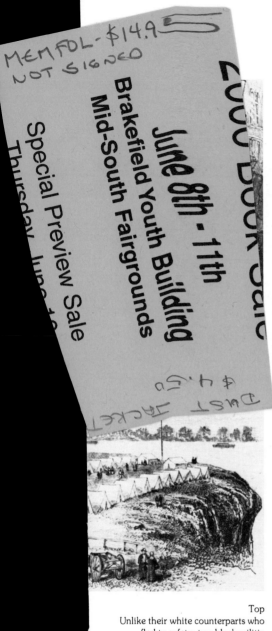

Top
Unlike their white counterparts who fled to safety, two black militia companies stayed and patrolled the streets to prevent looting. They also protected the city's store of supplies, even killing a fellow black when he tried to seize the food supply at the Court Square distribution point. Thereafter, their presence ensured order. From *Harper's Weekly*, 1878, Memphis/Shelby County Room (M/SCPLIC)

Above
The two black militia companies—the McClellan Guards and the Zouaves—put the town under a type of martial law as they protected both citizens and property. The seriousness of their task is attested to by the fact that they established campaign headquarters, pitched tents and all, on the bluff in front of the city. From *Harper's Weekly*, 1878, Memphis/Shelby County Room (M/SCPLIC)

the $700,000 worth of supplies which poured in from all over the nation. They collected and buried the thousands of corpses. Unlike their white counterparts, who fled to safety, two black militia companies stayed and patrolled the streets to prevent looting. They also protected the city's store of supplies, killing a fellow black when he tried to seize the food supply at the Court Square distribution point. Thereafter their presence ensured order.

The nightmare finally ended with an insect-killing frost on the night of October 18. The number of cases and deaths dropped rapidly, and 10 days later authorities declared the epidemic over. Of the approximately 20,000 citizens who had not fled, an estimated 17,000 contracted the fever, and 5,150 of these died. Virtually all of the 6,000 whites were stricken, more than two-thirds of them fatally. Among the 14,000 blacks who stayed, at least 11,000 were stricken, but of these only 949 died. Memphis was the hardest hit of more than 200 communities in the Mississippi and Ohio valleys, having suffered more than 17 percent of all the cases reported and more than 25 percent of the deaths.

The yellow fever epidemics of 1867 and the 1870s were financially calamitous for Memphis. Even before the onslaught of the worst epidemics, the city was staggering under an unmanageable $5-million debt. As early as 1874 there were calls for the city to renounce its charter and avoid payment of debts that most citizens believed were unethical and illegally contracted. City hall resisted any such move, which would have destroyed the city's credit and eliminated the jobs of officeholders. But the epidemic of 1878 made any discussion of the issue academic. With the city's population severely reduced, its tax base eroded by half, and many citizens unable to pay taxes on their property, Memphis was bankrupt.

In January of 1879 the state repealed Memphis' charter, and the city ceased to exist as a corporate entity. Declared simply a taxing district, the community was placed under state control, leaving the residents with little or no control in the management of public affairs. Under the supervision of a two-board commission, with half its members appointed by the governor, municipal functions were reduced to fire and police protection, health and sanitation protection, and public works. The former city would be on a forced austerity program until it cleaned up its environment and satisfied its creditors, perhaps at an adjusted rate. Memphis bondholders, resisting any attempt to discount the debt, attacked the legality of the taxing district scheme. They carried the battle all the way to the United States Supreme Court, where they finally lost.

With all that the local people had been through, it would seem that nothing more could befall the crippled ex-city. Not so. The summer of 1879 brought yet another yellow fever epidemic. This attack proved milder than that of the previous year, totaling only about 2,000 cases and claiming 595 lives. But the 1879 epidemic lasted longer, and it may have done even greater economic damage to the community. Many of the more prosperous citizens had already located elsewhere, and many others now proceeded to follow their example. With people so anxious to sell and move out, real estate values crumbled, with some property selling for as little as 10 cents on the dollar.

The un-city had reached the nadir of its fortunes. Even if the home-rule charter could one day be reclaimed, the community had lost thousands of its most productive citizens and destroyed its credit in the financial markets. There would be no capital or energetic entrepreneurs available for redevelopment. The locale had a reputation as the least healthy place in the nation. Out-of-town newspapers and some local citizens suggested seriously that the site be abandoned.

Would the community lose its physical as well as its corporate identity? The remnants of what had once been the fastest-growing city in the nation waited to see whether they had the intelligence and the grit to bring their city back. Those with faith would be rewarded as, like the phoenix of Egyptian legend, Memphis renewed itself from the figurative ashes of its devastation.

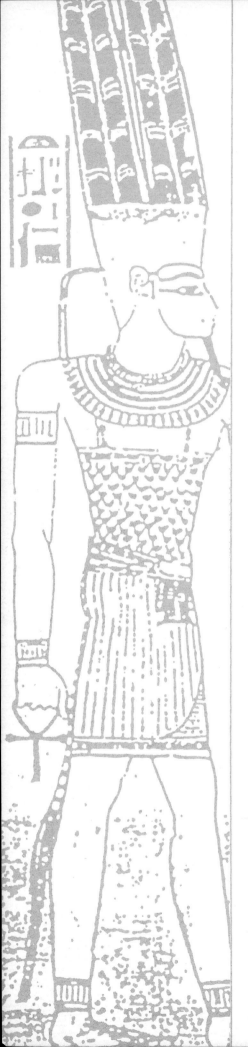

CHAPTER FIVE

BIRTH OF THE MODERN CITY: 1880~1908

Like the phoenix of old, Memphis rose again from disaster and near-destruction. Under the austere taxing-district administration the city restored itself to health and grew to become a 20th-century metropolis. As such it was destined to experience all the problems associated with expansion and industrialization in most of the nation's cities. Some of these problems could be solved with the aid of technology. Others were human problems, and these proved more intractable. Memphis fared reasonably well in addressing the problems of its white community, but the city's black citizens were shunted aside, their civil rights and their human dignity subordinated to a cult of white supremacy.

The Taxing District

Memphis began fighting its way back under a unique form of local government. Although the community no longer had home rule, some form of local organization was obviously needed to provide essential services and, above all, to combat the unsanitary conditions which had all but destroyed it. These functions were performed by a bicameral legislative council, composed of a three-member Board of Fire and Police Commissioners and a five-member Board of Public Works. Initially the governor appointed about half of the council's membership, including its president. Later all of the offices became elective, with vacancies being filled by the governor's office. The taxing district's budget and spending had to be approved by the state, and no frills were permitted.

Taxing-district officials were abler and more conscientious men than many of those who had previously ruled the city's fortunes. They were not politicians but men of substance

Metropolis of the American Nile

The rebirth of the city and its transition to modern metropolis is best symbolized by the construction of the first steel-skeleton skyscraper in 1895. The 11-story structure and its high-speed elevator thrilled visitors who paid a dime to ride to the top. After the Continental Bank folded near the turn of the century, the building was purchased and renamed the Dr. D.T. Porter Building. It remains one of the city's landmarks. From the Memphis/Shelby County Room (M/SCPLIC)

Above
Dr. D.T. Porter, a druggist turned businessman and developer, served as the first president of the taxing district after the city lost its charter. His direct methods were instrumental in cleaning up the city. In addition to being the president of a local bank and a wholesale grocer and cotton factor, Porter was active in many philanthropic causes. He is remembered particularly for his contributions to orphans at the Leath Asylum, now Porter-Leath Home. From the Memphis/Shelby County Room (M/SCPLIC)

Above right
The cotton factors or commission merchants were key figures in the Memphis area economy from the boom era into the 20th century. They financed the cotton growers' subsistence and operational needs from ground breaking until the cotton was shipped to the mills. Most factors derived substantial profits from the wholesale and retail grocery business and from banking operations for the farmers. Duffin Brothers and McGehee was probably a medium-sized cotton business and operated from this building at 72 Front Row at the turn of the century. From the Memphis/Shelby County Room (M/SCPLIC)

used to running business as they deemed best. With spending under strict state control, they were free from much of the political strife and pork-barrel bickering that had earlier prevailed. These hardworking men enjoyed a measure of good luck.

Two of the taxing-district officials deserve particular mention. Dr. D.T. Porter, a druggist turned businessman and developer, served as the district's first president. Working closely with the now permanent Board of Health, he made an excellent beginning in cleaning up the environment. David Park "Pappy" Hadden served as president from 1882 to 1889. By diligent and patient effort he carried recovery efforts to their completion. In his capacity as city judge, Hadden earned a reputation for being strict but fair with general miscreants and for firm enforcement of the city's new sanitary regulations.

Under such able men the filthy environment was effectively cleaned up. Not that the authorities knew precisely what they were doing. They did not. But in the general cleanup they succeeded in destroying most of the mosquito-breeding places. Between this happenstance and the enforced application of quarantine measures, yellow fever struck Memphis only one more time, and then without serious consequences. Although Memphis continued to have a poor health reputation, actual health conditions compared favorably with most other U.S. cities.

The taxing district also resolved the much more complex problem of the municipal debt. Doubtless some Memphians hoped that abrogation of the city charter would permit

David Park Hadden, usually called "Pappy," took up the reins of governing the defunct town when Dr. Porter resigned as president of the taxing district. Hadden served as president from 1882-1889, and was known for his diligence and patience in completing the reforms begun by Porter. He also served as city judge. To end scrapes rising from dice games, he invented a leather bell—known as Hadden's Horn—to insure a fair roll of the dice. From the Memphis/Shelby County Room (M/SCPLIC)

repudiation of the city's debts, a move that some citizens had been advocating since 1873. The city's creditors, also foreseeing this possibility, challenged the legality of the Taxing District Act in state and federal courts. Although the courts upheld the legitimacy of the act, in 1881 the state ruled that the taxing district was still responsible for the city's debts. After a tangle of lawsuits and hard negotiations, debts amounting to $5 million were adjusted and eventually repaid at between 50 cents and par on the dollar. Probably no creditors actually lost money, since the city's bonds had been sold at unfairly discounted rates.

Even after these adjustments, it took a long time to repay the debt. Because of the fever panic and the loss of business, the value of real estate had fallen by two-thirds, reducing the city's tax base accordingly. Property values did not return to their previous level until near the end of the taxing-district era. Final payment on this holdover debt was not made until 1908, and only then was Memphis again permitted to issue general-liability bonds. Even so, the national financial community's confidence in Memphis was not fully restored until the 1920s, and Memphis' financial reputation was questioned for years afterwards.

The good government of the taxing district ended long before the city had redeemed its credit. Historian Gerald Capers maintains that self-righteous citizens forced a return to "normal" government in order to suppress gambling, which taxing-district officials had only sought to regulate. If such was their aim, they only made a bad situation worse. But other Memphians, seeing the debt issue settled and local taxes entering state coffers, also wanted a return to home rule. The state legislature complied, authorizing restoration of the municipal corporation and the city's name in 1891 and returning its power to tax in 1893.

If the taxing district left Memphis a legacy of good government, it also left a legacy of citizen nonparticipation. This heritage did not bode well for the new government, which would face a complex set of new problems common to all the nation's cities. A new era of dramatic growth and change would bring both bright lights and cesspools calling for progressive measures. Memphis would require almost a generation to make the necessary adjustments.

Cotton: Still King

Underlying all the other types of growth that transformed Memphis into a modern city was the region's economic expansion. During the three decades from 1879 to 1909, as in earlier periods, the economy was dominated by the cotton trade. Despite continuous calls for economic diversification, and some modest attempts to achieve it, cotton remained king throughout this period.

One of the primary reasons for Memphis' addiction to cotton was the unique financial structure of the community. Capital-poor before the Civil War, the city was in much worse shape after its bouts with war, Reconstruction, and plague. Although Memphis attracted some Northern investment capital and entrepreneurial talent after the war, most of it was on a small scale. Thus risk capital had to be developed locally, and the only large-scale export from the area was cotton.

During this period, as in the prewar era, cotton was in the hands of the factor or commission merchant. In 1873 Memphis' leading merchants and factors established the Memphis Cotton Exchange to bring order and up-to-date information to the local cotton market. This innovation benefited both merchants and growers, and helped to make Memphis the largest "spot" cotton market in the world. The exchange limited its membership to 175 seats, and its leaders furnished the power elite that controlled the local economy for several generations.

The factor did much more than simply market cotton. He financed the cotton growers'

subsistence and operational needs from ground breaking until the baled cotton was shipped to the mills. Although the factor usually collected only a 2.5-percent commission on crop sales, most factors also derived substantial profits from the wholesale and retail grocery business and from banking operations for the farmers. These operations often led factors into other aspects of banking and wholesale business less directly related to farming, giving them even greater control over local capital. Many successful factors then moved into real-estate speculation and development, highly profitable during this period of growth, thereby gaining still greater control of local capital.

The most successful factors profited grandly from their numerous interrelated businesses and formed the core of the city's business and social upper crust. Families such as the Hills, the Norfleets, and the Fontaines intermarried with others who dominated the economic life of the city, thus strengthening the cohesiveness of the power elite and perpetuating its influence. The cotton brokers dominated the regional cotton market and the city's economy until World War I, and families of some of these continue to exert a strong influence to the present time.

Most of the Memphis commission houses were located on "Cotton Row"—Front Street between Jefferson and Beale. Initially chosen for its convenience to the steamboat landing, the location was retained even after railroads took over the bulk of cotton shipments. Some of the old companies are still there. Although the street now lacks the marvelous confusion and bustle of the late 19th century, a certain flavor of the picturesque old days remains.

The city's economic power structure was generally reluctant to invest its capital in building an industrial base for development. One reason was the stability of the factorage business. Even when the cotton growers lost money because of low market prices in the 1890s, the factors still received their commission and made profits on their diverse related enterprises. As cotton production continued to grow, some factors did get involved in cotton-related industries; but even when these industries became a significant segment of the local economy, they never rivaled cotton trading in value or prestige.

The most important of the cotton-related industries were ginning, loose baling, compressing, binding, transporting, and warehousing, all of which provided numerous jobs on the local scene. Warehousing protected the cotton, giving it a better appearance and higher selling price. By 1908 all of the cotton coming through Memphis was stored under a roof until transshipped.

Cottonseed, initially considered a waste product of the ginning process, created a host of allied industries. Crushing the seed yielded an extremely rich oil, which found extensive use in the manufacture of soap, cooking and salad oils, and margarine. The crushed pulp was compressed into cake to supplement livestock feed, and hulls became a fertilizer component. The combination of cotton by-products exclusive of cotton gave rise in 1881 to a local commodities market known as the Memphis Merchants Exchange.

Economic Growth

The Memphis Merchants Exchange strove to develop and diversify the local economy. But attempts at economic diversification had only limited success. Although capital investment in local manufacturing surged from $2 million to $9 million over the decade of the 1880s, most of this growth was tied to the cotton by-products industry and to lumber and related industries.

During this era the magnificent hardwood forests of the region began to be harvested, making lumber the second most important product in the local economy. The Memphis lum-

Above
S.R. Montgomery is a fitting symbol of a member of the power elite during Memphis' period of transition to a modern city. Handsome, wealthy, accomplished, and well connected, he reflects both the old and the new. He served as president of the New Memphis Jockey Club, which was headquartered at Montgomery Park, now the Mid-South Fair Grounds. He was also the general manager of the Merchants Cotton Press and Storage Company, which helped issue in the era of warehousing all of the cotton marketed in Memphis. From the Memphis/Shelby County Room (M/SCPLIC)

Right
Throughout the 19th century cotton remained king in the Memphis economy. Part of the reason for the supremacy of cotton rested with the unique structure of the city's financial community. The cotton factor, who financed the farmer's operations from ground breaking to crop sale, insisted on cultivation of this crop. Depicted here is the process from picking, hauling, and compressing to loading on a steamer. In recent decades, Mid-South agriculture has become much more diversified, although cotton is still extremely important. Courtesy, Charles A. Bobbitt

COTTON COMPRESS

DRAY LOAD OF COTTON.

COTTON PICKING.

UNLOADING COTTON STEAMER.

Above

Near the end of the 19th century the Mid-South became one of the world's major hardwood lumbering centers with Memphis as its leading market. As the picture indicates, blacks furnished most of the awesome labor required to bring down the giants of the forest. The picture is undated, but timbering methods did not change greatly in the early decades of this extractive industry. From the Memphis/Shelby County Room (M/SCPLIC)

Above right

The coming of the major railroads into isolated areas and the draining of swampy lands made possible the harvesting of the region's magnificent hardwood forests. By 1900 there were more than 500 sawmills within a 100-mile radius of Memphis. From the Memphis/Shelby County Room (M/SCPLIC)

ber industry grew from a capitalization of less than $200,000 in 1880 to more than $2.5 million by the turn of the century. By 1900 there were more than 500 sawmills within a 100-mile radius of Memphis, and the city claimed the titles of world's largest hardwood market and world's second largest lumber market. Memphis dealers shipped lumber and related products all over the globe.

Like cotton, the lumber industry gave rise to a host of allied manufacturing industries. Local manufacture of barrels, boxes, doors, blinds, wagons, farm implements, furniture, and other finished and semifinished articles consumed 12 to 13 percent of the region's lumber production. However, such enterprises, lacking the capital to become national concerns, stayed relatively small until well into the 20th century.

In addition to cotton, lumber, and their related industries, Memphis boasted a small number of other significant enterprises. The city was the largest snuff market in the world, the largest boot and shoe market in the South, and one of the largest wholesale grocery markets in the nation. Excellent beer from the Tennessee Brewery, minor iron and steel fabrication, distribution of hardware and dry goods, and the manufacture of paint also contributed to the local economy. Memphis also did a lively trade in livestock, especially mules, becoming the largest mule market in the world in the early decades of the 20th century. By 1900 the city's combined enterprises, limited in scope and size though they were, produced an estimated annual trade value of $275 million. Together they provided the employment that enabled the city to grow.

More significant than anything done in Memphis to boost the city's economy was the extension and development of the city's market-area hinterland. In the words of Gerald Capers, "Prosperity was almost thrust upon the city from without." Extension of the rail network and reclamation of swamplands provided the major thrusts in developing the hinterland and "forcing" prosperity on the city.

Changes Wrought by Railroads

In 1882 the rail network serving Memphis still consisted of the six railroads that had been in operation or under construction at the outbreak of the Civil War. By 1892 seven new lines entered the city. Several of these became part of the Illinois Central trunk line, providing service from Paducah through Memphis, the Yazoo Delta, Vicksburg, and Baton Rouge to New Orleans. Completion of this line was one of the most important economic developments prior to World War I.

The one development that rivaled the I.C. trunk line for railroading importance, and

Metropolis of the American Nile

In the economic boom that followed the fever decade, a host of secondary manufacturing enterprises blossomed. Henry Loeb's Shirt Company was among these. To insure the shirts were clean before going on sale, Loeb had them laundered on the premises. His methods were so good that soon his customers were bringing their shirts back to have them laundered at the factory. Later the laundry business took over, and became the first auto-delivery service in the city. Henry Loeb was also known for his many charitable acts and for purchasing many animals to give to the zoo. Courtesy, Charles A. Bobbitt

surpassed it for pure drama, was the construction of the "Great Bridge at Memphis." Up until 1892 there was no bridge across the Mississippi River below St. Louis, where the river was much smaller. East-west railroad traffic had to be shuttled across the river by railroad ferry boats, a cumbersome and time-consuming process. In 1892 the Kansas City, Fort Scott, and Memphis Railroad (later absorbed by the Frisco line) took the plunge and built the world's third longest bridge, at a cost of more than $3 million and several human lives.

Only the opening of the Memphis and Charleston Railroad some 35 years earlier ever rivaled the celebration in Memphis on completion of the Great Bridge. The festivities and fanfare lasted for four days and climaxed with a test of the bridge by 18 steam locomotives hooked together. By noon of May 12, 1892, 50,000 people had lined the bluff to watch the event. After young women ceremoniously kissed the crew members for luck, the engines rolled their hundreds of tons onto the span. Success brought a deafening cacophonous din as train whistles and bells were joined by the whistles of harbor boats and factories, cannon salutes, and the shouts of the excited multitude. The ribbon-cutting ceremony that followed proved an anticlimax.

After the grand opening, four railroads made use of the new bridge. Later called the Frisco Bridge, it extended the Memphis trade area farther west. It also opened through traffic between the Birmingham industrial complex in north central Alabama and the Missouri-Kansas region to the northwest.

Numerous other rail improvements followed. In 1895 the city's commercial interests formed the Memphis Freight Bureau to ensure that Memphis shippers received equitable freight rates. The bureau acted as an information clearinghouse, and within a few years it had reduced rates on all freight except cotton and lumber by an average of 40 percent. This factor, combined with the city's insistence that railroads cooperate within Memphis, helped make the city one of the nation's premier rail centers. By World War I Memphis was served by 11 trunk lines and probably handled more freight than any other Southern city.

In conjunction with the expanding rail network, there was a dramatic qualitative refinement of the Memphis hinterland. As railroads penetrated the swampy lowlands of the Yazoo Delta in Mississippi and the St. Francis Basin in Arkansas, their virgin forests were cut for timber. In conjunction with these timbering operations, and with the vital assistance of the Memphis District of the Army Corps of Engineers, levees were constructed and drainage programs implemented. The fertile bottomlands newly opened to agriculture produced the

PROCLAMATION

YOU ARE HEREBY COMMANDED to present yourself within the gates of "The Metropolis of the Great Valley," where the mighty ocean of commerce breaking over the bulwark of opposition is sweeping North, South, East and West, filling the reservoirs of the kingdom with the necessities and luxuries of the land; . . . . The faithful followers of his Majesty will pay homage to ISIS, the tutelary goddess of Memphis, on May 12th and 13, and in honor of this great event, his Majesty shall declare opened to his subjects a new cantilever structure — the greatest across America's inland sea — linking by bands of steel the shores of the mighty South and West on the spot where De Soto first saw the great "Father of Waters," facilitating uninterrupted commerce with all my dominion.

The war ships of the kingdom shall guard the entrance to the harbor while the great orators of the nation dwell upon the manifold advantages and beauties of the Southern Capital, where the majestic touch of the miner brings forth from the bowels of the earth all minerals known to science; where forests abound in all their pristine glory, giving abundant material for homes for the millions and for all manufactures; where the air is ever pregnant of the perfume of the sweetest and rarest flowers; where the purest and fairest women dwell; where all nature combines with the efforts of man in the up-building and strengthening of the greatest country of mother earth.

Come ere the sun hath risen and join freely in the festivities of the morn and of the noontime and of the evening and fail not. Given under the royal seal thin the XXVIII day of April MFVVVLCCCCII.

A-A-REX

— Announcement in the *Memphis Appeal-Avalance* of the public celebration of the official opening of "The Great Bridge" on April 28, 1892.

Memphis' Great Bridge, 1892. Courtesy, Memphis Pink Palace Museum

Facing page
Top left
Railroading made major strides in the
Memphis area in the 1890s. One of the
most important of these was the
development of the Illinois Central
trunk line providing service from
Paducah through Memphis, the Yazoo
Delta, Vicksburg, and Baton Rouge to
New Orleans. The depot of the I.C. line
stood at Front and Poplar. Courtesy,
Illinois Central Railroad. From the
Memphis/Shelby County Room
(M/SCPLIC)

Top right
In 1892 the Kansas City, Fort Scott,
and Memphis Railroad completed the
Great Bridge at Memphis, at a cost of
more than three million dollars and
several human lives. The festivities and
fanfare lasted for four days, climaxed
with a test of the bridge by 18 steam
locomotives. Success brought a
deafening roar of shouts, whistles, bells,
and cannon salutes. The picture shows a
line up of the decorated engines and
dressed-up employees at the event.
Courtesy, Memphis Pink Palace
Museum

highest cotton yields of any farmland in the country. This increased production was undoubtedly a major factor in the depressed cotton prices of the 1890s and pointed again to the need for agricultural diversification.

Toward the end of this period, another commercial crop was introduced into the Mid-South region. Beginning with the fledgling efforts of a grieving farm widow named Emma Morris, abetted by railroaders and land speculators, the successful cultivation of rice began in western Arkansas. Experimentation showed that the crop actually grew much better in the eastern delta regions of the state. There it became a very profitable crop and a boon to the Mid-South's economy. The Arkansas farmer and his Riceland Co-op eventually became the nation's number-one rice producers.

The spread of the Mid-South rail network also had another "fallout" effect. Despite great improvements in the Mississippi River navigation channels, especially after the establishment of the Mississippi River Commission in 1882, shippers opted increasingly for rail transport of their goods. By the late 1880s less than 20 percent of Memphis cotton was still being shipped by river, and by 1900 steamboat traffic in the Memphis harbor was less than half of what it had been in 1880. The glamour and romance of the floating palaces were headed for extinction. When river transport staged a comeback in the 20th century, it would be in mundane-looking towboats and barge traffic rather than the stately white river queens. Only a few of the grand old dames survive now, kept alive by the tourist trade and a yearning for the gracious time that is no more.

Technological Transformations

If changing technologies were altering the city's economic base, this was much less perceptible to the average citizen than the ways in which they were altering the quality of life. A latter-day Rip Van Winkle, going to sleep in 1880 and awakening in 1909, might have thought himself transported to another planet, so drastic were the changes. Not all of these changes were for the better, but in terms of health, comfort, and convenience, great strides had been made.

In 1880 the city's most pressing need was to clean up its filthy environment and establish and adhere to modern health standards. Taxing-district president Porter, working with the Board of Health and state and federal authorities, set out single-mindedly to do just that. Embracing an untried system of underground sanitary sewers and subsoil drains designed by Colonel George E. Waring, Jr., the city built more than 30 miles of sewers in 1880 and 1881. Made of relatively inexpensive expanding-diameter clay pipes and operating on a principle of continuous water flow, the sewer system became an immediate and enormous success. Known alternately as the Memphis System and the Waring Sanitary System, the sewer design was imitated by more than 200 other cities of the nation and the world. The city expanded the system to more than 50 miles by 1899, and then more than doubled its length when that year's annexation brought suburbs into the city.

Perhaps the city's next most important sanitary requirement was pure water. Until 1873 Memphis had no waterworks. Residents got their water from pumps, wells, or cisterns, often in the same yards with their privies. In that year the Memphis Water Company began supplying the city with a murky, polluted fluid from the Wolf River. This supply was needed mainly for the public cisterns used by fire fighters, but it was also a vital element in the daily flushing of the new sewer mains. Some people began drinking the Wolf River water, while others preferred the equally foul but cheaper products of their home cisterns.

Not until 1887 did Memphis discover that it was sitting only 400 feet above an aquifer system containing billions of gallons of perhaps the world's purest and clearest water.

Memphis had drilled for artesian water before, but these early efforts had failed. Then an ice company's exploratory drilling brought in pure water from a depth of 354 feet. Soon the newly merged water companies had constructed 40 wells with a daily capacity of 30 million gallons, far greater than the city's immediate needs. However, the water company's directors were much more interested in securing profits than in providing good service at reasonable rates to the public. The company's continued refusal to construct new water mains or to lower its prices prompted the city to buy the company. After years of delays and countless obstacles, the city purchased the utility in 1903 and was able to improve service and reduce rates by 20 percent the next year. The virtually inexhaustable supply of cheap, pure water was not only a boon to the city's health but also helped attract industry and population to Memphis.

During this period the Board of Health also clamped down on the sale of impure milk and food, destroying tainted products and forcing the dairies into compliance with regulations. By 1901 the board was able to impose compulsory smallpox vaccinations on the city's schoolchildren, despite considerable opposition to the program. Lastly, the city embarked on a comprehensive program of garbage collection and street cleaning. Like a converted sinner, Memphis had achieved a complete reversal on the issues of sanitation and public health.

Another utility that aided the city's growth was the street-railway system. Beginning in 1866 Memphis enjoyed (if that is the correct word) a mule-drawn street railroad. The initial tracks were expanded, and competing companies provided routine transportation at a nickel a ride, a considerable saving over the high rates of the hack drivers. This primitive system was still in use when the first electric streetcar was tested in 1891.

Two Chicago capitalists, C.B. Holmes and A.M. Billings, brought an efficient electrified street-railway system to Memphis. Consolidating competing lines and greatly expanding trackage and service, Billings and his son, C.K.G. Billings, built Memphis a first-rate trolley system. By 1900 the Memphis Street Railway Company had 100 miles of track spread over 17 routes and was running 75 cars.

The street railway gave working-class Memphians unprecedented mobility. Besides connecting the densely populated areas of the city with the business and industrial areas, the

General Sam T. Carnes was probably the city's greatest turn-of-the-century innovator. He introduced Memphis to the automobile, brought a Bell telephone franchise to Memphis only a year after Bell made his discovery public, and brought electrical lighting to the city as well. In 1890 Carnes merged with his main competitor to form the Memphis Light and Power Company. He secured a 10-year charter from the city and renewed this in 1900 for 35 years. He sold controlling interest in the company to a New York syndicate the following year. From the Memphis/Shelby County Room (M/SCPLIC)

rails ran to recreation areas beyond the city limits. Suburban communities sprang up along the streetcar lines, to be absorbed later into greater Memphis. These developments helped change the patterns of living in Memphis and enhance the quality of life of its citizens.

A.M. Billings died in 1897. C.K.G. Billings, who shared his father's special fondness for Memphis, continued the street railway system and other public enterprises until 1905. In that year, disgusted because a new state law would destroy his beloved horse racing in Memphis, the younger Billings sold the trolley company to a New York syndicate. The New York group recapitalized the system and continued to expand it to meet the needs of a rapidly growing city.

During this period of dramatic street-railroad improvements, the streets themselves remained the shame of the city. The city's past debts and its commitment to the sewer system exhausted revenues that might otherwise have been spent on the street system. In 1900 less than 10 percent of the city's 175 miles of streets were paved at all, usually with stones, bricks, and wooden blocks, and some of these were in bad shape. Finally, using the much less expensive asphalt paving, and imposing a frontage tax along the streets designated for improvement, significant progress began to be made. By 1908, when automobiles were still fairly rare, a comprehensive system of street improvement was well underway.

The man who introduced the automobile to Memphis was General Sam T. Carnes, probably the city's greatest turn-of-the-century innovator, who also gave the city electricity and the telephone. Carnes secured the Bell franchise for Memphis, making his first demonstration call in 1877, only a year after Bell had made his famous demonstration in Boston. He built up a small subscriber service for his telephone exchange, then sold out in 1883 to a Nashville company, which was later absorbed by the Southern Bell system.

Prior to selling his telephone company, Carnes acquired the rights to use the Brush electric-light patents in Memphis. He first demonstrated the use of primitive electric lighting in early 1884, and began commercial sale of the service shortly thereafter. In 1890 Carnes merged with his principal competitor to form the Memphis Light and Power Company. Building a much larger power plant, Carnes acquired a 10-year charter from the city, which he renewed in 1900 for 35 years. In 1901 Carnes and his local associates sold controlling interest in the company to the same New York syndicate that later purchased the Memphis Street Railway Company—a marvelous marriage for the stockholders, since the trolley company was the largest single user of electric power in the city. The combination also benefited the home user, since the MSR needed most of its power during the day and lighting was used principally at night.

Although gas and electric rates in Memphis stayed relatively low because of mergers and city regulation, the community resented the monopolistic ownership of its utilities by outside capitalists. This resentment bred intermittent agitation for public ownership and made the power company a tempting political target until the city finally purchased it in 1939. However, the city itself could never have begun electrification in the 1880s. If local entrepreneurs and outside capitalists made large profits from their investments, they also greatly improved the quality of life for tens of thousands of Memphians during the decades before the city could begin to cope with such complexities.

Social, Geographical, and Cultural Changes

Rebounding from the devastation of the yellow fever epidemics, the city's population soared in the last two decades of the 19th century. From the depleted figure of 33,592 in 1880, it surged to 64,495 in 1890 and 102,320 in 1900. But the disastrous decade had placed Memphis far back in the pack in its bid to become the South's premier city. Had the

County Trustee John Joseph Williams successfully challenged incumbent Lucas Clapp for the mayor's office just before the turn of the century and moved rapidly to annex 12 square miles, quadrupling the city's size. Although a "reform" mayor himself, Williams was a city politician who trafficked with the saloon interests. He was reputed to have stolen the election with purchased black votes. Ousted by a reform ticket victory a few years later, Williams stayed popular and a factor in politics until 1920. From the Memphis/Shelby County Room (M/SCPLIC)

city's earlier growth rate continued, it would probably have crested the 100,000 mark in the mid-1880s and had the advantage of momentum in the race with other Southern cities. Still, considering the blows of the 1870s, the degree of recovery was most remarkable.

In addition to retarding population, the fever experience drastically altered its cultural composition. It killed almost half of the Irish residents and caused about half of the Germans to locate elsewhere, principally in St. Louis. Because of its reputation Memphis failed to attract many new immigrants or many migrants from the North, as it had done in the immediate postwar years.

Yet people flocked in to populate the reviving city. The growth of the Memphis-area economy, the prospect of jobs, the glittering attractions of city life, and a high birth rate plus grinding poverty in the rural hinterland, all combined to bring in 50,000-60,000 rural migrants. These migrants, both black and white, had a profound impact on the values and mores of the city, giving it a distinctly provincial cast. The newcomers' conservative rural values were at odds with the urban conception of the "good life" with its conspicuous consumption and conspicuous leisure. The resulting sense of disorientation and alienation may have contributed to the high rates of crime and violence, which troubled Memphis well into the 20th century.

The white migrants reinforced the city's devotion to the "lost cause." Simultaneous with the growth of the New South, the Southern psyche created a parallel fantasy regarding the Old South. In seeking to keep alive the "noble traditions of bygone days," white Southerners embraced a complex credo, which included an uncritical Protestant fundamentalism, the assumption of and insistence on black inferiority, a belief in the innate purity of womanhood, and a "macho" justification for using violence in the protection of Southern ideals. White Memphians generally adhered religiously to this cult.

Although Reconstruction had been relatively mild in Tennessee, especially in Memphis, Memphians were bitter. With their world turned upside down, they could justify the actions of the KKK and deride all things Northern. When a group of Confederate veterans sought to establish a new Episcopal parish, they asked their bishop for permission to name it "Saint Lazarus." Asked to explain such an unusual choice, they responded, "Well, Bishop, like Lazarus, we were licked by the dogs." Whether or not the bishop agreed with this view of the Union Army, a St. Lazarus parish was established briefly in Memphis.

In 1900 the city honored the visiting Admiral Dewey, the hero of Manila Bay. Confederate veterans greeted him at the train station with a band playing "Dixie." Later he was taken on a tour of the city that included a visit to Miss Higbee's School. There, much as one might assure a visiting Frenchman that one did not despise frogs' legs or snails, Miss Higbee felt it necessary to inform the admiral that her students were loyal Americans. She assured him that these girls—most of whom had not been born until a generation after the war's end—sang the "Star-Spangled Banner" with the same ardor that they recited "The Conquered Banner." And this was 35 years after Appomattox!

Citywide devotion to the lost cause was best shown by the 1901 reunion of the United Confederate Veterans. Local citizens raised $50,000 for the celebration, decorated most of the downtown streets, and built an 18,000-seat Confederate Hall on the present site of Confederate Park. The ensuing parades, fireworks, concerts, speeches, and other entertainments provided the last truly great rally of the veterans. By the 1909 gathering most of the veterans were either dead or infirm, but the myth and the spirit of the cause lived on for generations. Such was the mental orientation of the new Memphis population.

Parallel to the growth of an idealized Old South, Memphis became a big new city in the real world of the New South. By 1890 all phases of growth engendered an optimism about the future that had not existed in the city since the 1850s. By 1895 citizens whose town had

nearly died 15 years before were translating the name Memphis to mean "good station." This translation would be altered in ensuing decades to "place of good abode," and finally to the promotional phrase "City of Good Abode." In a relative sense, and for the most visible segments of the city's population, the slogan was becoming increasingly true.

By 1890 more than half of the county's population lived within the city limits. Mushrooming suburbs meant that even this statistic did not accurately reflect the growth of the greater Memphis community. Such perceptions and a fledgling progressive spirit gave birth at the end of the 1890s to the "Greater Memphis Movement."

Progressive civic leaders in 1898 sought to annex the clustering suburbs for two major reasons. They wanted to extend the city's sanitation services into the peripheral communities to avoid the possibility of another bout with yellow fever, and they also wanted to add about 30,000 residents to the city's population to increase its rank and prestige in the forthcoming 1900 census. However, there was initial resistance to the movement both in the city and in its suburbs.

The issue was pulled into the political arena when County Trustee John Joseph Williams successfully challenged the incumbent mayor, Lucas Clapp. Although Williams seemed only lukewarm on the expansion issue, once in office he moved rapidly to effect the annexation. After overcoming some legalistic opposition from a few disgruntled suburbanites, Memphis annexed some 12 square miles surrounding the city, thereby quadrupling the city's size and changing its configuration from a rough rectangle hugging the banks of the river to a nearly square shape. The main thrust of expansion was eastward, taking in the communities of Madison Heights, Idlewild, and Manila.

This annexation was a major directional change for Memphis. Not only did it alter the city's thrust from north-south to east-west, but it set a precedent for subsequent annexations of eastern-perimeter communities. Not until the second half of the 20th century did the eastward trend end, as Memphis jumped the obstacles of Wolf River and Nonconnah Creek to annex the major communities of Frayser, Whitehaven, and even onetime rival Raleigh. The 1899 annexation was also notable for its sheer size. A jealous critic from another Tennessee city warned that should the U.S. take Cuba from Spain, Memphis would probably annex it!

New Buildings and Parks

Of course the 1899 annexation took in a great deal of empty farmland. The busy sub-

dividing and heavy residential development that had begun in the 1890s boomed following the big land grab. Some of these were shabby quick-buck operations, but others such as Annesdale Park Subdivision offered quality development and prestige to prospective residents. The building boom lasted from the 1890s until the Great Depression, more than tripling the number of housing units by 1920.

The annexation and building boom finally forced the city government to do something about its chaotic street names and numbering systems. Some names applied to as many as three separate streets, and the numbering of addresses defied the term system. The city's many attempts to remedy the numbering chaos met with passive resistance from residents, in spite of council-imposed fines ranging from $2 to $50 for violations. Finally, in 1903, the local postmaster's decision to discontinue mail delivery to violators forced residents to comply. The local history devotee has to be aware of these changes or, like the turn-of-the-century postman, he will get lost trying to find his way through the city's past.

Memphis' building boom was not confined to subdivision development. It also included the mansions and estates of the postwar wealthy, the physical transformation of the central business district, and the development of urban amenities to serve the aesthetic and recreational needs of its newly urbanized populace.

The mansions of the newly rich were not generally aesthetic gems. Spanning the architectural spectrum from Byzantine to Renaissance, some of these buildings were showy and expensive monstrosities, commodious though they might be. During this period American culture was characterized by ostentatious spending. Wealthier Memphians of this Gilded Age entertained lavishly, traveled widely, and sought, sometimes gauchely, to acquire the cultural baggage of aristocracy. If many of their homes reflected this social adolescence, it was in the American spirit of the times.

The city's new wealth also transformed the downtown landscape and the Memphis skyline in the period after 1890. The necessity of replacing drab, obsolete, and sometimes dangerous structures coincided with expanding demands for office and commercial space. The need was obvious, the capital available, and new technology ready to bring the skyscraper to Memphis. Starting with the 11-story Continental Bank (D.T. Porter) Building in 1895, a high-rise office building boom began. In 1905 the 15-story Tennessee Trust (81 Madison) Building became the city's tallest structure. High-rise construction continued until World War I, when supply caught up with demand. About a half-dozen of these turn-of-the-century landmarks survive and are being rehabilitated in the 1980s.

Turn-of-the-century renewal also included landmark buildings that were not skyscrapers. The Cossitt Library, the new Gayoso House, the Grand Opera House, and the Lyceum were among the dozens of imposing buildings constructed during this era. Nor was all construction new. Many structurally sound buildings, particularly those along Front Street, were expanded and refurbished.

All of this building, in Memphis as in other cities, was crowding people physically and cramping them psychologically, giving rise to a nationwide urban park movement. At its founding, Memphis' proprietors had donated a riverfront promenade and the downtown squares. However, encroachments on the donation had reduced it from 40 acres to about 10. Later, donations by private citizens and the city's conversion of other lands to park use added about 20 more acres to its parklands, but these were all relatively small, formal parks. The national trend was toward large, naturalistic parks, and in this respect Memphis lagged far behind most other progressive cities.

Mayor Williams and other strong advocates of a modern park system sought to remedy this situation. They pushed the necessary legislation through the general assembly, established a park commission, and authorized the issuing of $250,000 in bonds for park use.

THE MEMPHIS PYRAMID

The Tennessee Centennial and International Exposition, held at Nashville in 1897, was Tennessee's first world's fair and Memphis' first chance to sell its economic and cultural virtues to a world audience. The city's pavilion, built in the shape of a pyramid, created an architectural sensation.

The fair had been postponed for one year, from 1896 to 1897, giving Memphis and Shelby County a chance to look at all the other buildings' designs and hold a design competition for a truly dazzling edifice in which to exhibit the products of its agriculture, industry, commerce, education, and culture. The winner was Memphis' leading architect, James B. Cook. Explaining that there was no way to rival the Parthenon with another Grecian design, or the various Roman, Gothic, Renaissance, American colonial, and Oriental designs that would be represented at the fair, Cook proposed instead a classical Egyptian design, evoking the city's ancient namesake. The

480-foot-high Pyramid of Cheops was scaled down to 100 feet, symbolizing the state's 100 years.

The exhibit area inside was 83 feet square, with a 50-foot-high Egyptian column six feet in diameter supporting a coved ceiling. The wooden structure was stuccoed on the outside to look like stone, and each of its four faces had a portico painted with Egyptian motifs in red, yellow, and blue. The four pyramid edges were outlined in electric light bulbs. Electricity was one of the leading themes of the exposition, symbolizing the wondrous new age of the coming 20th century.

The exposition was by no means all seriousness and high culture, aptly represented by the fine arts collection in the Parthenon next door to the Memphis pyramid. It was lots of fun, too, with boat rides, a Gettysburg cyclorama, the great seesaw, a carousel, shooting the chutes, an ocean-wave swimming pool, and the immensely popular hot-air balloon rides over the exposi-

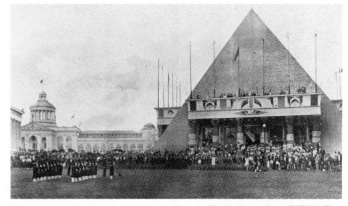

Memphis Pyramid on Memphis Day. From the Memphis/Shelby County Room (M/SCPLIC)

tion area.

The fair opened on May 1, 1897, with elaborate ceremonies, and President William McKinley officially switched on the exposition's equipment with a Morse key. In the course of the exposition, which ran until November 1, there were 100 special days, each designated in honor of some locale or organization. September 24 was Memphis and Shelby County Day, and thousands of people arrived in Nashville by special trains to attend the ceremonies, speeches, and parades.

The pyramid cost nearly $9,000 to build, plus another $14,000 to operate. The original plans for constructing it so that it could be disassembled and brought back to Memphis for reerection on the bluffs at Monroe and Front had been rejected as too expensive. Once the exposition was over, the lumber was sold for $250, some of the exhibit cases were donated to the new Cossitt Library, and that was the end of the city's most exotic creation.

— David Bowman

Acting on recommendations from the Olmsted firm, which had designed New York's Central Park, the city purchased two large wooded tracts at the northeastern and southwestern corners of the city and built a broad greenbelt boulevard to connect them. This timely "civic miracle" became an object of local pride and furnished the foundation for a magnificent urban park system.

Because of the city's financial situation, the parks were developed slowly, with the emphasis being placed on the eastern tract, named after founding proprietor John Overton. George Kessler, a gifted landscape architect, laid the original design for Overton Park, utilizing fully the tract's natural beauty and advantages. Serpentine roads and bridle paths crisscrossed the park, preserving virgin trees and other natural features of the landscape. Along the roads rustic bridges spanned creek beds, creating picturesque scenes. Turns in the roadways brought charming glades into view suddenly and dramatically. A golf course, a shallow lake, a zoological garden, athletic fields, a playground, pavilions, and an art gallery would all be added in time, making Overton Memphis' premier park. As the city grew it encircled this bit of Eden, converting its fringe location to one near the center of the city.

The slightly larger southwestern park, named Riverside for its location, now called Martin Luther King, Jr.-Riverside Park, was even more beautiful because of its river vistas and its more undulating terrain. Developed to a lesser degree than Overton Park and remoter in location, Riverside received less use and remained even more of a nature park. These two large parks gave the newly urbanized citizens of Memphis some of the open green space for which they yearned.

The demand for outdoor entertainment was clearly there. It had been reflected in the 1890s rage for bicycling and in the success of the city's private entertainment parks, East End and Montgomery parks. With the rise of the public park system and other turn-of-the-century popular amusements such as movies, the private parks could not compete and eventually closed.

For a short time at the turn of the century, Memphis became one of the nation's horse-racing centers, with saddle and harness racing at Montgomery Park and world-class harness or sulky racing at the North Memphis Driving Park. The latter, a private project of street-railway magnate C.K.G. Billings, became the home of the Memphis Gold Cup and was reputed to be the world's finest harness-racing track. Here the legendary Dan Patch drew national attention to Memphis when he set a mile record (1 minute, 57.5 seconds) that stood for nearly 20 years. Memphis might have become even more famous as a racing center, but a state law outlawing pari-mutuel gambling effectively killed the sport locally in 1905. The racing parks languished, and the park commission later bought Montgomery Park as a permanent home for the regional agricultural fair.

The public parks served the recreational needs of tens of thousands of Memphians. For those not interested in golf or baseball there was always hiking, bicycling, or picnicking. People rode bicycles, carriages, and even automobiles to get to the parks. By 1903 there were about 40 horseless carriages terrorizing the city's streets, forcing the council to impose an eight-mile-per-hour speed limit and to require registration of the strange vehicles. The most popular form of transit to the parks, however, was the street railway. At the turn of the century as many as 4,000 people would crowd the Sunday streetcars to escape the heat for a free concert in the park, where Professor William W. Saxby's orchestra played the popular tunes of the day, free to all who attended.

Black Memphians were not among those who could attend. Blacks comprised 49 percent of the city's population in 1900, but they were not welcome in the city's public parks. In 1899, however, black millionaire R.R. Church invested $100,000 in a six-acre private park and amusement center on Beale Street. Church's Park was a magnificent enterprise for the time, with formal walks and gardens, picnic grounds, a playground, a bandstand, and stroll-

ing peacocks. The 2,000-seat Church's Auditorium served black Memphians as both entertainment and civic center, hosting personalities as diverse as Theodore Roosevelt, Booker T. Washington, and W.C. Handy. Despite Church's philanthropy, his park was not usually free, and even the nominal charge was out of the reach of some urban blacks. And of course there was the question of equity. If blacks were not allowed to use the same public parks as whites, at least they deserved comparable park facilities for their exclusive use.

The issue of providing a public park for blacks had become a political football by 1910 and remained so even after 1913, when the city bought a 53-acre tract northeast of the city and began developing Douglass Park. That black Memphians valued their park is attested by the fact that a very cohesive community grew up around it. Although the city later provided other recreational facilities for blacks and initiated "Negroes only" days at the zoo and the art gallery, equity in public facilities did not occur until after 1963, when the Supreme Court struck down racial barriers in public facilities. The beginnings of the city's racial alienation are more difficult to pinpoint, but they are to be found in the city's post-fever decades.

Blacks on the Fringe

The turn-of-the-century period of resurgence and reform may have been an uplifting era for whites, but it proved a degrading and disheartening time for many of the city's blacks. During this period the North turned its back on black Americans while the South strangled their civil rights and reduced most of them economically to a helot class. Although the Memphis record during this period was better than that of most of the South, it followed the general trend of promoting white racial supremacy and included widespread discrimination and considerable oppression.

During the 1880s blacks and whites were still working together in civic endeavors. They served together on the police force, on the school board, and in lesser offices of city hall. They rode together on the same streetcars and lived in the same neighborhoods. Black leader R.R. Church, Sr., was liked and respected by most whites. He displayed his faith in Memphis when he purchased some of the early bonds issued to fund payment of the

city's disastrous debt. Although still voting, most blacks had abandoned political militancy and the overt quest for white acceptance as equals.

The old-guard white conservatives did not cynically betray their tacit agreement with blacks, symbolized by the biracial July Fourth celebration of 1875. Rather this leadership was supplanted by a younger generation of whites who moved to exclude or control black political participation and establish absolute white supremacy. Pockets of resistance to white supremacy had led to "incidents," and these in turn led to lynchings.

Black accommodation with the conservatives had included a renunciation of political power, rendering them helpless to effectively resist lynching or demand justice in the aftermath. The number of lynchings in Memphis was lower than in many Southern cities or the region as a whole, but even one was unconscionable.

In 1892 commercial competition between black and white grocery stores in south Memphis resulted in violence, and although a white merchant started the incident, three

Metropolis of the American Nile

Beginning in 1875 many black leaders
adopted a policy of accommodation
with white conservatives. In abandoning
political militancy they renounced office
holding, rendering their race politically
helpless to resist injustice. Lymus
Wallace, pictured here, was one of the
last blacks to hold major office, serving
as city alderman during the 1880s.
From the Memphis/Shelby County
Room (M/SCPLIC)

Left, bottom
Native Memphian G.P. Hamilton was
one of the city's early advocates of
black pride. An honors graduate of
LeMoyne Normal Institute, he served as
principal of Kortrecht High School and
Booker T. Washington from 1892 until
shortly before his death in 1932. He
also authored two books dealing with
black achievements, noting that all
things derogatory about blacks were
publicized excessively "and
achievements passed over in silence."
Hamilton High School is named for this
educator and author. From the
Memphis/Shelby County Room
(M/SCPLIC)

Right
This Memphis scene, captured near the
turn of the century, tells a good deal
and implies more. The fact that the
black youth's clothing seems
comparable to that of the white boy,
and that he is included in the picture,
may tell something of his social status.
In pre-Jim Crow days they may have
been sharing the use of the bicycle.
From the Memphis/Shelby County
Room (M/SCPLIC)

blacks were arrested. Four days later the blacks were marched out of the jail and gunned down in cold blood, evidently with the connivance of the deputies. Not only was there no chance that the murderers would be punished, but some members of the white community actually condoned the lynching of blacks. This sublime insult, added to capital injury, proved too much for many blacks and brought on a racial crisis.

When the *Appeal-Avalanche* actually defended lynching as a suitable punishment for black men who raped white women, the black press fought back. Miss Ida B. Wells, militant associate editor of the *Free Speech and Headlight,* pointed out in an unsigned article that only one person of every three lynched was even accused of rape. As for the remaining third, she declared, there was more seduction by white females than rape by black men. White Memphians were collectively incensed over these aspersions cast on the purity of their womanhood. They wanted to brand and castrate the perpetrator, whom they mistakenly assumed to be a man. They did burn the *Free Speech*'s press.

The upshot of the crisis was that most of the known militants and more than 2,000 other blacks left the city. Reverend Benjamin Imes prevailed on white and black leaders to restore sanity. United endorsement of a resolution denouncing mob violence signaled an acceptance of the white supremacists' position and set a precedent for accommodation that would last for decades, sublimating problems rather than solving them.

Miss Wells, however, did not accept the accommodationists' view. She continued her crusade against lynching from the North and from England, where her efforts were so successful that they reached all the way back to Memphis. The local press and business leaders, sensitive to outside criticism and to the fact that British textile mills were among the city's best cotton customers, strongly condemned lynching. When six more blacks were lynched in 1894 for alleged barn burning, the town focused on the incident and recoiled in horror. Thirteen local whites were indicted in an apparently genuine attempt to bring the murderers to justice. White supremacy triumphed over justice and there were never any convictions, but the mere attempt to convict whites for the mob murder of blacks very nearly brought an end to lynching in Memphis.

Although Miss Wells' strong stand against lynching helped to end the reprehensible practice in Memphis, the status of blacks continued to erode as the heavy hand of Jim Crow descended across the South. Although black Memphians were never victimized by the race baiting that characterized the Vardaman era in Mississippi, by the turn of the century Tennessee's segregation laws were beginning to be enforced in Memphis. Starting in 1905 blacks were forced to sit separately on streetcars and were excluded from the city's parks. The suburban movement reinforced old patterns of residential segregation and established new ones, including black subdivision developments such as Douglass Park and Orange Mound.

Actual conflict between the races remained minimal after the crisis of the 1890s, and many black families enjoyed cordial relations with white families who assisted them in times of trouble. But even these paternalistic and sometimes hypocritical relationships began breaking down as segregation precluded physical contact and hampered interracial communication. After 1900 Memphis no longer seemed a mecca for rural blacks. In the first decade of the new century, the city's black population increased by only 2,500, thus reducing the black share in the city's population to about 40 percent. This proportion remained relatively constant until 1970.

For all its faults and injustices, Memphis was probably a better home for black Americans during this era than many other Southern cities. If this was true, or perceived as true, surely part of the reason was the magic of the legendary Beale Street. Part of Beale Street had initially been a high-fashion residential street. During the 1880s and '90s the commer-

cial leadership of R.R. Church transformed its western end into the "Main Street of Negro America." George W. Lee, who coined this phrase, described it as "a mile of vice and commercial ambition ... owned by the Jews, policed by whites, and enjoyed by the Negroes." In fact only the block between Fourth and Hernando made up the honky-tonk strip. Most of the rest of the black section was devoted to business purposes, although Church's Park added to the entertainment atmosphere.

The Beale Street phenomenon began with the black roustabouts whose strong arms and backs handled the freight from the steamboats moored at the Beale Street landing. Restaurants, boardinghouses, and saloons grew up along Beale from the wharf to Front Street to cater to the needs of this vital work force. Their work songs of blue music incorporated much of the Afro-American heritage and became the source and inspiration for the "blues," which W.C. Handy would give to 20th-century America and the world.

Not many blacks lived on Beale, but it was the street where both urban and rural blacks took their triumphs and their troubles, to celebrate or lament as the occasion demanded. It was where the action was. Its pool halls, barrooms, pawnshops, and dance halls catered to a mix of colorful street characters, gamblers, entertainers, and prostitutes. Its sensuous, vibrant life helped mask the social and economic misery of many blacks—which the blues transmuted into personal and emotional terms. The heyday of Beale Street lasted only from about 1880 to 1916, when enforcement of state prohibition ended some of its wilder life. However, its legend lives on in song and story, a testimony to the exuberance and the pathos of black life at the turn of the 20th century.

The Impulse Toward Reform

Beale Street was hardly the only segment of Memphis life that was wild and in need of reform at the turn of the century. Memphians had enjoyed relatively honest and frugal government during the taxing-district period. Afterward, inefficiency, cronyism, and stagnation crept back into government. Although the election of John J. Williams ended the city's standstill, Williams was reputed to have stolen the election with purchased black votes and to have had the political support of the city's underworld.

That the saloon keepers had strong influence in Memphis government was beyond doubt, but this association neither started nor ended with the Williams administration. In 1903 Memphis was a "sin city," with a total of 504 saloons, most of them cheap dives. Violence and murder abounded, with the police either unwilling or unable to enforce the laws. The city's fire-fighting equipment was so inadequate that insurance companies raised the city's premium rates 25 percent, forcing the city to upgrade the system. Firemen and policemen were political appointees, more valued by the administration for their political loyalty than their abilities or dedication to their jobs.

The city's failures also carried over into the educational system. Because of the financial drains of the lingering debt and the sanitation system, public schools in Memphis were of poor quality until 1900 and not greatly improved in the years immediately following. In the decade prior to 1910, the city did build 13 new grade schools for whites and four for blacks, but until 1911 Memphis had only one public high school. Because the public schools were so poor, affluent citizens supported more than a half-dozen fine private schools, some of which survive today.

Memphis had not even provided its citizens with a free public library. Until 1893 the only thing close was a small free library on the second floor of the Odd Fellows Hall. After the death in 1887 of Frederick H. Cossitt, a Northern businessman who had made his initial fortune in Memphis, his daughters decided to memorialize him with a library in Memphis. Their donation provided the grandiose building from which the present excellent public library system has evolved, but the initiative was taken privately and by outsiders.

The social and political reform movement in Memphis also had its origins in affluent private groups. A multitude of reform and charitable organizations, including the King's Daughters, the Nineteenth Century Club, the WCA, and the Anti-Saloon League, lent their voices to the Protestant clergy's clamor for social and political reform.

Mayor Williams, elected on a reform ticket himself, soon came under fire for his refusal to enforce laws against vice. When a disgruntled citizen named Walker Wellford insisted, in 1903, on looking at the city's financial books, Williams resisted until a court order forced compliance. A private audit of the books, paid for by Wellford, did not reveal any corruption, but it did show sloppy fiscal administration. The incident united the city's reformers and gave them purpose.

Bowing to political expediency, Williams sought to enforce the laws against all violators, including the affluent club set. His efforts seemed to be calming public passions when, in July 1904, a raid on a De Soto Street gambling dive resulted in the shooting of five special deputies. Two of the deputies were killed, including one black deputy. The murderer got off on the grounds that the black had baited him into shooting.

This tragic event refueled the fires of the reform movement, which now enlisted the help of the conservative business element. With the aid of activist groups such as the Jackson Club, the reform element captured the country's legislative delegation in 1904 and the city administration in 1905. The new mayor, James H. Malone, was totally honest and hardworking, but he lacked political astuteness, had no organization of his own, and faced monumental problems of long standing. What Memphis needed was leadership with courage, political adroitness, reform goals, and personal flair. These it would find in the person of Edward Hull Crump, to whom the city would give unprecedented political power for about half a century.

CHAPTER SIX

THE CRUMP ERA: 1909~1954

Unlike most 20th-century histories, whose demarcations naturally coincide with the two great wars of this century, the history of Memphis is more appropriately demarcated by the domination of one man—Edward Hull Crump. Crump not only dominated local politics from the first decade of the 20th century until his death in 1954, but his activities penetrated the woof and warp of the total social fabric. His impact on life in Memphis challenges that of the wars for importance and surpasses them in duration.

For all of Crump's importance, his visibility, his power, and the controversial nature of his rule, he has never received adequate, balanced treatment in the histories of Memphis. Detractors and glorifiers alike have recounted their version of events, yet Crump remains a giant, enigmatic sphinx to those who would understand the man and his era.

"Pharaoh" for 45 Years

Horatio Alger himself could not have applied his formula for success plot better to paper than E.H. Crump did to life. Scion of a northern Mississippi family impoverished by the Civil War and reared by a mother widowed by yellow fever, Crump grew up in and near Holly Springs, Mississippi, about 45 miles southeast of Memphis. A tall, lean, redheaded youth, Crump had a reputation for learning quickly and getting into mischief, but showed no particular promise of greatness.

Young Crump left school at about age 15, worked at a series of make-do jobs, and took a course in bookkeeping. Half man, half boy, he spent nearly five years trying to get enough experience and save enough money to try his fortune in the big city. The extreme rural poverty of the time prevented Crump from saving a stake, but he decided to meet his fate head-on and moved to Memphis in 1894.

Arriving in the city in deep winter with only 25 cents in his pocket, Crump took a succession of temporary jobs until he got a permanent bookkeeping position at a carriage and saddlery business in 1896. Within four years Crump was secretary-treasurer of the company and was considered a young leader of business groups in the city. Soon after achieving these successes, he courted and wed a young socialite named Bessie Byrd McLean. The marriage

Metropolis of the American Nile

Early 20th-century life in Memphis was exciting, and not without its impact on the larger historical scene. This collage depicts the spirit and the landmarks of that era. In it are E.H. Crump, Clarence Saunders, W.C. Handy, the Cossitt Library as it was then, the Porter Building, and the Great Bridge. Perhaps depicting Crump so large was intentional, for he dominated the Memphis scene for 45 years. Courtesy, Pat McCarver

was a love match, but Crump's new family connections also enabled him to borrow $50,000 to take over the foundering carriage business, from which he had recently resigned because of a policy dispute. Crump quickly turned the business around, made it the leading buggy company in the city, and from the profits was able to buy out his partner within three years.

Thus, within a dozen years of arriving near penniless in the city, Crump seemed to have achieved financial success, family, and social position. Here Alger might have ended the story, but for Crump it was only the beginning.

With the casting of his first ballot at age 21, Crump became irretrievably hooked on politics. In addition to his successes in local businessmen's groups, he also involved himself for business reasons in the city's rough-and-tumble ward-level politics. Not averse to using his fists to settle business or political disagreements, by 1902 Crump was on his way to mastery of the city's very tough Fourth Ward.

With his passion for order and efficiency, it was almost inevitable that Crump would be drawn into the larger arena of municipal politics. In 1905 he ran successfully as part of a reform ticket for the lower legislative council. Disappointed at the relative powerlessness of this position, he resigned in 1907 and won a seat on the upper council. There, in a dramatic, grandstanding power play, Crump precipitated a crackdown on the city's illegal gambling. In the aftermath of this episode Crump tried unsuccessfully to get the police chief fired for incompetence.

The battle lines were now drawn between Crump's followers and the Walsh-Malone faction. Embracing the issues of restructuring municipal government and achieving more equitable representation, Crump fielded an independent Democratic ticket for the Shelby delegation to the state legislature and scored a decisive victory in November of 1908. Going to Nashville personally to lobby the Commission Government Act through the legislature, Crump achieved another resounding success.

Commission government was in many ways a return to the municipal structure of the taxing-district era. Since then it had been used successfully by Galveston and other cities to bring efficiency and reform to municipal politics. This innovation combined the legislative and administrative functions of city government under a single, five-member body. The mayor would preside over commission meetings and direct the divisions of administration and public health. Other commissioners, each of whom had an equal vote with the mayor, would be responsible for fire and police; accounts, finance, and revenue; streets, bridges, and sewers; and public utilities, grounds, and buildings. The new structure was to go into effect after the 1909 election, and no one was surprised when Crump announced that he would head a ticket of officials to initiate it.

Crump's major opponent in the race was the still popular machine-connected ex-mayor, Joe Williams. Crump, a distinct underdog, ran on a progressive, anti-utilities platform. Concentrating on paid political advertisements and personal contact with the voters, he left all speech making to friends with greater oratorical ability. Crump's supporters also hired W.C. Handy's band. Among the tunes played for the campaign was the one that Handy would later publish as "The Memphis Blues." Perhaps the music was decisive, for Crump won the election by the slender margin of 79 votes. After a recount the results still remained uncertain because of court challenges involving unethical tactics at the polls by both factions.

Notwithstanding the tentativeness of his victory, Crump took office in January of 1910 and proceeded to consolidate his political power. The Crump faction already had at least nominal control of the Shelby legislative delegation, which had put through the Commission Government Act. In 1911 this delegation pushed through a restructuring act for Shelby County government, reducing the number and power of the magistrates serving on the Quarterly Court and placing the lion's share of county power in the hands of a three-member commission board. Not surprisingly, when elections filled these offices, it was with people friendly to the Crump interests.

Crump now had control or at least extremely strong influence over all three elements of local political power—city and county governments and the county's legislative delegation. These three mutually reinforcing legs of the Crump pyramid of power assured and perpetuated nearly absolute control. The organization's control of city and county jobs gave it the automatic votes of employees and their families and friends, as well as a dependable source of campaign workers and funds. These factors plus the large black bloc vote enabled the machine to pick almost all city and county officeholders.

Control of offices meant control of regulatory and police functions of both governments. It also meant control of the election machinery countywide, ensuring *at least* a fair shake in registrations, poll-tax receipts, and ballot counting. With hard work at ward and precinct levels in civic and social groups, plus reasonably good administration, the organization's position appeared unassailable. Only unfavorable action at the state or federal level and/or through the courts could damage this interlocking tripod of political power.

Crump easily won reelection in 1911, this time to a four-year term, defeating his old adversary Williams by more than 7,000 votes. Crump's landslide victory was due to his good administration record, his organization's effective control of the city's wards, and to a

Metropolis of the American Nile

change of allegiance by the city's black voters. Although Crump promised black leaders less than his opponent, he convinced them of his sincerity and actually delivered more real benefits to the black community than other white politicians had. Crump's followers registered and voted blacks in this election, and officials eased up on the saloon keepers as well.

To claim that the Crump organization did not indulge in political chicanery and extralegal voter manipulation would be a patent falsehood; it did. Presumably these methods had at least Crump's okay, if not his blessing. But that was the way the political game was played when Crump arrived on the scene. He simply learned the ground rules, got into the game, and played it harder and more astutely than anyone else. He also did not use it to line his pockets, something that was more or less expected of politicians at the turn of the century.

In the six years between 1905 and 1911, Crump rose from political nonentity to political mastery of city and county and strong influence statewide. He had come very far very fast and had stepped on a number of people in his climb. Given the rapidity of his rise and the extent of his domination, it is not surprising that he tried to overreach himself and then received a major setback.

Upon becoming mayor Crump had given up his carriage business. The mayor's salary was small, and whether or not that was his reason, Crump announced he would run for sheriff in 1914. Discovering he could not hold both offices simultaneously, Crump offered a substitute write-in candidate in the sheriff's race. This obvious machine power play was made more glaring by the fact that Crump's man won with the equally obvious manipulation of black votes. Crusading *Commercial Appeal* editor C.P.J. Mooney was aghast at Crump's power. While admitting that Crump was personally and scrupulously honest, and that his

Chapter Six: The Crump Era: 1909-1954

administration had done many good things, Mooney abhorred some of his organization's tactics. He also saw very great potential danger in the absoluteness of Crump's control. Mooney determined to do all in his power to stop the "machine." Others doubtless shared Mooney's views, but some who did not had in any case become Crump's political enemies.

In 1915 the blow fell. A combination of anti-Crump interests struck at him through the channels where he was most vulnerable—the state government and the courts. The issue was the state's new prohibition law. Most Memphians did not want prohibition, and Crump believed the law would be unenforceable even if they did. These factors, plus the political support that Crump received from the saloon interests, gave him sufficient reason to ignore the new law. His enemies, together with the drys, then succeeded in passing another law, providing for the ouster of public officials who failed to enforce state laws.

The state attorney general brought suit to oust Crump from the mayor's office. Since Crump had never made the slightest pretense of trying to enforce prohibition and had never denied nonenforcement, the state won its case. The state supreme court, in an appeal that carried over into Crump's third term, upheld the decision. The court ruled that Crump could take office for his new term, but that the same evidence of nonenforcement could be used in a new ouster proceeding. In the face of this situation Crump resigned, and one of his organization's men was made mayor.

The incident was a sore point with Crump for the rest of his life, and he always claimed that the syndicate that owned the local utilities company was behind it. Crump had been re-elected in 1915 with a mandate to buy the company out or build a city-owned power plant. While the utility interests doubtless desired Crump's removal, it is impossible to determine the extent of their actual influence in his ouster.

Crump's removal from office encouraged his enemies to write his political epitaph prematurely. He promptly ran for and won the office of county trustee, the most lucrative of all local offices, and served in this capacity for eight years, until he voluntarily left to enter the private sector. Meanwhile, he continued to exercise strong influence in city politics. A succession of mayors found that, though they could not get along with Crump, they could not stay in office without his support. In the 1920s Crump reluctantly backed reform mayor Rowlett Paine for two terms, first against his old rival Joe Williams and then against a Ku Klux Klan slate of candidates. In 1927 Crump threw his direct political might back into city politics, defeating the popular incumbent, and thereafter kept control of city hall virtually until the day he died.

Memphis in the Teens and Twenties

Crump's story, dramatic and important as it is, was not the sum total of the city's history during this epoch. It was a colorful era for the nation and the world, and Memphis and Memphians played some not insignificant roles on the larger stage of history. Blacks and women emerged from the chorus for the first time to play larger roles, some of national prominence.

The first thing for which Memphis became nationally prominent was its violent crime rate. Memphis had been a wide-open city in the 1890s, and the reform efforts of the early 20th century did not dent the crime rate. Based on insurance-industry statistics, Memphis was the per capita "murder capital" of the nation. The homicide rate was about twice as high as that of the next highest city and in some years was nearly 10 times the national average for larger cities. If the murder rate can be taken as indicative of all crime, Memphis was indeed a sin city in the early 20th century.

Memphians rankled at what they considered their unfair reputation for violent crime. They blamed the high rate on the black population and the large percentage of undesirable transients of both races who flocked to the city. Although there was doubtless some merit in these arguments, lax law enforcement and lenient courts were also factors. The murder rate remained high well into the 1920s, and the reputation clung until a general vice cleanup in 1940 pushed the murder rate below that of several other major cities. By 1960 the rate was the lowest of any major Southern city.

If it took reformers far too long to make headway against crime, the city fared much better in two other areas of social reform—medicine and education.

Memphis had had medical colleges and hospitals in the 19th century, but these were primitive by 20th-century standards. St. Joseph Hospital, founded in 1889, grew into a 300-bed facility by 1919. The University of Tennessee Medical School moved to Memphis in 1911, at the same time that Baptist Memorial Hospital was being built. These institutions, together with the existing city hospital and the facility that became Methodist Hospital in 1918, formed the nucleus of what would become one of the largest medical complexes in the nation.

Memphis had its full share of medical heroes in the first half of the 20th century. Doctors and nurses such as Richard B. Maury, Lena C. Angevine, Edward C. Ellett, Willis C. Campbell, Eugene Johnson, William Augustus Evans, and Joseph LePrince won justifiable acclaim for achieving significant medical breakthroughs, carrying Herculean work loads or both. Many others, less well known or completely unsung, also made important contributions.

The transfer of the state medical colleges to Memphis may have given a boost to the general educational environment of the city. After making a good beginning in the 1840s, public education had suffered greatly during the four decades following 1860 and in the 1890s clearly played second fiddle to the city's 31 private schools. From a school-age enrollment rate of only 40 percent in 1890, education fought its way back to a rate of 70 percent by 1920. Even so, most children left school after age 14 to seek employment. Memphis teachers were poorly trained and underpaid, and primitive teaching methods rivaled miserable facilities as obstacles to education. These lamentable conditions were nearly universal in the South and would require decades before they would be totally eradicated.

Perhaps the biggest boost to local public education was the state's decision to place one of three proposed teachers' colleges nearby. Amid fierce competition with other West Tennessee cities, in 1911 Memphis claimed the plum. Donations of land, subscription donations of money, and $300,000 in bond pledges from city and county governments convinced state officials to place the facility at Buntyn, just east of Memphis. Opening in 1912 with an initial enrollment of 330 students, West Tennessee State Normal School ultimately grew into Memphis State University, whose annual enrollment in the 1970s was about 23,000. Although the college grew slowly at first, it prepared thousands of teachers for the task of improving education in the city, the county, and the Mid-South region.

One of the unsung educators associated with the fledgling Normal School in its earliest years was a young woman who taught there for two years before becoming superintendent of Shelby County's backward educational system in 1914. Miss Charl O. Williams, a handsome, imposing woman from a family of Shelby educators, turned the rural school system around. She modernized the curriculum, made classes more interesting, and initiated numerous other improvements, with the result that the system's daily student-attendance

Like the surrounding countryside, some low-lying areas of Memphis were subject to inundation when the mighty Mississippi neared maximum flood stage. In this 1912 scene Bayou Gayoso had backed up a half mile into the city and overflowed its banks, giving rise to the cynical imprint "Market Street Landing." From the Memphis/Shelby County Room (M/SCPLIC)

rate doubled. Building the system's funding base, she replaced more than half of the county's primitive one-room school buildings with modern, functional buildings. In the brief seven years of her tenure, she raised the system's ranking to among the six leading county school networks in the nation.

Such executive and administrative talents did not go undetected at the national level. After serving for a year as president of the National Education Association, she was hired away from Shelby County to serve as national field secretary of the NEA. Miss Williams moved to Washington, D.C., where she put her abilities to work for rural schools nationwide. Not limiting her efforts to the educational sphere, Miss Williams also became a leader in national business and political circles.

The social-reform sentiment that manifested itself in local medical and educational improvements was part of a national trend which crested with World War I. Initially the war itself had little effect on Memphis other than disrupting cotton shipments to England, but as the United States became increasingly involved, Memphians vented their typical patriotic outpourings. When war actually came in 1917, almost 9,000 men entered the military service, more than one-third of the county's eligible population. The government established an aviation training station at Park Field, north of Memphis near Millington. Although closed after the war, this site later became the home of the extensive Memphis Naval Air Base.

The indirect effects of the war on the Memphis area may have been more important than its direct effects. The price of cotton soared from prewar lows of less than five cents a pound to highs of more than 35 cents. High prices brought prosperity to the region's farmers, with additional economic benefits and consequent growth for Memphis. The war also fostered an interest in aviation that would aid Memphis in becoming a major air-transport center in later years.

At least as important as the economic stimulation of the war was its psychological effect. Although still considering itself very much a Southern city, Memphis began to lose some of its "lost cause" fervor. Traveling more and mixing more with people from other regions eroded some of the parochial attitudes of Memphians. The parts that women and blacks played in the war effort altered their self-images and their positions in local society.

Women in the Postwar Era

The woman-suffrage movement came to fruition in the United States during the immediate postwar years. Tennessee proved to be the critical swing state in ratifying the 19th Amendment to the Constitution, and the Shelby County delegation and local lobbyists were a crucial element in Tennessee's ratification.

The groundwork for this momentous event had been laid much earlier. Elizabeth Avery Meriwether, a remarkable woman in many areas and by any standards, was Memphis' first forceful advocate of suffrage for women. The first Southern woman to lecture and write widely on the topic, she forced her way into the polls and voted in the 1870s. She suspected that her ballot was never counted, but it gave her a claim to being the first woman to vote in U.S. elections. Mrs. Meriwether served as vice-president of the National Woman Suffrage Convention in 1876 and continued her largely unpopular suffragist work in Memphis until 1883, when she moved to St. Louis.

Elizabeth's move left local leadership of the movement in the hands of her sister-in-law, Lide Meriwether, who became Tennessee's outstanding suffragist leader for the next two decades. When she failed to get the attention that she thought the issue deserved, she tied it to the prohibitionist movement of the Woman's Christian Temperance Union. Enjoying moderate success through this connection, she helped prepare for the state's stand in the crucial test in 1920.

By the end of the First World War, women had dispelled many myths of their inferiority, and Memphis had ardent male advocates of female suffrage. Senator Kenneth McKellar and Representative Hubert Fisher worked tirelessly to push the 19th Amendment through Congress, and Memphians McKellar, Gaston Fitzhugh, and Joseph Hanover worked equally hard to push a female-enfranchisement act successfully through the state legislature in 1919. Memphis women first exercised the right to vote in that fall's election and provided the margin of victory for progressive, reform mayor Rowlett Paine. The national amendment was still pending, however, and Tennessee's antisuffragist forces were mustering their total strength to defeat it.

In 1920 Tennessee was the only uncommitted state with its legislative machinery in place to ratify the 19th Amendment in time for women to vote in that year's national election. The state's political factions were badly divided on the issue, with Shelby County's Crump-McKellar group standing as ratification's most forceful supporters. The battle itself was so bitter, complex, confused, dramatic, and humorous as to seem fictionalized, but it was too weird to be untrue.

The entire Shelby delegation introduced the ratification resolution to a joint session of the General Assembly. Educator Charl Williams and Senator McKellar made forceful speeches supporting the resolution's passage. The state senate had little problem with the measure and passed it overwhelmingly after only three hours of debate.

The house, however, was where the antis planned to defeat ratification. Lobbying was fierce as the opposition offered money, jobs, whiskey, and "many other temptations" to uncommitted or wavering representatives. Threats were made, kidnappings allegedly took place, and prosuffragist floor leaders had to have police protection to ensure their safety. The antis delayed the vote for six days through parliamentary jockeying and trickery. Meanwhile the suffragists mustered their full strength, including calling one legislator back from a trip to California and physically carrying into the chamber another sympathetic legislator who had just undergone major surgery.

House Speaker Seth Walker moved to table the resolution. After the Honorable Speaker nearly became involved in a fistfight with one of the honorable members of the Shelby delegation, the motion was defeated. A motion to reconsider the resolution then passed by the required 50 votes, and the suffragists staged a wild outburst. The antis tried more dirty tricks and parliamentary foul play, with 36 of their number at one point fleeing the state to prevent a quorum. The suffragists won the day anyway, and Tennessee became the 36th state to ratify, making the 19th Amendment part of the highest law of the land and enfranchising 26 million American women.

Metropolis of the American Nile

THREE MEMPHIS BLUESWOMEN

Memphis in the 1910s and '20s was bustling with creative musical activity. The city was headquarters for the leading blues artists of the day—singers, musicians, composers, and lyricists—and many of them were black women. Three of the best were Alberta Hunter, "Memphis" Minnie McCoy, and Lillian Hardin Armstrong.

Alberta Hunter was born, appropriately enough, on Beale Street. Her mother was a chambermaid for Miss Myrtle and Miss Emma's sportin' house on Gayoso Street. Her father, who died when she was an infant, was a Pullman porter. At the age of 14 she hopped a boxcar and wound up in Chicago, where she was to become the "Idol of Dreamland."

Unlike almost every other blueswoman, Alberta Hunter was a soprano. Memphian George W. Lee, in his *Beale Street Sundown,* gives this description:

Her voice, high pitched ... drifted through open windows over the silent park. A sorrowful voice, breathing of love and hate; a melodious voice, laughing of lazy days, of happy nights, of gin, women and dice. Blind men

on the corner heard it and rested their itching fingers on the strings of their guitars. Church folk heard it and forgot their revival songs.

W.C. Handy considered her one of the best and chose her to introduce some of his classics, among them "Loveless Love." She replaced Bessie Smith in the Broadway musical *How Come?* in 1923. In 1929 she appeared as Queenie with Paul Robeson in the London production of *Show Boat.* She recorded prolifically for Paramount Records, Black Swan, Gennett, and Victor. Like Handy, she later turned from blues writing and barrelhouse music to hymns and sacred themes.

In the 1950s she retired to care for her ailing mother. She took nursing training and started a new career. But her performing days were not over. In 1977 Barney Josephson, owner of the New York nightspot, "The Cookery," heard her singing at a party and asked her to appear at his club. She was, and still is, a smash hit. She wrote the musical score for Robert Altman's film *Remember My Name.* She has performed more frequently on the "Today" show than any other singer and has made two triumphant appearances at White House concerts.

"Memphis" Minnie McCoy, born in Algiers, Louisiana, moved to Memphis at the age of seven. Her first instrument was the banjo, which she mastered at the age of 10. She bought a guitar when she was 15, and soon she was playing on the street corners of Memphis. A recording company talent scout discovered her in 1929, playing in a

Beale Street barber shop. She went on to make a great many recordings in the 1930s and 1940s, some of them solo and others with her husband, Kansas Joe McCoy, and brother-in-law, Charlie McCoy.

Her style of singing was unlike that of most female blues singers—"rougher," with more of a country flavor. She was also a formidable guitarist, one of the very best in the blues-jazz genre. Bill Broonzy, in his book *Big Bill Blues,* recalled a guitar-playing contest held in a saloon in which he took on his rival, Memphis Minnie—and lost. Many male musicians paid her the ultimate chauvinist compliment: "A lot of gals can play the guitar, but Minnie plays like a man."

Lillian Hardin Armstrong was a woman of many talents—pianist, vocalist, arranger, and composer. She was born in Memphis and educated at Fisk in Nashville. The

public first became aware of her brilliant playing through the classic recordings of Louis Armstrong's Hot Five in 1925 and '26. Since the group had no bass or percussion, Lil's piano set the beat as well as carrying its share of the melodic line.

She became Louis Armstrong's second wife, and many blues historians, including Harry E. Godwin of Memphis, credit her with persuading him to stop playing second cornet for his mentor, King Creole, and strike out on his own. Lil taught Louis the rudiments of reading music and wrote many of his songs, including "Struttin' with Some Barbecue" (one of his greatest hits) and "Original Boogie." Their friendship survived divorce. Lillian Hardin Armstrong died in 1971 while performing in a concert in honor of her former husband, Louis Armstrong.

— Berkley Kalin

Top left
Memphis Minnie McCoy. Courtesy, Berkley Kalin

Left
Lillian Hardin Armstrong. Courtesy, Berkley Kalin

Above
Alberta Hunter. Courtesy, Berkley Kalin

Blacks in the Memphis Scene

The war and its moral fervor also worked a profound, if less measurable, change in Southern black society. The war brought many local blacks into military service, some of them serving as officers and seeing action in France. Numerous other blacks went north or west to work in war-related industries. The question "How ya gonna keep 'em down on the farm after they seen Paree?" applied to blacks as well as whites, and it applied to New York, Cleveland, Detroit, and Chicago as well as Paris. Eventually the question would change to "How ya gonna keep 'em down," period, after they had traveled and found out that the whole world was not wedded to white supremacist notions of segregation and subordination. But this would require time and another world war before coming to fruition.

The war era had altered blacks' self-image and perceptions of their own mobility. Blacks migrating to the North began to create a labor shortage in Memphis that was viewed by local businessmen as a genuine threat to the city's continued growth and prosperity. The Chamber of Commerce and individual business leaders responded with a campaign to make Memphis "the best town in the country" for blacks to live in—including white support for black community centers and educational and recreational facilities—and with efforts to promote the leadership of accommodationist blacks. These efforts enjoyed a measure of success prior to the onset of the Great Depression.

Despite white efforts, many blacks still moved north. At the same time Memphis became a sort of halfway house for rural and other blacks moving out of the Deep South. They would come first to the relatively tolerant atmosphere of Memphis, working long enough to get a stake to help them get established in a Northern city. No story illustrates this pattern of migration more simply, graphically, or dramatically than Richard Wright's classic autobiographical novel, *Black Boy*.

Wright, whose early life was similar to that of many other Southern blacks, lived in a variety of locales before moving to Memphis in 1925 at age 17. Blessed with great sensitivity and perception, Wright found Memphis less oppressive than the other places he had lived. He secured employment and a place to stay and began saving money to bring his family to Memphis and then move them north. Eschewing the fleshpots and other tempta-

Metropolis of the American Nile

tions of the big city, Wright stumbled across the literary personality of H.L. Mencken and began his intellectual awakening.

Driven by an inner urge to find out more about this white man who freely criticized other whites, Wright needed access to books. Perhaps not knowing that there was a public library for blacks, or more likely because the black library did not have books by the authors that he wanted to read, Wright resorted to a ruse to get hold of the books he craved. With the aid of an Irish co-worker who had also felt the sting of Anglo-Southern discrimination, Wright began to use the white man's Cossitt Library card on the pretext that he was simply a messenger. The young man became positively addicted to serious reading.

Wright's passion for reading built him up, broke him down, and forged him anew. Having no one with whom to discuss his ideas, and in constant fear that his secret intellectual life would be discovered and cause him harm, Wright more than once tried to quit. He found that he could not, and in the turmoil of his agonies and ecstasies he began to write. He left Memphis after less than two years and eventually became the greatest black novelist in American history, with the possible exception of James Baldwin.

Black Boy describes episodes from Wright's life in Memphis, many of them unflattering. It depicts the limited economic scope for blacks and their interactions with whites. The novel portrays the roles that both races played in their manipulation of each other, to their mutual shame and degradation. Wright's fear that he might forget or abnegate his "Sambo" role, and get himself killed, forced him to leave Memphis sooner than planned. Unable to take all of his family with him, he sent for them later. His negative impressions were not limited to Memphis, for Wright also found New York and Chicago unsatisfactory places to live. Once he became successful, he moved to France and lived there as an expatriate.

Thousands of blacks less sensitive than Wright also made their way north during the teens and twenties. Others stayed and fought to make Memphis more livable for their race. Among them were black ministers and teachers such as T.O. Fuller and Sutton E. Griggs, who attempted to do what they could through the policy of accommodation. This group also included a new breed of black businessmen, like Robert R. Church, Jr., and George W. Lee, who entered the political process to try to redress inequities for their race.

Memphis was the only major Southern city where blacks were never disfranchised after Reconstruction. Memphis' political leaders, including Williams and then Crump, protected the black franchise because it favored their interests to do so. Black leaders such as Church gave their support to Crump during his 1909-1915 mayoralty and extracted valuable concessions for their race in return.

Church became the preeminent political and business leader in black Memphis. As the moral fervor of World War I hastened the demise of the old Beale Street, blacks replaced it with a business district as respectable as Main Street. During this transition, Church enlisted the black middle class in the Lincoln League for political action and urged all blacks to register and pay their poll taxes. Supporting Crump candidates in local elections and fielding Republican candidates for national and state offices, Church built a machine as effective in its way as Crump's. By 1920 young Church had filled the spot once held by Booker T. Washington as the foremost black adviser to national Republican leaders.

The leadership represented by Church and Lee was more vigorous and protest-oriented than that of the ministers. According to Lee, too many of the ministers were advocating peace at any price; "too many [were] preaching about the glories of the other world and too few pointing out the hell" in this one. To Lee it was a gross distortion of priorities that blacks were spending $90 million annually to support 40,000 black preachers to teach them to depend on God, whereas nothing was being done to teach blacks to depend on themselves.

Chapter Six: The Crump Era: 1909-1954

With the secularization of black political leadership, it was almost inevitable that a branch of the NAACP would be established in Memphis. Incorporated in 1917 under Church's leadership, the Memphis chapter achieved some notable early successes. Participation by Church and other black leaders including Lee, who became active after the war, meant mortal risks in the South at that time. After its initial gains the Memphis chapter began faltering in the face of KKK resurgence in 1923. Church withdrew from its leadership, and it sputtered along ineffectively until revived in 1933 by Dr. J.E. Walker. It is unclear why Church left the NAACP—perhaps he was placing all of his hopes for racial equality in the Republican party—but he remained cool to the local chapter until he left Memphis.

In the period of Republican resurgence between 1920 and 1932, Crump and Church enjoyed a mutually beneficial political relationship. Church's Republican influence kept Crump free of federal interference in local matters, and his control of federal patronage gave some federal appointments to Crump supporters. In return Crump distributed minor local appointments to Church's black supporters, and his organization supported Church against lily-white Republicans in Tennessee politics. Crump also minimized racial harassment in the city and county. Frequently their interests simply coincided, as in the city elections of 1923 and 1927.

The election of 1923 represented a vital choice on the part of Memphians regarding the direction in which their city would move. The early 1920s saw the rise of the new Ku Klux Klan, and disparate elements in Memphis joined hands to meet the common threat. Leading personalities as diverse as editor C.P.J. Mooney, Rabbi William H. Fineshriber, Episcopal Bishop Thomas F. Gailor, Edward H. Crump, and Robert R. Church made common cause to defeat an all-out Klan election drive in 1923. With this support the "clean-government mayor," Rowlett Paine, returned to another four years in office. By the next municipal election the Klan had been discredited nationwide, and its political threat in Memphis was dead. The 1923 election had not been very close, with the Paine ticket winning by almost 5,000 votes, but years later stalwarts of the Crump organization would claim it was the way that the ballots were counted, rather than the way they were cast, that saved the city from Klan government.

The Crump organization had not had a strong candidate to field in the elections of 1919 and 1923. Although Crump and Mayor Paine stood for many of the same things, Crump was unable to influence Paine's governing of the city and seems to have been constitutionally unable to let somebody else run things. As the election of 1927 approached, Crump's organization fielded a strong, balanced slate of candidates led by a young man named Watkins Overton, a candidate with impeccable credentials.

In addition to the attractiveness of the Crump slate and the power of the organization, the black community felt that Paine had failed to keep his promises to them. Determined to vote him out of office, Church launched an election drive that raised the number of registered black voters from about 3,500 to 11,000. Paine claimed that the Crump group was trying to reestablish the "Negro rule" of Reconstruction as soon as black leadership endorsed Overton, but to no avail. The organization won by a larger majority than the number of black votes.

The 1927 election marked the beginning of more than 20 years of absolute political control of Memphis and Shelby County by Crump. Because of the associative connotations given to the words "boss" and "machine," Crump disliked having them applied to his operation. But in their literal sense, they were accurate. In his largely uncritical, authorized biography of Crump, William D. Miller writes:

> In the thirties he brought his political organization to the peak of its effectiveness. It ran with well-oiled efficiency, so smoothly balanced that the energizing

Metropolis of the American Nile

force behind it could almost stand aside and watch it work from its own momentum. If dissonance developed, the trouble was quickly corrected. A telephone call, a word, a hint from Crump restored the balance.

With his local power base firmly consolidated, thanks in part to black voters, Crump increasingly turned his attention to state and federal matters. Although Crump's political activities and battles afield would have their effects on the local scene, in many instances they had less impact than other local developments on the economic front.

Economic Boom Times

The Memphis growth rate had slowed from its earlier pattern of nearly doubling every 10 years, but it was still significant. The population, just over 100,000 at the turn of the century, had swollen to more than 250,000 by 1930. Although Memphis was falling behind some other Southern cities in its rate of growth, changes in technology and the economy were greatly enhancing the quality of life for its citizens.

One Memphian played a very important part in one of the most dynamic yet understated revolutions ever to hit the country. Clarence Saunders, another rural migrant to Memphis, virtually invented the supermarket and modern food-marketing technologies. Although he neither gave Memphis its first chain food store, nor the nation its first self-service market, Saunders put existing practices and techniques together, expanding and systemizing them. In the process he contributed more to the nation's food revolution than any other single individual.

Saunders launched his first Piggly Wiggly store in Memphis on September 11, 1916. His methods included self-service, cash-and-carry, high volume, low profit margin, consumer-sized packaging, and, after some growth, massive wholesale discount purchasing. In addition Saunders was an authentic advertising genius, whose psychological perceptions and marketing techniques were decades ahead of his time. His first store was a huge success, and within six weeks he had opened a second. By 1923 there were 2,600 such stores nationwide, with a gross income of $180 million annually.

It was from a store laid out like this one that Clarence Saunders launched one of the most dynamic, yet understated, "revolutions" ever to hit the country. He virtually invented the supermarket and modern food-marketing technologies. By putting the idle labor of the customer to work assembling the family's market basket, Saunders was able to reduce costs and raise volume dramatically. Between 1916 and 1923 Piggly Wiggly grew to 2,600 stores, grossing $180 million annually. The result was much lower grocery prices. From the Memphis/Shelby County Room (M/SCPLIC)

Chapter Six: The Crump Era: 1909-1954

What Saunders had done was apply the assembly-line technique to the American family's food larder, as Frederick W. Taylor and Henry Ford had applied it to the machine shop and the automobile. Introducing the market basket, he took the idle labor of the customer and put it to work assembling the daily or weekly food purchases. He got the customers' labor free, but they did not mind because self-service gave them a real choice and lower food costs. The concept is so simple, and the practice has become so commonplace, that it is difficult to realize what a truly revolutionary innovation it was.

Saunders, now a multimillionaire, had to go public with his company to finance its rapid expansion. In 1923, victimized by Wall Street stock manipulators and determined to fight them, Saunders lost control of his company. His genius fought its way back more than once, again with innovations ahead of the times, though none had the simplicity or the impact of his 1916 breakthrough.

It is difficult to overemphasize the impact that Saunders had on American life. Between 1915 and 1925 the proportion of family income that went for food decreased by two-thirds. Other factors besides Saunders' innovations figured into this drastic reduction—among them, improved systems of distribution, reduced spoilage, increasingly mechanized farming, and real growth in family income. But these all interacted with Saunders' contribution, which may have been the most important of all.

The food revolution and rises in real wages freed a fantastic amount of capital for consumer purchasing. This, in turn, helped to revolutionize more of the American economy, build a tradition of enterprise and efficiency, and introduce a period of unprecedented productivity and plenty. Working-class families became mass consumers of such "luxury" products as radios, cameras, record players, vacuum cleaners, refrigerators, and automobiles. It was the beginning of the consumer age, and it drastically altered life-styles in Memphis as it broadened the city's economic base.

Not all of the traditional grocery stores went under in the face of Saunders' food revolution. Some, like Seessel's, maintained their high quality of products and services and adapted to meet new consumer demands. The Seessel family is now in the fifth generation of food-retailing service in Memphis. From the Memphis/Shelby County Room (M/SCPLIC)

In the late teens and twenties, Memphis began to attract national companies and to build up industries of national scope. Memphis Packing Company, opened in 1919 and later absorbed by Armour, would become the largest locally owned meat packer in the South. E.L. Bruce, founded in 1921, would become the largest hardwood-flooring producer in the world. Fisher Body Works and Ford Assembly Plant opened in Memphis in the mid-1920s.

Metropolis of the American Nile

Above
E.L. Bruce, Sr., was the founder of the world's largest hardwood floor manufacturing company. The huge plant that Bruce opened in Memphis in 1921 was so large that it revolutionized the industry. Bruce's methods were so effective that the company developed nearly a dozen plant locations. Later the company was also involved in the production of termite protection, furniture parts, prefabricated housing, doors, plywood paneling, and floor-care products. With changes in technology, the use of hardwood floors declined and in 1965 the big plant that had once employed a thousand workers closed. The company was later bought by Cook and Company and the idled plant burned in 1977. From the Memphis/Shelby County Room (M/SCPLIC)

Above right
Who says that industrial buildings have to be ugly? Memphis Steam Laundry, the city's largest commercial laundry, built its large plant on Jefferson north of Russwood Park and gave it a Venetian Gothic facade copied from the Doges Palace. This beautiful building was a Memphis landmark for many years until 1973 when it was demolished to make room for the expansion of the University of Tennessee Center for the Health Sciences. From the Memphis/Shelby County Room (M/SCPLIC)

Buckeye, Swift, and Humko all grew into national producers and distributors of cooking fats and oil products. Federal Compress and Warehouse, formed by the merger of 28 corporations, became the world's largest warehouser of cotton. In 1927 Sears Roebuck opened a mammoth retail and catalog store outside the downtown area, presaging a trend that would nearly destroy the central business district 40 years later. But in the 1920s downtown construction more than proceeded apace. Developers built large office structures, including the Sterick Building, luxury-class hotels like the Peabody, and gigantic movie palaces such as the Lowe's State and the Orpheum. Meanwhile the suburban residential building boom continued as well.

All of this growth and change meant new problems for a city that, as of 1920, had no zoning laws. The advent of the streetcar and the automobile, and spot encroachments of industry into traditionally residential areas, created a need for and an acceptance of city planning. Pressure from local civic organizations, eloquently spearheaded by prominent attorney Wassell Randolph, led to the establishment in 1920 of a city-planning commission consisting of Randolph and seven other prominent citizens. Under the guidance of this able group, Memphis became a national leader in urban planning.

Since commission members lacked the technical skills to order the city's future development, in 1922 Mayor Paine hired St. Louis planner-engineer Harland Bartholomew to create a comprehensive city-improvement design. Largely following Bartholomew's recommendations, submitted in 1924, the city mandated zoning restrictions, widened and improved its street system, and expanded and improved park and recreational facilities. Such planning was particularly important because during this era the city annexed additional huge areas, doubling its size again.

In 1929 the city completed its municipal airport, established a harbor commission to facilitate a reviving river trade, and converted the mansion of Clarence Saunders into the Pink Palace Museum. By the end of the 1920s, Memphians could take justifiable pride in their progressive, modern city, and in the prosperity that was trickling down to the working class. Little did they realize that the roller coaster that the city seemed to ride throughout its history was about to take another downward plunge.

The Great Depression and World War II

Largely as a result of overproduction during World War I, the nation's farmers had suffered an economic depression since the summer of 1920. Although Mid-South farmers fared better than the rest of the agricultural community throughout most of the 1920s, cot-

Chapter Six: The Crump Era: 1909-1954

THE RIVER AND RAIL TERMINAL

Late in the 19th century the railroads took most of the heavy freight-hauling business away from the steamboats and other river craft. During the First World War, however, there was so much freight to be moved that the U.S. government decided to revive inland waterway traffic with newly designed steel barges and powerful new towboats. Memphis was a major beneficiary of this river revival.

In 1917 a group of business and civic leaders formed the River and Rail Terminal Association of Memphis and went to Washington to talk with the Army Corps of Engineers, who were in charge of river improvements. The result was a 50-50 matching agreement of local and federal funds. In August 1917 Memphis voters approved a $450,000 bond issue, guaranteeing the local funding component.

Part of the money was used to acquire and renovate the River and Rail Storage Company, located where Ashburn Park and the Rivermont Hotel are today. This facility had a conveyor system to move small freight wagons up the steep bluff from river barges to warehouses and railroad cars at the top of the bluff. But the system was not equipped to handle bulk freight of any kind—lumber, steel, pipe, coal—and it was too slow to transfer the volume of freight required for the city's busy port.

Unlike most other ports, Memphis had to design a terminal to accommodate the dramatic rise and fall of the Mississippi River—as much as 50 feet between flood and low-water levels. Fixed piers or quays were out of the question. Some kind of floating terminal was the only answer.

The new facility involved an inclined railroad track that descended southward along the bluff edge from what is now Martyrs' Park down to the river's edge. Two "car floats," steel barges 270 feet long and 56 feet wide, were connected to the inclined track by a "cradle," a wooden framework hinged to the car float at one end and riding the rails up or down at its other end by means of wedge-shaped "feather rails." Moored alongside the car floats were two "transit sheds," 240-foot-long sheds resting on concrete barges.

When barges arrived at the terminal, they were moored to the transit sheds. The freight was then trucked across gangplanks into the sheds for temporary storage, or directly on through to the railroad cars on the car floats. Similarly, Memphis products began their river journey here by being unloaded from rail-road cars through the transit sheds and onto barges.

The port's freight tonnage climbed from 84,000 tons a year, before the terminal opened in 1923, to 1.6 million tons by the end of the decade. Major commodities coming into Memphis, as of 1922, were sugar (36 percent), burlap and bagging (17 percent), coffee (10 percent), and prepared roofing (5.6 percent). Outbound shipments were dominated by cotton (74 percent) and wood (5.6 percent).

The River and Rail Terminal was both a significant engineering achievement and a major contributor to the Memphis area economy. The port's present volume of 12 million tons a year owes its beginnings to the farsighted entrepreneurs of the 1910s and '20s.

— David Bowman

Memphis riverfront, 1925. From the Memphis/Shelby County Room (M/SCPLIC)

If the world was becoming too tame, too civilized, and too convenient in the 1920s, this handsome and daring young Memphian gave readers a look at "an alternative life style." Richard Halliburton, traveling and living most of the adventures he described in his books, became a national sensation with the publication of his *Royal Road to Romance* in 1925. His sense of personal freedom and childlike wonder came through in his writing. He continued adventuring until the 75-foot junk he was sailing from Hong Kong to San Francisco was lost at sea. From the Memphis/Shelby County Room (M/SCPLIC)

ton prices dropped off too. Meanwhile the rest of the nation, largely ignoring the plight of its farmers, indulged in a speculative binge unprecedented in American history. Unknowingly, the recently urbanized country was about to join the farmers in the worst case of economic and physical distress its people had ever known.

The stock market crashed in October of 1929, losing $26 billion almost overnight. For Memphis, primarily an agricultural and distribution center, there was a lag before the full effects were felt. It was not until 1931, writes Robert Sigafoos, that "the visible evidence began to show up dramatically among Memphis residents in terms of joblessness and human misery."

By mid-1932 the number of unemployed in Memphis, fewer than 4,000 in 1930, had risen to more than 17,000. Though this was the official figure, the actual number of jobless and underemployed Memphians was probably much higher. Thousands upon thousands of people lost their jobs, their health, and their self-respect. Some of the weaker ones even lost their lives because of exposure, malnutrition, and disease. Others, unable to face a crumbling world, committed suicide.

Although the suffering in Memphis was severe, it was probably not as bad as in most other cities, thanks in large measure to the political organization's sensitivity to constituent needs. City employees donated a portion of their salaries to help the needy. The Mayor's Employment Committee created make-work jobs, initiated other job programs, and furnished food, fuel, and other necessities to thousands of families. Community kitchens served tens of thousands of meals weekly. The Unemployed Citizens' League bartered labor for food, clothing, and furniture.

But for all the good intentions and hard work, local relief was not enough. Families lost their homes and either doubled up with others or moved back to the farm with relatives. Depression was psychological as well as economic, and both worsened. Massive federal relief seemed a necessity, but it would have to wait for the inauguration of Franklin D. Roosevelt.

During this time of uncertainty and doubt, Memphians fought back in another way. When the bottom fell out of the cotton market in 1930, it badly hurt the economy of Memphis, as of the whole Cotton Belt. Just as in the 1870s, in another time of economic distress, Memphians had instituted a Mardi Gras celebration, so in 1931 a group of men— including A. Arthur Halle, Hubert Jennings, and Everett Cook—put together the Cotton Carnival. The first festival featured a parade of 86 floats, costumes with an Old South theme, elaborate balls, and bands playing all over town. The festival was very much a success, both in heartening the people and in drawing favorable national and international attention to Memphis and cotton products.

The Cotton Carnival was repeated the following year, but later in the spring and even more elaborately. After that the celebration became an annual event, marking its 50th anniversary in 1981. At the half-century mark the carnival revamped its secret-society participation and, for the first time, included black social organizations in its high-society affairs. Ironically, the festival, which was initiated with an Old South theme, is now becoming an agency for racial dialogue and harmony. The continued success of the Cotton Carnival over the years has helped make Memphis a city of festivals in the late 20th century.

The carnival helped pull the diverse cotton-producing interests together in other ways. One outgrowth of this cooperation was the establishment of the National Cotton Council in Memphis in 1938. Designed to aid the faltering cotton industry, its wide variety of programs and promotions did not cure all ills prior to World War II, but it did give the cotton interests both organization and leadership. These would be sorely needed again when competition with synthetic fabrics emerged after the war.

Chapter Six: The Crump Era: 1909-1954

LLOYD T. BINFORD

Next to Crump, himself, Lloyd T. Binford was probably the most famous (or infamous) Memphian of his day. *Commonweal, Time, Variety, Collier's,* the *New York Times,* columnists such as Hedda Hopper, movie moguls such as Samuel Goldwyn, theater owners, and members of Congress ridiculed his mentality, taste, and judgment and decried his power. But to censorship boards and city officials in Shreveport, Little Rock, Covington, Charlotte, Birmingham, and many other Southern cities, his word was as good as law.

Censorship in Memphis began long before Binford became chairman of the board of censors. As early as 1914 the Memphis board had banned the motion picture *Uncle Tom's Cabin* on the grounds that it might create racial tension. But it was not until Binford took the reins in January 1928 that the full regulatory potential of local censorship was realized.

The job of chief censor was a Crump-approved political appointment. Binford must have pleased the machine, for he was appointed 28 consecutive times. An insurance magnate with a fifth-grade education, a Baptist deacon who bred racehorses and owned his own track, Binford was for nearly three decades the moral and aesthetic arbiter of Memphis.

Among the films that Binford banned because of excessive sex or violence were *Duel in the Sun* ("the foulest human dross"); *Miss Sadie Thompson* ("Everything in it is raw, but not as vulgar and obscene as the dance part of it"); *Forever Amber* ("There isn't a decent thing, there isn't a decent line in it"); and Marlon Brando's *The Wild One* ("the worst, the most lawless bunch I ever saw and the most lawless picture I ever saw"). Other films, including James Dean's *Rebel Without a Cause,* Humphrey Bogart's *Dead End,* and *Jesse James,* were banned because they "encouraged juvenile delinquency."

Another of Binford's criteria was "maintaining community racial standards." *Brewster's Millions* was banned because black comedian Eddie "Rochester" Anderson "was too familiar and the picture presents too much social equality and racial mixture." Louis Armstrong's *New Orleans* never showed in Memphis because Binford threatened to cut Armstrong's scenes. Lena Horne's appearances in MGM movies were limited to isolated songs so that she could be scissored out in Memphis and other Southern cities without destroying the continuity of the films.

Biblical films were favorite Binford targets. The 1928 *King of Kings* offended because scenes of Jesus' scourging and crucifixion were too graphic. Others were proscribed or cut because they distorted the "sacred chronicles of the Bible."

The personal lives of actors could constitute grounds for prohibiting exhibition of their works. No other actor invoked the wrath that Binford directed toward "the London guttersnipe," Charlie Chaplin. All his films were barred because of his "Communistic leanings" and because he was "a traitor to the Christian American way of life, an enemy of decency, virtue, holy matrimony and godliness in all its forms." All films produced by him were forbidden, even those in which he did not appear, including a film of the opera *Carmen.* Ingrid Bergman's private life was also the basis for banning her films. "It would be inimical to the public morals and welfare," Binford explained, "to permit the public exhibition of a motion picture starring a woman who is universally known to be living in open and notorious adultery."

Theater and stage shows were also subject to his scrutiny. Several sketches in the 1933 road show of Earl Carroll's *Vanities* were deleted as "inimical to the public welfare." Mary Martin's Broadway hit *Annie Get Your Gun* was censored on the grounds that three black actors "were lurking in the cast disguised respectively as a trainman, a waiter, and a porter."

Objecting to language reportedly used onstage by Alfred Lunt and Lynn Fontanne, Binford ordered that in the future they submit their scripts for his approval. The Lunts announced they would never again appear in Memphis. Extending his control even to sporting events, he refused to permit three white acts to perform before a black audience during a Harlem Globetrotters appearance.

Binford was criticized and condemned by Memphis newspapers throughout his long reign, but to no avail. Protests and court challenges notwithstanding, he and his board had the support of the political establishment, and that was all that counted. Films banned in Memphis were shown in West Memphis, Arkansas, and Memphians crossed the Mississippi River in droves to see them.

When the Crump machine was voted out of office, it was time for the 85-year-old movie censor to resign at last. He did so in October 1955, lamenting as he left, "Things are different now. The way it looks, there may not be any censor boards soon."

— Berkley Kalin

Lloyd T. Binford. From the Memphis Room, Memphis Public Library

Top

Memphian C.R. Knouff (third from left) was 19 years old when this photograph of 97th Infantry Division soldiers was made in Germany in 1945 during a lull in the fighting. The flag had been captured during a street-to-street engagement in Siegburg, Germany. After Siegburg, the 97th Division met heavy resistance pushing on to Solingen and then Dusseldorf. The fall of Dusseldorf marked the elimination of the Ruhr Pocket. Next, the 97th moved into Czechoslovakia with General Patton's Third Army as the European theater of war ended. Courtesy, David Knouff

Above

The B-17 bombers, popularly known as Flying Fortresses, were among the major factors in allied victory in the European theater of World War II. This one, the *Memphis Belle,* was the first to complete 25 missions over Europe and keep her original crew alive and together. Discarded after the war, the *Belle* was purchased and brought to Memphis for display. Courtesy, Charles Bobbitt

Once FDR's relief measures got under way, Memphis received a disproportionate share of federal relief. Crump, who was elected to Congress in 1931, and his longtime ally, Senator Kenneth D. McKellar, exerted their tremendous influence to get a huge variety of large-scale federal programs and projects centered in Memphis and Shelby County. Mammoth public-works programs were undertaken under the aegises of the RFC, the WPA, and the PWA. These included public housing projects, hospital and school buildings, slum clearance, home gardening programs, and health and beautification projects. These efforts and many others pumped tens of millions of dollars into the local economy and gave tens of thousands of jobs to the unemployed. The Depression awaited the coming of World War II before giving up its last hold on the city, and even then it left psychological scars on Memphians, which never completely healed.

The war in Europe was already boosting the American economy in 1940, and U.S. industrial production was playing a vital role in the British defense effort for many months before Pearl Harbor. After the Japanese attack, the nation's war economy boomed. The effects rapidly penetrated the local economy, and aspects of total war entered every fiber of the social fabric. Memphians went to war with an optimism that utterly belied the pessimism of the preceding decade.

Shelby Countians participated directly in the war in unprecedented numbers. Of the 160,000 selective-service registrants, some 40,000 actually served in some branch of military service. Tens of thousands of others participated less directly through war-bond drives, scrap-materials collections, USO service, civil-defense organizations, and numerous other volunteer causes.

While Memphians went off to the military, the military also came to Memphis and Shelby County. Perhaps again because of the political influence of Crump and McKellar, the federal government located several major military installations in and near Memphis. The Second U.S. Army made its headquarters at Memphis from 1940 to 1946. Other military facilities included a major quartermaster supply depot and an air force depot in Memphis proper as well as an extensive naval air base complex at Millington. Kennedy General Hospital, located on the southeast border of the city, opened in 1943 and grew to a 4,600-patient capacity. The Fourth Ferrying Group centered its global aircraft-ferrying operations at the Memphis Airport. All these facilities and operations brought military and civilian personnel to the locale, and their payrolls contributed tens of millions of dollars to the local economy.

War production became a major part of the Memphis business scene. DuPont's Chickasaw Ordnance Plant, Firestone Rubber, Ford Motor Company, Fisher Aircraft Division, and Continental Can Company all produced munitions and machinery for war. Their swollen payrolls, which included thousands of women, added to the already booming local economy. At the same time this war production helped the city reach the elusive goal of diversified manufacturing.

As beneficial as the war's forced growth was to the local economy, it also brought severe problems. In addition to the concern and sorrow for loved ones separated by the war and lost in battle, the war on the home front meant sacrifices and adjustments. Rationing of tires, gasoline, shoes, sugar, coffee, meat, and other items became part of the war effort. Items that were not rationed, such as cars and housing, became increasingly scarce as war production precluded their manufacture and construction.

The Memphis housing situation became particularly critical prior to 1943 as 30,000 to 40,000 persons arrived in the city to work in the war effort. Rents were frozen at 1942 levels to minimize profiteering and to hold the line on inflation. In lieu of new construction, Memphians made do with rehabilitating and converting existing structures, and they partici-

Chapter Six: The Crump Era: 1909-1954

pated in programs to share existing housing. Still the shortage remained critical, and much of what housing could be found was substandard. Virtually no housing was available to incoming blacks.

Despite nationwide shortages and sacrifices, the industrial capacity of the nation, once geared up, did its work well. In full production the United States produced more war materials than all other belligerents combined. Memphians were proud to be part of this Herculean effort and were overjoyed when Axis resistance crumbled in 1945. Now Memphians had to face a new set of adjustments as war production and military service came to an end for many thousands of local citizens.

Federal postwar programs, especially those for veterans, helped ease the transition to a peacetime economy, and by 1947 unemployment had leveled at about 5 percent. The Crump organization also bent every effort toward aiding the city's postwar economic recovery, most notably in the Tennessee Chute project for the development of Presidents Island into a major industrial-freight complex. Although the project was not completed until after Crump's death, it and the four-lane Memphis-Arkansas Bridge, completed in 1949, were major factors in the city's postwar growth.

Probably the most important element in the city's postwar economic recovery was the housing boom. The pent-up demand from the Depression and war years created nearly 10,000 construction jobs as low-cost single-family units and public housing projects mushroomed. Memphis seemed on the move into a new era sparked by war-related technologies—an era very different from what previous generations had known.

The End of the Crump Era

Depression, war, and quiet control of local politics did not take Crump out of the limelight. After his consolidation of power in the 1927 election, he became more visible than ever. He was perceived as a kingmaker in Tennessee politics, supporting certain candidates for governor, then sometimes cooling toward them once they were in office. Although Crump did not actually control the state, he carefully chose strong candidates to back and gave the impression that he did control it. Crump also served two terms in Congress in the early 1930s, helping to get federal relief for the local area.

In Crump's work as liaison with national Democratic leaders, he had an extremely valuable ally in Senator Kenneth D. McKellar. Crump and McKellar had been young reformers together in 1905 and had supported each other generally afterward. Contrary to the sometimes voiced opinion that McKellar was a Crump stooge, the Senator was not. Although Crump was in many ways the dominant partner after the 1930s and deliberately embarrassed McKellar more than once, the two men usually got along and saw things in the same light. When they did not, Crump usually won McKellar over. Together the two arch-politicians did a great deal for the city, the county, and the state. McKellar's seniority in Congress grew until he was perhaps the most powerful Senator in Washington. After Roosevelt's death in 1945, as president pro tem of the Senate, McKellar was acting Vice President—"only a heartbeat away from the Presidency." He and Crump remained political allies until McKellar's defeat in 1952.

Among Crump's local achievements during the Depression and war years were securing public ownership of local power and gas utilities, major flood-control measures through the Army Corps of Engineers, and a complete cleanup of the city's lingering vice problems. He also sponsored a physical cleanup of the city through the City Beautiful organization, which also operated as a political arm of his organization. By the end of World War II Memphis was one of the cleanest, quietest, healthiest, most law-abiding, and most beautiful cities in the nation. Memphis became noted for its extensive parks, numerous churches, fine hospitals, model fire and police departments, and low tax and utility rates. Indeed, in many ways the muddy, pestilential little hamlet atop the Fourth Chickasaw Bluff had become like its namesake—stable and beautiful and a place of good abode.

No truly satisfactory explanation has yet been offered as to why Crump allowed vice to flourish from 1909 until about 1940, and then crushed it utterly. Some claim that he "found religion" after the accidental death of his son John. Others maintain that he knew Memphis would never get the massive military facilities it wanted without a cleanup of its sinful ways. Still others point to the potential threat of federal intervention in local matters and the fact that the organization no longer needed political support from the shady side of town. Crump's decision may have resulted from a combination of these factors, or it may have been motivated by some reason as yet unguessed. At any rate, not only were gambling and prostitution run out of town, but the cleanup even extended to a nearly comic censorship of local movie houses.

While most Memphians accepted Crump's rule without question, he did have some critics. By the 1930s Crump's longevity, effectiveness, and exotic appearance invited both criticism and caricature. Sensationalist journalists from outside the area attempted to paint him as a semiliterate backwoods demagogue who was absurdly benevolent. His influence in Tennessee politics excited derogatory comment in other parts of the state; after one Crump-influenced election a headline proclaimed, "The People Be Crumped." Finally World War II brought analogies between Crump and the fascist leaders, Hitler and Mussolini. But with rare exceptions, whether because of the extent of his control, a general satisfaction with it, or some combination of the two, there was little criticism or complaint about Crump locally.

One major exception to this generalization, during Crump's later years, was Edward J. Meeman. After the death of C.P.J. Mooney in 1926, Crump had no articulate critic or opponent with staying power until 1931, when Meeman arrived as managing editor of the *Memphis Press-Scimitar*. Meeman epitomized the hard-hitting, idealistic, crusading news editor. While giving Crump grudging credit for all the good he had done, he lamented the extent of Crump's control and saw it as potentially catastrophic. Beginning in 1931, Meeman fought the "dictator" and the organization in his paper until Crump's demise more than two decades later. Much of Meeman's early protest fell on deaf ears, but after about 1940 things began to change.

Above
One major exception to the general lack of criticism of the Crump regime during the 1930s and 1940s was Edward J. Meeman, managing editor of the *Memphis Press-Scimitar*. While much of Meeman's earlier criticism fell on deaf ears, after the war things began to change. A citizens' interest group led by Meeman and two friends, Lucius W. Burch and Edmund Orgill, formed around the issues of international democracy and world peace. Its emphasis on personal freedom put it on a collision course with the Crump forces. In 1948 it dealt Crump his first statewide defeat in more than 20 years. Courtesy, *Memphis Press-Scimitar*

Right
One of the major postwar developments for the Memphis area was the Tennessee Chute project. By building a causeway-dam across the Tennessee Chute to Presidents Island, the island was developed as a major port facility and a major industrial-freight complex. The backwater area behind the dam was named McKellar Lake and became a recreational facility, as shown in this picture. Courtesy, Shelby County Public Affairs Office

Following Gordon Browning's election as governor in 1948, Memphis finally traded in the paper ballot for voting machines. Although the Crump forces had long opposed the use of voting machines, this picture of Crump-supported congressman Cliff Davis in 1954 seems to indicate that Davis was pleased with the change. Davis had been an opponent of the Crump group in the 1920s, but like many able outsiders he was absorbed by the system. Courtesy, Shelby County Public Affairs Office

This picture of Mr. Crump and members of his family shows him in one of the few instances when he was not "mugging" for the camera. Crump was devoted to his family and the simple pleasures of family life. From the Mississippi Valley Collection, MSU

In the early 1940s a nucleus of opposition to the Crump organization began forming around the issues of international democracy and world peace. Influenced by Clarence K. Streit's *Union Now: The Proposal for Inter Democracy Federal Union,* a citizens' interest group developed under the leadership of Lucius W. Burch and Edmund Orgill. The group's emphasis on personal freedom put it on a collision course with the Crump forces, but it would take years of patient work to develop the inevitable confrontation.

The 1948 primary election saw the battle lines drawn in Shelby County for the first time in two decades. A coalition of the Burch-Orgill-Meeman group, aggrieved labor unionists, offended blacks, and the League of Women Voters threw their combined weight against the organization, supporting Harry Truman for President, Gordon Browning for governor, and Estes Kefauver for U.S. Senator. Crump's influence in Shelby County carried the area against the liberal triumvirate, but the margin was so much narrower than usual that all three candidates won statewide. This defeat at the state and national levels did little to disturb Crump's hold on the city and the county, however. The old political master simply altered his tactics to perpetuate his control.

Browning's election as governor seriously weakened the organization's control of the local election machinery. Abolition of the poll tax, permanent voter registration, and a referendum approving voting machines ended the use of methods through which the machine had long maintained its power. But Crump was far from down and out. A majority of people in the county as a whole still supported him and kept his local candidates in office.

In 1952 Crump's candidate, Frank Clement, beat the incumbent Gordon Browning for the governorship. But like his friend McKellar, who lost in the same primary, Crump was old and tired. He had not even campaigned actively in the 1952 election. The 1954 election saw "Big Shelby" give a 40,000-vote majority to Clement, who again defeated Browning, indicating that Crump was about as strong as ever in his home county. Physically stricken by the summer of 1954, the 80-year-old Crump wasted away as he monitored this last election. He died at home on October 16, 1954.

What is history to do with this character who played such a dominating role on the local stage for more than one-third of the city's life up to that time? In the first place, how did he do it? How did he control a major American city from its horse-and-buggy days into the era of jet airplanes and hydrogen bombs? And what was he like, this modern-day autocrat? While the answers to these questions are elusive, a few observations about this man of paradox can safely be made.

Crump could present warmth and aloofness simultaneously. Having very few confidantes and identifying with no particular group, he generated respect, loyalty, and genuine affection in many people. Most groups, be they blacks, Catholics, Jews, or others, considered Crump to be their special friend. In addition, Crump's allies and organization people controlled civic, social, and fraternal groups which lent their active support to him.

Crump was extremely good at attracting and keeping able lieutenants. Men such as "Roxie" Rice, Will Hale, Tyler McLean, and Will Gerber worked effectively for the organization for decades. Crump also showed a unique talent for allying with and then absorbing opposition. Lastly, his mayors, notably Watkins Overton and Walter Chandler, were very effective administrators.

Crump understood and epitomized the intense personalism that had pervaded Tennessee politics since the days of Andrew Jackson and John Sevier. He knew what made the common people tick, and what they would respond to. Crump's task was rendered easier by the one-party system that followed Reconstruction, but which had also characterized the Jackson-Sevier era a century earlier. Without the legacy of Reconstruction, the Crump phenomenon could never have taken place.

Metropolis of the American Nile

Like all truly effective leaders, Crump could make unpleasant decisions, and be ruthless if necessary, without losing sleep over it. He knew how to take credit for a favor granted or a successful project and also how to pass the blame for a favor refused or a policy that did not succeed.

Yet Crump was much more complex and paradoxical. To characterize him further, one might well borrow from James Parton's summary of the paradox of Andrew Jackson. He was a demagogue who never made a major public speech. He was a white supremacist who catered more to the needs of blacks than political expediency demanded or even permitted. He was a deeply religious man who almost never attended church or made public display of his feelings. He was a patriot whose family never served in the military after the Civil War. He was a 19th-century throwback who, alone of all Southern Congressmen, voted for every piece of New Deal legislation in the early FDR program. Considered a buffoon by some, he had the courtliest of manners and the personal chemistry and resolve to win, awe, or intimidate the most powerful of figures. A self-made millionaire, he had simple if not Spartan tastes and habits. Although he married into a socially prominent family, he eschewed the attractions of "society." Characterized as a bumpkin, a hick, this high-school dropout was a voracious reader with a truly phenomenal memory and a genius' gift for analysis and decision. Yet even these contradictory attributes only scratch the surface, for Crump contained multitudes.

Even Crump's backers and friends admit that the organization's methods were frequently unworthy, and its tactics sometimes absolutely ruthless. Even his enemies admit that Crump was personally honest and that he accomplished a great deal that was good for the city and the county. All admit that his power in local affairs was very nearly absolute, but they disagree on its effects.

The basic question about Crump seems to be one of motivation. Was Crump a man of high purpose who grabbed and held power for the betterment of the community at large? Or was he a megalomaniac who felt a relentless drive to wield power at any cost, throwing a few crumbs of civic betterment to the populace to retain power? Biographical treatments of the man point in both directions, but these and other questions about Crump and 20th-century Memphis history will remain unanswered until his papers are made available for objective historical research.

Chapter Six: The Crump Era: 1909-1954

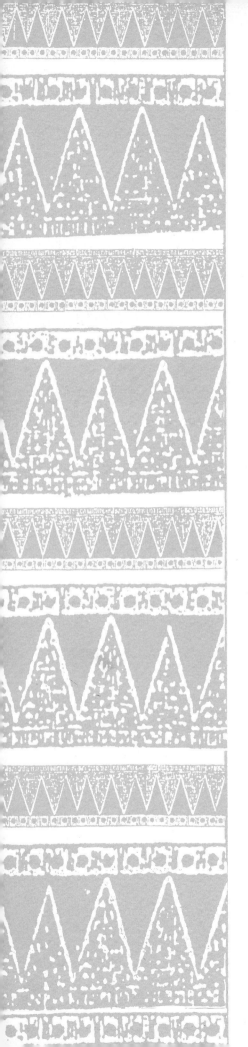

CHAPTER SEVEN

MODERN MEMPHIS: 1955~1981

Historians are generally timid about writing recent history, and for good reason. Events and personalities that seem vitally important to contemporaries often fade and vanish in time. The full explanations for and consequences of truly important events frequently take decades to manifest themselves. Many personages who were principal actors on the historical stage may still be alive, to resent interpretations ascribed to their actions. Readers remember many of the happenings in their lifetimes, and historians are sometimes reluctant to contest their memories. For all these reasons, historians prefer to write about the more distant past.

The factors that make the recounting of recent history risky in general are especially true for the last quarter-century in Memphis and Shelby County. Only two major historical works, by David Tucker and Robert Sigafoos, deal with this period to any significant degree. Even with the aid of these books, recent local history is so complex and contradictory that putting events and personalities in perspective is a most hazardous undertaking. Nonetheless so many dramatic and important occurrences and trends cannot be ignored, so an attempt must be made to at least highlight the story of the past 25 years.

Some of the city's recent history can be ascribed directly to the Crump legacy. Because E.H. Crump had been *the* decision maker for so long, Memphians and other Shelby Countians had to learn anew how to begin governing themselves. Blacks' aspirations on many fronts in society, held in check for so long, nationally as well as locally, broke loose, and blacks and whites had to learn to deal with each other on the basis of human equality. Economic changes, changing life-styles, central-city decay, and urban sprawl all accelerated greatly, requiring adjustments and comprehensive professional planning. In each of these areas Memphis has achieved some notable successes, as well as some notable failures.

Mayor Frank Tobey was Crump's last "appointee" chief executive for the city. Miss Juana Hendricks, the 1954 "Spirit of the Cotton-Makers Jubilee," called at the mayor's office before leaving on a goodwill tour to the Caribbean. Mayor Tobey's flexibility regarding the directions that the city should take made him acceptable to the reform element. When Tobey died suddenly in September of 1955, however, the CRC had to scramble to field its own candidate. Courtesy, *Memphis Press-Scimitar*

A New Political Maze

The most evident, immediate effect of Crump's death was that the organization very nearly died with him. Since Crump had made no provision for a successor and none of the organization's lieutenants or officeholders were strong enough to bring the others under control, the machine began faltering in the very next municipal election. Although some Crump men would continue to hold office for a time, and a few would remain important on the political scene well into the 1970s, they had no unity of purpose and rarely presented a united front to challengers.

The first challenge to the remnants of the Crump faction came from the Orgill-Burch-Meeman group which had contributed to Crump's statewide defeat in 1948. This group had founded a citizens' fact-finding body which they incorporated as the Civic Research Committee. The CRC was reform- and planning-oriented, rather than anti-Crump as such. Its major goals were a council-manager form of city government, city-county consolidation and the use of voting machines and permanent voter registration as antidotes to the political machine's methods. Realizing that the organization was too strong to be attacked head-on, the CRC eschewed direct political action and concentrated on informing the electorate on directions in which it thought the city ought to move.

When Crump's last "appointee" mayor, Frank Tobey, proved amenable to CRC programs, the reformers planned to support him in the 1955 municipal election. The opposition candidate was Watkins Overton, Crump's two-time appointee who had twice been ousted for being too independent. Tobey's sudden, fatal heart attack in September of 1955 forced the reformers to offer a candidate if their goals were to have any chance of realization.

139   Chapter Seven: Modern Memphis: 1955-1981

Edmund Orgill was a successful business executive who, with his friends Burch and Meeman, had opposed Crump's state and national choices in the 1948 election. Drafted by his friends and co-reformers after Mayor Tobey's death, Orgill defeated Watkins Overton and initiated major improvement programs for the city. A moderate and a gradualist on racial issues, he encountered brick-wall obstruction in his efforts to bring blacks into the governing process. Health considerations forced him out of the race for reelection. From the Memphis/Shelby County Room (M/SCPLIC)

The reformers' clear-cut choice was Edmund Orgill, a successful business executive whose family had owned a major wholesale hardware business in Memphis since before the Civil War. Drafted by his friends and co-reformers, Orgill entered the race on the assumption that the machine holdovers would field a candidate of their own. When they did not, the race became a duel between the untried Orgill and the twice-tried Overton. Although Overton was a good administrator who had operated with some independence within the Crump framework, he was seen by some as having been a figurehead mayor. He bore his association with the old order, yet he did not have the support of the machine remnants. His attempts to brand Orgill a reckless radical also probably worked against him. Orgill, with the support of local blacks and an eager coterie of liberal and conservative reformers, won the election overwhelmingly, receiving 61 percent of the vote.

The Orgill reformers, however, unsure of their strength, had not fielded a slate for other offices on the city commission. This meant that Orgill would have to try to work with three holdovers from the Crump era and one new face on the political scene, that of Henry Loeb. The reform element would come to rue its lack of support within the commission as it strove to enact its programs.

Orgill began his tenure with characteristic energy and enthusiasm. A large number of problems and needs had not received attention since 1930, first because of the Depression and World War II and then because of Crump's insistence on fiscal stringency. Orgill worked tirelessly in his efforts to have local government catch up with the city's needs. However, because of his lack of support on the commission, his inability to persuade the masses, and his lack of diplomacy, he would achieve only limited success.

Another factor that doubtless hurt Orgill's effectiveness with many whites was his racial views. He was not pro-integration as such, but he saw integration as preferable to its alternatives. A moderate and a gradualist on this issue, he encountered brick-wall obstruction in his efforts to bring blacks into the governing process. However, his determined work for balance maintained at least surface racial harmony, and there were no major confrontations during his administration.

Orgill was able to achieve consolidation of city and county planning for physical improvements, but not much more, in his efforts to consolidate the two local governments. He sought to implement a new Harland Bartholomew *Comprehensive Plan,* which projected $200 million in expenditures for public improvements. Although the city could have afforded it, such sums were an anathema to old-line politicians. Raising the tax rate became the key issue of Orgill's administration, followed closely by the race issue. The pro-Orgill reformers reorganized under the name Good Local Government League and opposed a briefly reunited group of Crumpites under the misnomer Citizens for Progress. The CP's conservative and racist appeals in the state legislative contest of 1956 hit their mark and gave the Orgill program a major setback. Thereafter, bickering and delay became standard fare at city hall, and obstructionism kept achievements modest.

Orgill, distressed at the difficulties in enacting his program, bowed to the wishes of his friend Estes Kefauver and ran for governor in 1958. Losing narrowly, he recommitted himself to his Memphis capital-improvements program and began campaigning for reelection to the office of mayor. To his surprise, his opponent was not one of the Crumpites who had been thwarting his programs, but young Henry Loeb. Health considerations forced Orgill out of the race, and Loeb won overwhelmingly.

In view of the opposition, Orgill's administration had actually achieved substantial capital improvements for the city. In addition to upgrading the inadequate street system, it had completed the $163 million Allen steam generating plant, annexed the northern community of Frayser, begun construction of an expressway system and the civic center, and en-

Metropolis of the American Nile

tered upon a major expansion of the airport. Participating in the mixed blessing of federal urban-renewal programs, it had cleared off many acres of slums, made progress in public housing, and begun rehabilitation of the city's medical center. These ambitious projects would require much of the 1960s to complete.

The Orgill administration also had its failures. It did not begin work on revitalizing the riverfront area, and more important, it was unable to solve some basic problems in race relations. Black leadership was passing to a younger, more militant, and less patient generation, and black aspirations would dominate the political scene after the 1959 election. The Orgill group also failed to streamline city and county government and to consolidate them into a single, metropolitan government. However, the reform group had made a good beginning, and under the Citizens Association it hoped to press these goals to completion.

Blacks into the Mainstream

Blacks had been part of the Memphis political scene since the Civil War. Never disenfranchised, they threw their votes where they were calculated to do the black community the most good. During the early Crump era this meant voting with Crump in local elections and voting Republican in national and some state elections. This tradition lasted until the 1930s, when it began to break down.

During the 1930s significant numbers of black Memphians began deserting the party of Lincoln and Reconstruction for that of Franklin D. Roosevelt and the New Deal. Democratic ascendency in Washington also freed Crump from his dependence on Robert Church's national Republican connections. By 1939 Crump was secure enough in power to end his political relationship with Church, and the city confiscated Church's vast real-estate holdings for nonpayment of property taxes. Church felt forced to leave the city, leaving control of the local Republican party to be taken by George W. Lee, who continued to cooperate with Crump. Church later returned to Memphis, planning to resume leadership of black Republicans, but he suffered a fatal heart attack soon after arriving.

Blacks continued to vote with Crump in local elections and increasingly supported Democrats in national elections. They strongly backed Truman in the 1948 election and voted overwhelmingly for John F. Kennedy in 1960. During the same period many conservative white Memphians began voting Republican in national elections, giving majorities to Eisenhower and Nixon in 1956 and 1960.

Crump died in 1954 with his Shelby County organization essentially intact. Five months previously the Supreme Court rendered its landmark decision regarding racial segregation in *Brown* vs. *Board of Education of Topeka*. This ruling, in conjunction with attitudinal and demographic changes wrought by World War II, marked the beginning of a process that would galvanize black Americans into a "revolution of rising expectations." The resulting civil-rights movement was national in its scope. Once it began, local racial problems would never be truly local again. Nor would racial events elsewhere in the nation be without their impact on Memphis and Shelby County.

Memphis had long had its unofficial contacts between black and white leaders. Cooperation between the races was formalized in 1940 under the Memphis Interracial Commission (MIC), a ministers' group that provided a structure for biracial communication. The group's major achievement was raising funds for a black hospital, completed in 1955. MIC was superseded in the late 1950s by a broader-based organization with wider objectives: the Memphis Committee on Community Relations (MCCR), which had strong ties to the Orgill-Burch-Meeman reformers.

The MCCR was largely responsible for the peaceful and successful desegregation of Memphis in the early 1960s. After an NAACP lawsuit, Memphis State University was inte-

141 Chapter Seven: Modern Memphis: 1955-1981

grated in 1959. The next year a group of LeMoyne and Owen College students began sit-in demonstrations at the public library. The demonstrators' decorum and restraint won the support of older, more conservative elements in the black community, and this plus the liaison work of the MCCR kept the demonstrations nonviolent. In a relatively short time buses, parks, museums, and other public facilities were integrated quietly, with movie theaters following soon afterward. It required a little longer to integrate the city's restaurants and to persuade local companies to begin hiring blacks, but with patient work the biracial MCCR won some success here too. By 1964 there was at least token-level integration of all local public facilities and services.

This racial integration, reversing habits of more than 50 years' standing, was a remarkable achievement, and it was accomplished in less than five years. Memphis alone among major Southern cities could claim such advancement. Its citizens had made most of the changes voluntarily, without violence, the destruction of property, and white racist demonstrations such as cross burnings. The city was lauded nationally as an example of reason and decency in the South. Local white liberals and moderates were justifiably proud of the biracial achievement, and especially of its implementation before federal law mandated it.

Black leaders, however, if they were satisfied at all, did not remain so for long. Some claimed that the advances made were insubstantial and had taken too long. Others wanted to push forward more rapidly on educational and economic fronts. All were dismayed by subtler forms of racism and continuing reports of police brutality to blacks. Emboldened by past successes, the spreading mantle of federal support, and a new perception of black unity, these leaders resolved to push forcefully for further concessions from the white establishment.

Politics and Polarization

These far-reaching changes in the social arena had their impact on local politics. Henry Loeb, a racial moderate while serving as public-works commissioner, became mayor in a landslide victory in 1959. During the campaign he appeared to be increasingly anti-integration. Although he worked with the MCCR to smooth the transition from segregation to integration and proclaimed himself anxious to serve all the people, Loeb's tightfisted fiscal policies, insistence on merit for reward, and other conservative views were construed as

Metropolis of the American Nile

being antithetical to black aspirations.

To the student of local history, Loeb is nearly as paradoxical and enigmatic as Crump. Large, handsome, and personally charming, he enjoyed unprecedented popularity, particularly with middle- and lower-class whites. He emphasized old-fashioned virtues—pride, thrift, hard work, decency, and patriotism. He had the ability to use cliches and aphorisms effectively and to convey sincerity and enthusiasm. Many of Loeb's critics called him an opportunist and a demagogue, yet he remained a political independent and built no political organization as such. However, his appeal to the white voters was so successful that he acted as a one-man political machine.

A dark-horse candidate, Judge William B. Ingram, won the election after waging an unconventional, anti-establishment campaign. Ingram, who had appealed to black and working-class white voters, also proved to be an unconventional mayor. His frequent differences with other members of the city commission were sometimes humorous. Moreover, they furnished part of the impetus for civic leaders to push for a restructuring of city government.

If Memphis seemed to be moving unevenly and uncertainly during the mid-1960s, certainly the rest of the nation did likewise. Technology had shrunk the size of the nation and removed Memphis from the isolation that had long characterized the town. Television news coverage gave Memphians front-row seats for such major events as the forced integration of the nearby University of Mississippi in 1962, the murder of civil-rights leader Medgar Evers in 1963, and Martin Luther King's 1963 freedom march of 250,000 in Washington, D.C. While events such as these raised the consciousness of some white Memphians and caused them to reexamine their attitudes, they confused and irritated others.

When Henry Loeb dropped his plans to run for reelection in 1963, the race for mayor opened up and Judge William B. Ingram won the election. Shown here with his family and supporters at what appears to be a victory rally, Ingram proved to be an unconventional mayor. Ingram's antiestablishment attitudes built more support for him in the black community, but cost him support with whites. He lost in a bid for reelection in 1967 to his predecessor, Henry Loeb. Courtesy, *Memphis Press-Scimitar*

ABE FORTAS

Abe Fortas, the youngest of five children of a Jewish cabinetmaker who came to Memphis from England, had a long and distinguished career of public service, culminating in four years (1965-1969) as a justice of the Supreme Court—the highest appointive office in the land.

Fortas was born in Memphis on June 19, 1910. Working his way through school in a variety of jobs, he gained the nickname "Fiddlin' Abe" by playing with local bands. He earned top academic honors at Southwestern College in Memphis and at Yale, where he was editor in chief of the *Yale Law Journal*. Graduating first in his class in 1933, he immediately joined the faculty of Yale Law School and that same year became one of the "bright young men" of the New Deal.

Fortas served in many capacities in the Roosevelt administration, becoming Assistant Secretary of the Interior under Harold Ickes from 1942 to 1946. Known as a tough but extremely capable administrator, he did not shrink from taking on controversial political causes that might jeopardize his future in government. He fought in vain to stop FDR's Japanese relocation program on the West Coast, but he and Ickes were successful in getting the administration to moderate the harsh martial law imposed on Hawaii.

In 1946 he left government and became the dominant figure in a new law firm, Arnold, Fortas & Porter. The firm guided top blue-chip corporate clients through the intricate antitrust, tax, and regulatory maze, and Fortas

himself was an officer and director of several major corporations. His wife, Carol, also a member of the firm, was recognized as one of the best tax attorneys in the country.

In 1948 Lyndon B. Johnson won the Texas Democratic primary for U.S. Senator by the narrow margin of 87 votes. His opponent, charging voting irregularities, obtained a court order removing his name from the ballot. Fortas, representing Johnson, boldly brought the matter before Justice Hugo L. Black of the Supreme Court, who reversed the order, and Johnson went on to win the election. It was the beginning of a lifelong relationship, with Fortas becoming the future President's closest confidant. He was the first person Johnson telephoned after President Kennedy's assassination, and it was he who organized the Warren Commission.

Fortas and his colleagues gained national attention during the McCarthy era when they defended many individuals accused of being "security risks," the most publicized case being that of Owen Lattimore. They offered their services free to destitute people in trouble. In 1954 Fortas was the court-appointed counsel in *Durham* v. *United States,* which led to a more scientific definition of criminal insanity. He was also unpaid defense counsel in the precedent-shattering *Gideon* v. *Wainwright,* which established that any person accused of a serious crime must be represented in court by a lawyer.

Fortas refused several positions in the Johnson administration, including that of At-

Abe Fortas, wife, and friends. Courtesy, Esta Fortas Bloom

torney General. Finally, in 1965, he reluctantly accepted appointment to the Supreme Court. In 1968 President Johnson nominated him to succeed Earl Warren as Chief Justice, but the appointment was blocked by a filibuster in the Senate. His outside financial interests drew widespread public criticism, and in May 1969 he resigned from the Court and returned to private practice.

In his four years on the Supreme Court, Abe Fortas became one of its most active and influential members. His vote made possible the 5-4 *Miranda* decision that extended the Fifth Amendment's privilege against self-incrimination to include police interrogation. In his oral argu-

ments and written opinions (including several notable dissents), he demonstrated scholarly breadth, judicial wisdom, and precision of language. He made significant contributions to the development of constitutional law in the areas of civil rights, loyalty-security checks, the rights of criminal defendants, juvenile-court law, and reapportionment. Sympathetic to big business on the issue of government control, he broke with his liberal colleagues in this area of the law. "The courts may be the principal guardians of the liberties of the people," he wrote. "They are not the chief administrators of its economic destiny."

— Berkley Kalin

Among the sweeping changes in the post-Crump era was the entry of women into politics and leadership positions on a more than token basis. Gwen Awsumb, who had been a leader in the League of Women Voters, was the first woman elected to serve on the new city council and the first to serve as its chair. Mrs. Awsumb left the council to direct the agency of Housing and Community Development, from which she has since retired. She remains active in civic affairs and in efforts to develop new leadership. From the Memphis/Shelby County Room (M/SCPLIC)

The mid-1960s was a difficult era. With the country bogged down with the war in Viet Nam, children revolting against the values of their parents, and drug abuse becoming commonplace, the world seemed to be turned upside down. President Johnson's Great Society poured billions into social programs, yet to many this seemed a policy of appeasement. The "long hot summers" came—with black-instigated race riots in Watts in 1965, Chicago in 1966, and a half-dozen other cities including Newark and Detroit in 1967. Television cameras zoomed in for close-ups of burning and looting.

To many whites, the entire social structure appeared to be breaking down, with black aggression viewed as a major part of the problem. The rhetoric of black militants seemed to them as senseless as the destruction and lawlessness. The fiery speeches of black nationalists such as Malcolm X were incomprehensible to white Memphians, but they saw the rhetoric taken up and intensified by young black leaders. Stokeley Carmichael, Rap Brown, the Black Panthers, and others proclaimed the slogan "Burn, baby, burn," advocating violence as a solution to their race's problems. Even the relatively moderate local black leaders broke with the white liberals who had worked with them and aided their cause. Some began demanding 40 percent of all local wealth because blacks comprised about 40 percent of the local population.

Many white Memphians were somewhat bewildered by these developments. Skepticism of the justice of the black cause increased as they saw that what they regarded as repeated concessions made to blacks met only with increased demands and the threat of lawlessness. The races were becoming increasingly polarized ideologically and politically. In David Tucker's words:

> The civil rights movement had gone far enough to threaten the vast majority of white Memphians who voted Republican, and they no longer tolerated politicians who compromised with blacks. They demanded toughness. Racial confrontation was almost inevitable now that whites had united in resistance while blacks had grown impatient and united in pressing for more dramatic change.

One of the last things that black and white leaders worked together to achieve was the restructuring of municipal government. This had been part of the old liberal coalition's program, and the unrest of the Ingram years hastened its implementation. A civic group calling itself the Program of Progress drafted a new city charter and lobbied for its passage in a 1966 referendum. The new charter provided for a strong mayor to run the executive branch and a 13-member body (7 chosen by district and 6 at large) to serve as a legislative council. Blacks supported the change because it would give them several voices in city government for the first time since Reconstruction, and Memphis became the last major city to discard the commission form of government.

Strike and Tragedy

The year after Memphians chose their new form of government, they voted on the candidates who would run it. Henry Loeb came out of political retirement to run for mayor in a crowded field. The election resulted in a runoff between Loeb, who had endorsed the new charter, and Mayor Ingram, who had opposed it. Loeb captured almost 90 percent of the white vote, beating Ingram who had the nearly unanimous support of the city's blacks. Three prominent blacks had won district seats on the council, but the city's racial polarization had been reinforced and intensified.

By the time the election was over, Memphis had become a racial powder keg. The summer of 1967 had seen sporadic incidents of race-related violence and destruction. Wild

Chapter Seven: Modern Memphis: 1955-1981

rumors were rife, and white Memphians had made unprecedented purchases of arms and ammunition in anticipation of possible race warfare in the streets. All that was lacking was a major incident to light the fuse; then all hell would break loose.

The incident came from an unexpected quarter, and the fuse proved to be a slow one. Memphis, being underindustrialized, had had relatively little labor-related strife prior to the 1960s and almost none in the ranks of public employees. The largely rural migrant sanitation workers seemed the least likely of municipal employees to organize and engage in a job action. Although the American Federation of State, County, and Municipal Employees (AFSCME) had chartered Local 1733 in Memphis in 1964, the union was not recognized by the city and had fewer than 40 dues-paying sanitation-worker members.

Except for supervisory personnel, the ranks of sanitation workers were filled overwhelmingly by rural blacks. The near-minimum wages and the working conditions of these men were certainly far from optimum, but compared favorably with those of their counter-

parts in other Southern cities. T.O. Jones' efforts at union organizing over a 10-year span had been largely unsuccessful, when suddenly in February of 1968 a mundane grievance caused his efforts to bear fruit.

Twenty-two sewer and drain workers had their workday canceled because of rain. They were paid for only two hours, while their white supervisors would be paid for the whole day. This incident, combined with the fact that two other workers had been accidently crushed to death in a garbage compressor, aroused sufficient anger for Jones to try calling a strike meeting. Surprisingly, more than 400 of the city's 1,300 sanitation workers attended the meeting. Jones' rhetoric persuaded the workers to issue a list of demands to the Sanitation Department, which ignored them. The next day more than 1,100 members of

Metropolis of the American Nile

the sanitation work force engaged in a wildcat strike, shocking the national union leadership as much as it did city officials.

The workers had little in the way of reserve resources, and the strike would probably have ended quickly if black leaders had not rapidly converted it into a civil-rights issue. The local NAACP and black ministers threw their support and resources behind the strikers and joined in their protest marches. The police department's perhaps too-ready use of chemical mace radicalized many black moderates and solidly united the black community behind the striking workers. Increasingly, black ministers, under the auspices of the Inter-denominational Ministers Alliance, took over leadership of the protest. Even the oldest and most conservative ministers were willing to fight city hall on this issue. Younger, more militant ministers were not above hinting at violence as a solution to the stalemate.

Stalemate it was. Mayor Loeb declared the strike illegal, which it was under existing laws, and insisted that the workers return to their jobs. Blacks, who had been practicing civil disobedience for years now, refused. The city began replacement hiring and tried to maintain minimal levels of garbage collection. When militant blacks harassed and attacked garbage trucks in some black neighborhoods, collections there ceased. Open garbage piled up and became breeding places for rats and other vermin. The city, which had long claimed to be the nation's cleanest, rapidly became among the filthiest.

Loeb viewed the strike issue as a matter of principle. Although he talked with union leaders and members of the MCCR, his views on this point did not change. As the black boycott of downtown stores shrank sales by 35 percent, some of the city's white solidarity began breaking down. Still most white Memphians did not see the magnitude or complexity of the city's racial problems, ascribing them to a few activist troublemakers and outside agitators.

Local black leaders brought in nationally known figures, including Roy Wilkins and Martin Luther King, Jr., to participate in the protests. With integration being achieved nationwide, moderate leaders such as King and Wilkins were turning increasingly to the pursuit of economic goals for their race. Even so, they seemed to be losing their leadership of the black masses. Young radicals were belittling the value of their monumental achievements, and some actually referred to them as "Uncle Toms." Participation in the nationally newsworthy economic struggle in Memphis would give media exposure to their activism and their cause.

The situation had by now escalated out of all proportion to the sanitation workers' grievances. The strike had become a symbol of the city's two races deadlocked in a test of will. Negotiations had reduced differences between the city and the workers. The major point holding up an agreement was whether the city would permit union dues to be deducted from the workers' paychecks. Such a concession would not only imply de facto recognition of the union, it would also give the union leverage for building its membership.

Although most of the white council members still agreed with Loeb regarding the principle involved, several of them were keenly aware of the damage that was being done to the city's spirit and of the potential that it could become far worse. They did not think the issue of prohibiting municipal unions was as important as the risk of permanently impairing chances for racial harmony if the situation blew up. Joining with the three black councilmen, they attempted to override Loeb's refusal to concede the dues checkoff. They failed. The seven-member majority, like most white Memphians, wanted the strike broken and the union discredited. The two halves of the city were on a collision course.

Martin Luther King, Jr., had spoken at a Memphis rally in mid-March and had received such a welcome reception that he promised to return to Memphis to lead a protest march. He kept his promise, but during the course of the march vandalism broke out. A downtown

The sanitation workers' strike quickly transformed Memphis from one of the nation's cleanest cities into one of its filthiest. Open garbage piled up in many areas and became breeding grounds for rats and other vermin. Courtesy, *Memphis Press-Scimitar*

Chapter Seven: Modern Memphis: 1955-1981

petty-criminal element apparently started the window smashing and looting, but some protesters left the line of march to join in the riot. Once the demonstration was out of control and the law had been breached, the police used tear gas and force to try to break it up. In the process one young black was killed, 60 persons were injured, and about 300 were arrested. King's ability to lead a nonviolent protest came under serious and nearly universal question.

King was planning a summer of major civil-rights activity, including a mammoth poor-people's march on Washington. He felt that he had to reassert his ability to lead nonviolent protest, and that he had to do it in Memphis. He had returned to Memphis to lead a second march when, on April 4, 1968, a sniper's bullet struck him down on the balcony of his motel. Then all hell did break loose.

Shock waves of anger, grief, remorse, and guilt smote the nation. Riots broke out in 172 American cities, resulting in 43 deaths, 3,500 injuries, and 27,000 arrests. Memphis was in the forefront of the rioting, and a curfew had to be imposed to curb the lawlessness which King's murder unleashed.

In the aftermath of King's murder, more than ever, national attention focused on Memphis and its problems. Mrs. Coretta King took up her husband's struggle. Here she leads a protest on South Main Street with her two children, Reverend Ralph Abernathy, and entertainer Harry Belafonte. Such demonstrations were peaceful and many white Memphians began to reexamine their attitudes regarding race. Courtesy, Ernest C. Withers Photographers

Yet King's martyrdom did aid the civil-rights cause. The television networks flooded the nation with days of sympathetic coverage of King's life and the whole civil-rights movement. This saturation coverage caused millions of whites, including many Memphians, to face the issue of racial injustice squarely for the very first time. Club women and businessmen, some of whom had assumed that King was a communist or worse, and that the NAACP was communist-backed, were rudely awakened. White Memphians who earlier had despised King in their ignorance and referred to him in derogatory terms, acquired a new understanding and now referred to Dr. King as a martyr. They reexamined views they had held for decades, and many wanted to do something to improve race relations.

The garbage strike, which had gone on for two months, reached a compromise settlement 12 days after the King murder. It involved de facto recognition of the union through a memorandum of understanding, a 10-cent-per-hour raise for the workers, and a provision for collecting union dues through the employees' credit union. Union recognition and dues payroll deductions were later regularized. Thus at great cost, victory, if it can be called that, went to the blacks. Later, however, many blacks were outraged when the increased cost of sanitation service was charged to individual users on their utility bills, rather than being passed to the more affluent in the form of higher property taxes.

Both Henry Loeb and the city of Memphis endured a great deal of adverse publicity and criticism stemming from King's death. Loeb had remained intransigent regarding the strike, but he viewed it as an economic and administrative matter rather than a racial one.

Metropolis of the American Nile

He certainly did not want King killed, least of all in his town. On the question of his "racism" as the cause, Loeb was not a racist in his personal life, and his segregationist orientation represented the views of much of his white electorate. His sincerity on the question of principle in the strike has been challenged by some, who claim it was merely a cover for racism, yet even his political enemies who knew him well admit that he would have taken virtually the same position had the striking workers been white.

Memphis has been called the city that killed Martin Luther King. Although conspiracy theories abound, none of them has proved convincing. Evidence indicated that James Earl Ray had been following King for some time and might have killed him in Atlanta or elsewhere, had the opportunity presented itself. In a sense Memphis was the victim of a capricious fate. Two outsiders, each with a mission, happened to collide on its streets, to set off a blast that rocked the nation and the world. The effect on Memphis was a drastic heightening of racial tension and polarization that destroyed the city's momentum.

Some blacks embarked on a new era of militancy that included campaigns of systematic harassment and property destruction aimed at the white establishment. And there were those who embraced a double standard of values. Any whites who did not make the achievement of black goals their first priority were branded racists, while acts or expressions of black racism toward whites were excused because of past injustices. Black unity on any issue was equated with racial solidarity, soul brother- or sisterhood, and laudable loyalty, while white solidarity was racism, irrespective of the issue or its merits.

Twelve days after King's death, the sanitation strike reached a compromise settlement. It involved de facto recognition of the union, a small raise, and a provision for collecting union dues through the employees' credit union. This photograph shows the union leaders and ministers reacting to the news. Those pictured are from the left: the Reverend James Lawson, Dr. Ralph Jackson, Jerry Wurf, international union president, an unidentified striker, and local union president, T.O. Jones. Courtesy, *Memphis Press-Scimitar*

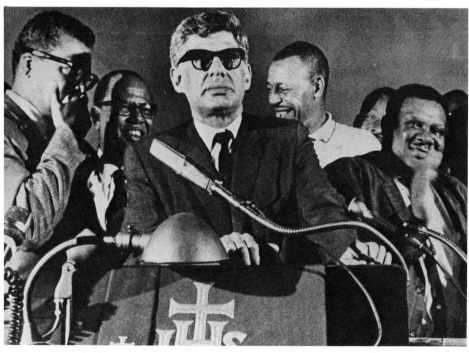

Racial considerations became the overriding factor in most aspects of local politics. Councilman Wyeth Chandler, son of a former mayor and protege of Henry Loeb, became mayor when Loeb chose not to run in 1971. Chandler has won three mayoral elections, the last two by narrowing margins over a black former judge, W. Otis Higgs, Jr. Significantly, in the last race Higgs hardly campaigned in the white community and lost by only a few percentage points.

149   Chapter Seven: Modern Memphis: 1955-1981

A POLITICAL FAMILY: THE FORDS

fices in Memphis-area politics.

As a man who admired the politics and personal style of the late Senator Robert Kennedy, Harold Ford ran a vigorous campaign in 1974 and beat the Eighth District incumbent Dan Kuykendall by only 744 votes out of 136,000 votes cast. Political analysts argued that the Eighth Congressional District had been redrawn by a Democratic-controlled legislature to make it difficult for a Republican to win. Kuykendall had defended Nixon until near the end of the Watergate affair, so probably suffered from that political connection. But it is difficult to argue that this district with a 53 percent white majority would have elected the city's first black congressman without a very powerful performance from Harold Ford, his family, and the capable political organization that the Fords had created.

Like the Kennedys, the Fords have a great depth of political talent. They have retained the offices that they have won against challengers of both races. Their very effectiveness has aroused some criticism, but such controversies do not appear to damage their voter appeal. Even if none of Newton Ford's other children enter the political arena, in a decade or more, his grandchildren may be running for office in Memphis.

— David Bowman

Harold Ford. From the Memphis/Shelby County Room (M/SCPLIC)

Ebony magazine in 1974 called Newton J. Ford's family "one of the nation's most politically astute families." In that year Ford's 29-year-old son, Harold, became Tennessee's first black congressman.

Newton Ford grew up on a wooden shack south of Memphis. He worked hard to get an education and learn about business, and in time established what is now one of the city's leading funeral parlors, N.J. Ford & Sons. In 1966 he ran an unsuccessful race for the Tennessee House of Representatives. Since then, however, four of his 12 children have been winning political races.

Harold Ford moved quickly from being voted "Mr. Esquire" at Tennessee State University, the student body's most coveted title, to winning a seat in the Tennessee House of Representatives in 1970. His older brother John managed to serve simultaneously in the General Assembly in Nashville and on the City Council in Memphis. When John Ford moved up from the State House to the State Senate, his younger brother Emmitt ran successfully for his House seat. When John decided not to seek re-election to the City Council in 1980, his brother James ran and won handily. Thus the Ford brothers hold four major of-

James Ford. From the Mississippi Valley Collection, MSU

After King's death the city seemed to have lost its momentum. Amid racial divisions on nearly every issue, the city's leaders (black and white/public and private) have rarely to agree on either larger goals or the programs and priorities for reaching them. Because of such divisiveness, economic and population growth have nearly ceased.

The local business elite, reacting to the trauma of King's death, made genuine efforts in the 1970s toward solving racial problems in the economic area. As part of the Greater Memphis Program, they attempted to redress discrimination against blacks and women and to bring the community together. Such leaders and the Chamber of Commerce spent several million dollars attempting to get Memphians "to believe" in their city and trying to stimulate job-creating investment from outside. But all of the sloganeering and positivism produced little in the way of tangible results. By mid-1977 the Chamber of Commerce was on the verge of economic collapse, and some business leaders had withdrawn from trying to help solve the city's problems. The city appeared to be neither any less divided nor any more on the move than when the business community had plunged in to help.

During the 1970s the Sunbelt city of Memphis grew less than 4 percent in population—down from figures of from 20 to 36 percent for the three preceding decades. Crime accelerated, and streets became less and less safe. The local economy remained sluggish, characterized by low wages and underemployment. Worst of all, some Memphians seemed to have lost their sense of identity, purpose, and local pride. By 1981 this seems to have reversed, for a poll in that year showed 71 percent of Memphians preferred living in Memphis to anyplace else in the world.

Physical and Economic Changes

The most noticeable change in the city in recent decades has been in its physical makeup. The postwar construction boom continued into the 1970s, when overdevelopment caused a collapse in the real-estate market. The changes have been qualitative as well as quantitative. A combination of center-city decay and suburban sprawl has drastically altered the physical character of the city.

Much of the center city had become run-down during the Depression and World War II. The immediate postwar pressure was for single-unit housing, and literally acres of subdivisions were rapidly created to satisfy the hunger for homes. Most of the initial expansion was eastward, moving farther out from the downtown area. The city's 50.9 square miles in 1945 grew to 280 square miles in 1978, and annexations included the major communities of Frayser, Oakhaven, Whitehaven, Fox Meadows, and Raleigh. The city also annexed a great deal of vacant land, giving it a very low density of population and long distances between settlements. This urban sprawl rapidly began altering retailing and shopping patterns for the city.

Among the major problems facing downtown were inadequate streets. The system which had served 60,000 vehicles in 1940 became woefully congested by the 140,000 using it in the early 1950s. Downtown parking was even worse. The obvious need for more convenient retailing gave birth to the shopping center in Memphis.

The first experiment with a shopping center was the Poplar Plaza complex built about six miles east of downtown in 1949. Viewed as highly risky by some and derided as positively foolish by others, Poplar Plaza became an almost immediate success. It started a boom of satellite shopping complexes that reduced the downtown share of the city's retailing from 28 percent in 1948 to 5 percent in 1972.

The 1950s, '60s, and early '70s saw the steady physical and economic decline of the

downtown area. Middle- and upper-class white shoppers had largely deserted the downtown stores prior to 1968. Then the sanitation workers' strike, Dr. King's murder, and the ensuing racial hostility dealt a mortal blow to the already prostrate commercial area. The result was a wholesale flight of businesses from downtown and a noticeable drop in property values. Many retail stores and business offices, all of the movie houses, and most of the hotels closed. Some retailing survived because of custom from blacks, downtown office workers, and rural shoppers. But the central city had become nearly an empty shell.

Another factor that changed the physical characteristics of the downtown area was federal urban renewal. Accepted by planners as sacred writ after 1955, urban renewal went on a 20-year binge in Memphis, from 1957 to 1977. In 11 designated project areas spread over 560 acres, 3,000 structures were demolished. Although the program did rid the city of many genuinely blighted areas, it was applied somewhat indiscriminately and did not make a careful distinction between baby and bath water. It destroyed many of the city's landmarks, including much of the historic Beale Street district. Although some of the cleared areas were put to immediate reuse, others were left vacant. As a result downtown now has the luxury of green fields among its buildings.

One of the most important uses made of the cleared land was construction of public housing. Between the late 1930s and 1978, the city built more than 7,000 public housing units and leased almost 1,000 more, providing low-cost, adequate shelter to about 28,000 persons. Desegregation of public housing in 1965 resulted in white flight, and the units became increasingly black-occupied.

Other uses of the cleared land included the medical and civic centers. The medical center has more than 7,000 beds, employs more than 15,000 people, and has an annual payroll in excess of $100 million. Clearance enabled the hospitals to expand and improve their facilities. The civic center plaza occupies the north end of downtown and includes city, county, state, and federal office buildings, the Cook Convention Center, and the Criminal Justice Complex. All of these large, modern landmarks were constructed between 1960 and 1981.

Other landmark public buildings were built during the same period in various parts of the city, notably the Avery Street complex in the midtown. Nearby in the fairgrounds city and county governments constructed a major recreational complex, including the 11,000-seat Coliseum, the 51,000-seat Liberty Bowl Stadium, and a more modest baseball park, later named McCarver Stadium, for the hometown minor-league team. As a prelude to the nation's bicentennial, the amusement park was refurbished and expanded into the Liberty Land theme park.

These ambitious building programs were intended to benefit the city as a whole, but they did little to help the central business district. A multitude of varied schemes were proposed for revitalizing downtown. The most notable of those actually undertaken was the conversion of 4,000 feet of Main Street into a pedestrian mall. The Mid-American Mall is a modern, tree-shaded, fountain-lined walkway. Paved largely in a brownish gray tile, it was completed in 1974 at a cost of approximately $7 million. Unfortunately, so far it has not been the success its backers claimed it would be, and the cost of upkeep is steep. It may have enabled the few remaining major retailers to survive, and it has attracted a few new, smaller businesses, but it has not yet revived the downtown retail economy.

Competition from suburban office facilities dealt downtown business real estate as harsh a blow as the shopping centers dealt the retail stores. William B. Clark revolutionized business-office development in 1966 with the completion of his high-rise White Station Tower, 10 miles from downtown. The building, which conventional wisdom proclaimed would be a "white elephant," had the advantages of adequate free parking and proximity to the homes of affluent business people. Within two years Clark was constructing a larger tower close by, and other developers soon followed his lead. A variation on this theme was the executive office park plaza. All these developments damaged downtown rentals, while new downtown office buildings constructed by the major banks delivered the death blow to rentals in most of the older structures.

Metropolis of the American Nile

Another major factor in the decline of downtown was the continuing inadequacy of transportation. Memphians' love for the automobile, combined with postwar prosperity, brought the number of cars in the city to 450,000 by 1976, putting a severe strain on the street system and leaving the city's transit system in trouble. An expressway system designed to ease the flow of traffic was begun in the 1950s, but unfortunately the plan involved bisecting Overton Park with the major east-west throughway. A group calling itself Citizens to Preserve Overton Park fought for 24 years against cutting this expressway through the park. The issue was finally decided in their favor by the courts and state and federal agencies, but no referendum was ever held to find out what the majority of Memphians actually wanted.

Yet all has not been gloom and stagnation in the post-Crump era. Memphis has made genuine progress in a number of areas, and the city has enjoyed its brighter moments in the national limelight.

One of the brightest, although fleeting, was in the music industry. Memphis had its own blues tradition, and rural white migrants brought in their love for country music. At some point in the early 1950s these two elements came together, took on a beat similar to that used for jitterbug dancing, and the synthesis produced a new musical form. Known at first simply as "bop," it was later refined and renamed rock and roll.

Memphis was not alone in the development of this new music, but the city produced perhaps its most noteworthy artist. Crump had been out of the picture a scant two years when he was supplanted as the personality who most represented Memphis to the world by another young northern Mississippi transplant named Elvis Aron Presley. The shy but sensuous young singer combined aspects of both black and country music with something uniquely his own. He staged a meteoric rise to fame and wealth, becoming a sex symbol and cult figure of unprecedented dimensions. Surprisingly perhaps, despite his wealth and career commitments in Hollywood and Las Vegas, Elvis chose to keep Memphis as his home. His death in 1977 made that home a shrine to his fans, who continue to come here from across the nation and around the world.

Memphis celebrated its sesquicentennial in 1969, giving its citizens a renewed appreciation of the city's history. This float in the Rose Parade shows a riverboat bedecked with pretty girls who wave an invitation to the rest of the nation to join in celebrating the Bluff City's 150th birthday. From the Memphis/Shelby County Archives (M/SCPLIC)

Chapter Seven: Modern Memphis: 1955-1981

ELVIS PRESLEY

A long wall covered with gold and platinum records stands today at Graceland as permanent testament to a career that spanned more than two decades. Those records still sell, DJs still play them, and Elvis fans by the thousands still come from all over the world to visit his home, his grave, and the places he frequented.

When Elvis Presley burst upon the music scene, he was only 19 years old—the first of a whole new generation of young pop stars that would follow his lead. Discovered by Marion Keisker and Sam Phillips, he launched his meteoric recording career with "That's All Right [Mama]," released by Sun Records in August of 1954.

His style was unique—a white boy who "sang black," expressing emotions freely, liberated from the conventions of American popular music. He used his voice like an instrument, incorporating falsetto, mellow baritone, shouting, growling, staccato phrasing ("I l-o-o-o-o-ve you"), and breathless quivering, with a unique tremolo that many would try (unsuccessfully) to mimic. His mentors and models included groups such as the Ink Spots, R.H. Harris's Soul Stirrers, and the Swan Silvertones, as well as soloists such as Sister Rosetta Tharpe, Fats Domino, and Clara Ward, and he was a frequent visitor on Beale Street, where soul music could practically be absorbed by osmosis. He had an almost incredible ability to absorb styles, yet out of them he developed an utterly distinctive style of his own.

Through the years Elvis recorded a tremendous range of music—blues, rock, country, gospel, and even light

Above
Elvis strikes a handsome pose in the 1960s. From the Jerry Hopkins Collection, MVC Special Collections, MSU

Left
Oscar Carr and Clare Mallory, 1956 Cotton Carnival king and queen, meet new recording star Elvis Presley. From MVC Special Collections, MSU

Below
Elvis, MSU Dean R.M. Robison, and Mayor Frank Tobey at MSU in 1954. At the time Elvis was just another unknown with a guitar. From MVC Special Collections, MSU

opera ("O Solo Mio"). His voice appealed to people of all ages, and as he matured his following grew worldwide. His best work expressed a relaxed, unconscious, intuitive feeling for music, matched by a voice of tremendous range and power.

Throughout the 1950s and '60s Elvis also made a great many movies. His films contained wholesome, good-humored entertainment that appealed mainly to the younger generation. Some, such as *Jailhouse Rock, Viva Las Vegas, Wild in the Country, King Creole,* and *Flaming Star,* were good enough to impress fans and tough critics alike, demonstrating—especially in the last two—a talent as an actor that was never to be fulfilled.

Elvis never forsook his region and his roots. Born in Tupelo, Mississippi, he moved to Memphis at the age of 13, and he always considered it his hometown. Most of the people who worked for him were Memphians, their rowdiness and prank-pulling earning them the nickname "Memphis Mafia." Graceland was the dream home he bought for his mother, and, despite the entertainment establishment of East and West coasts, it was here that he chose to remain.

Elvis Presley's rags-to-riches story has all the elements of triumph and tragedy. Certainly there were flaws in his character, but above all stood the tremendous talent, the genuine spontaneity, and the personal appeal that made Elvis truly "the greatest entertainer of his time."

— Berkley Kalin

Above
An impassioned Elvis performs in the 1970s. From the Jerry Hopkins Collection, MVC Special Collections, MSU

Right
"The King" and Kang Rhee, his karate instructor and confidant from 1971-1974. Courtesy, Kang Rhee Institute

Below
Elvis, with Sonny West and Jerry Schilling, visits President Nixon in 1970. From the Jerry Hopkins Collection, MVC Special Collections, MSU

But the "Memphis sound" included more than Elvis Presley. It also involved Sun Records and artists such as Carl Perkins, Johnny Cash, and Bill Justice. Stax Records—with artists that included Otis Redding, Muddy Waters, and Rufus and Carla Thomas—also contributed. In the late 1960s it was big business, bringing the Memphis area an estimated $100 million a year in outside income. Music in Memphis continued through the heyday of Isaac Hayes, the "Black Moses" of American soul music. Mismanagement of Stax ultimately ruined the company, and the Memphis music industry has not yet recovered.

Metropolis of the American Nile

If Memphis was found wanting for entrepreneurial talent in the music business, this has been far from true in other local businesses. The mid-20th century had produced a large number of giants, particularly in the service industries. Among the most notable businesses whose founders have created national empires are Holiday Inns Inc., Federal Express, Dunavant Enterprises, Inc., Malone & Hyde, Inc., Dobbs House, Belz Enterprises, Fogelman Management Corporation, Cleo Wrap, and Guardsmark, Inc. These and many other businesses, large and small, are the economic lifeblood of the city. (Some of their contributions are presented in greater detail in the "Partners in Progress" section of this book.)

Individual companies aside, post-Crump Memphis produced one other field of enterprise that can hardly be omitted. During the early 1970s the Bluff City was moving toward a leading position in the nation's municipal-bond business. With a total of about 35 bond-investment houses, some of them large companies with more than 100 employees, Memphis became the third largest municipal-bond brokerage city in the country. Unfortunately there were also some fly-by-night outfits, and the unethical practices of a few dealers gave the whole city a bad name in the business. As a result many of the better houses left the area to escape the onus of association, and the opportunity for Memphis to grow as a national investment center was lost.

Back to the River

When urban-renewal projects were initiated in Memphis, they met little resistance until well under way. But then, in reaction to the destruction of the city's architectural heritage, a bunch of self-declared "little old ladies"—some in tennis shoes, some in white gloves—determined to stop the bulldozers and save what they could. By dint of hard work and grit, these *femmes formidables* saved a number of landmark homes on Adams Street, now known as Victorian Village. Under the sponsorship of the Memphis chapter of the Association for the Preservation of Tennessee Antiquities, and the Daughters of the American Revolution, they are turning some of the homes in the village into museum showplaces.

Perhaps more important, they have inspired an interest in historic preservation, and now there are other groups and agencies involved in the movement. Memphis Heritage, Inc., the Memphis Landmark Commission, the Shelby County Historical Commission, and the Center City Commission are all involved in some aspects of preservation and rehabilitation. Their cumulative efforts, along with more enlightened government policies and special bank loans for restoration projects, seem to be taking a giant step in reversing downtown decay.

Perhaps the most important aspect of the preservation movement is the adaptive reuse of downtown buildings. Tax breaks and other financial incentives are making renovation attractive to investors. Convenience, rising transportation costs, a declining crime rate, and the river atmosphere all make living downtown attractive to apartment dwellers and condominium owners. The movement to live downtown is escalating, with businesses beginning to compete for the remaining vacant buildings. If the current momentum continues, it will be a truly great step toward revitalizing downtown. Strong neighborhood associations have already made the midtown residential area pleasantly livable. Homes are being well kept again, and during the past decade real-estate prices have soared.

Whether inspired by the preservationists' efforts or just coincidental to it, there is a general flowering of interest in local history throughout Memphis and Shelby County. Neighborhood, community, and town histories are being written in profusion, oral histories of individuals, families, and enterprises are being systematically recorded, and significantly larger numbers of people are participating in historically oriented organizations. It seems

Top
Mr. Paul R. Coppock has doubtlessly done more than any other individual to build awareness of and appreciation for local history in the Memphis area. Journalist, editor, and historian, he has been educating the local citizenry for almost four decades on their history. His newspaper columns are so good that they have been compiled twice for hardcover publication. From the Memphis/Shelby County Room (M/SCPLIC)

Above
Oral history interviews, such as the one being conducted here by Ronald Walter and Alma Booth, are one of the many ways in which the area's heritage is being preserved. In this photograph longtime church and educational leader Reverend Blair T. Hunt answers questions. Courtesy, *Memphis Press-Scimitar*

Right
City government's recognition of the vital role of history to the tourist industry and to the revitalization of downtown has resulted in the building of a unique recreational and educational complex on Mud Island. Courtesy, Mississippi River Museum, Mud Island

ironic that a growing sense of the city's past is contributing so strongly to its prospects for a brighter future.

The city government has recognized this anomaly and is hoping to make maximum effective use of it. The city has allocated more than $60 million to convert the southern end of Mud Island into a major facility that will include a large park, an amphitheater, recreation facilities, restaurants, and a Mississippi River Museum. This large investment is expected to draw tourists from across the nation, as well as playing a major role in attracting locals to the downtown area. It should prove a good fit with the convention center, the mall, and Beale Street, whose redevelopment is currently under way.

Besides looking to the past, Memphians are also working to shape their city's future. Since 1979 Memphis has launched an annual Jobs Conference to prepare strategy for economic growth. As of 1981 these efforts have been successful in getting $20 million in state appropriations for the development of several of the city's potential resources.

Among the major developments still in drafting-board or ground-breaking stages, as of this writing, are an agricenter complex, to be developed on the 4,400-acre Shelby Farms property on the northeastern edge of the city, and a uniport complex designed to ensure maximum effective use of the city's excellent air, rail, river, and trucking facilities. Appropriately enough, in their reliance on location and agriculture, these ultramodern, future-oriented projects hark back to the days of the city's founding.

In its fall 1981 session, the Jobs Conference changed its emphasis to concentrate on settling the city's detrimental divisiveness and on developing attainable objectives toward which the city should try to move. Three propositions that emerged from a series of town-hall meetings dealt with the issues of local-option taxation, school busing for integration, and consolidation of city and county governments. Although questionnaires indicated that the biracial participants were in essential agreement on solving these problems, it still remains to be seen how that agreement will be translated into community action on these complex and controversial issues.

The city of Memphis stands today at another junction on what has been its roller-coaster ride through history. Many elements seem to indicate an upswing in the city's fortunes, but the outcome at this point is far from certain. The future of modern Memphis, like the past of its ancient Egyptian namesake, remains shrouded in mystery. But we can be sure of one thing: Memphis' fate will rise, or fall, depending on human aspirations that require effort and cooperation and continued goodwill from all its citizenry.

Metropolis of the American Nile

Above
A sharp contrast between the old and the new is evident in a view of Memphis' Southwestern College as seen through this geodesic sculpture on the campus. Photo by Bob Milnes

Right
The Memphis skyline is an arresting sight, especially at sunset. Courtesy, Shelby County Public Affairs Office

To show the world what the Beale Street area was once all about, this mural depicting the street's heritage faces toward the river. The National Blues Foundation intends to see that blues music returns to Beale to stay. Photo by Bob Milnes

Metropolis of the American Nile

Above
The Goldsmith Civic Gardens in Audubon Park contain some of the most beautiful sights in the city. This pond, its lovely Japanese bridge, and its colorful, exotic fish are for the contemplative moments. Courtesy, Memphis Board of Realtors

Right
Memphis' three great building eras—the turn of the century, the 1920s, and the 1960s—are all represented in this view taken from the Mid America Mall. Photo by Bob Milnes

Far right
Memphis and Shelby County still retain a great deal of the area's natural beauty. Subdued rural and suburban scenes can be as captivating as the more dramatic landmarks. Courtesy, Memphis Board of Realtors

Metropolis of the American Nile

Business is the very reason for Memphis' existence. The city's elevation made it a natural haven from the floodwaters of the Mississippi, the "inland sea" of the Great Valley's commerce. In addition, its advantage as a crossing point to the trans-Mississippi West made it a natural railroading center, which in turn brought more commerce. The establishments depicted here—E. Keck and Brothers Livery Stable (top, left), Coonley's Photograph Gallery (top, right), Williams and Company (middle), Lownes, Orgill and Company (bottom, left), and J.S. Levett and Company (bottom, right)—suggest the diversity of Memphis' business community in the 19th century. From the Memphis/Shelby County Room (M/SCPLIC)

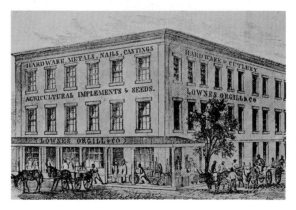

CHAPTER EIGHT
PARTNERS IN PROGRESS

This history of Memphis was made possible by select representative business, health, and historical "partners in progress" who supported and helped fund the project. Their individual histories reveal the multiplicity of achievements which have enriched Memphis and Shelby County. Business was the reason for Memphis' existence. In fact, the city was founded as a proprietary town, a business enterprise.

The Mississippi River always has been Memphis' greatest asset. The city is the second largest inland port on the Mississippi and one of the largest shallow-draft inland ports in the United States. In 1980, 14 million tons of cargo moved through the port on the way to Chicago, Pittsburgh, and New Orleans, as well as the Gulf of Mexico, Europe, Asia, Africa, and South America.

Industries concentrated within a 100-mile radius of Memphis use its port to ship a host of products including grains, soybeans, corn, cottonseed, lumber, chemicals, raw metals, and petroleum. Incoming goods include coal, crude oil, textiles, fertilizer, cement, plywood, and raw rubber.

Water has always been the cheapest and most efficient means of moving goods and the recent energy crunch has enhanced its desirability. The Mississippi carries more freight than any other river in the world.

Because the city is located within one of the nation's most productive agricultural regions, a substantial percentage of its citizens are employed in food manufacture. Agriculture, or "agribusiness," is still the basis for the city's economic stability. Likewise, its chemical industry has roots in Mid-South agriculture. A tremendous variety of chemical products is developed and produced in Memphis and sent all over the world.

The area has always been the hub of regional economic developments. Memphis still holds the title of "the hardwood capital of the world," and the cotton merchandising capital, as well. Because the city is in a noncongested area and has ample room for expansion, it is attractive to new industry. Memphis has many excellent industrial sites due to the foresight of private and public planners, high-quality storage facilities, transportation facilities (water, air, highway, and railroad), and superior public utilities. Other incentives for new industry include a relatively low tax rate, abundant and high-quality water, and cheap power, including TVA.

Memphis has a huge and outstanding medical center. The hospitals employ a large number of the people of Memphis. The city has many outstanding private medical organizations, and is a leader in medical technology.

Home-based national and international firms have played a large role in the building of the Memphis economy. Recently old and new financial and investment institutions have demonstrated new vigor, which has stimulated Memphis-based corporate activities.

Not only has business created the city's financial vitality, but it has also made significant cultural, social welfare, medical, and sports contributions.

— Berkley Kalin

ANDERSON-TULLY COMPANY

Seneca B. Anderson and Christopher J. Tully acquired controlling interest in the N.B. Hall Company of Benton Harbor, Michigan, on December 31, 1887. The company operated box and basket plants at Benton Harbor and Greenfield, Tennessee. The Greenfield plant was built and managed by Tully. They renamed the partnership the Anderson-Tully Company. In 1887 Anderson took a boat trip down the lower Mississippi River and was impressed with the cottonwood timber along the river in Tennessee and Arkansas, and decided that a veneer mill in the area would have an excellent supply of soft hardwoods. Tully had the knowledge and experience to build such a mill; Anderson was better suited to sales and payrolls.

The Anderson-Tully Company was incorporated on February 16, 1889. Tully and Anderson, who was mayor of Benton Harbor at the time, moved to Memphis on May 27, 1889. They bought a lot on the Wolf River from Collis P. Huntington, the

railroad tycoon. It was bordered on the east by the Memphis, Paducah and Northern Railroad (later the Illinois Central) and the Randolph and Big Creek roads (later North Second Street). On this site they built a veneer mill, box plant, and warehouse. They manufactured veneer boxes for everything from crackers and macaroni to eggs and bottles.

In 1895 another tract was acquired east of the railroad on which another box plant and large mule barn were built. Until 1930 the company used mules and wagons to move lumber and veneer on the yards. The mules were bought from the Southern Horse and Mule Company of Memphis.

In 1904 the firm bought the Wisconsin Hoop Company plant, which joined the original company lot on the south. The company also acquired the Patterson-Busby Company hoop plant on Henning Island (now Mud Island), and its machinery was consolidated with that of the Wisconsin Hoop plant to manufacture wood barrel hoops. In 1906 company stockholders purchased the Memphis Stave Company

plant, which manufactured slack barrel staves on Henning Island.

Anderson-Tully began operating circle sawmills to assure a supply of lumber for their boxes in 1900. They operated the C.W. Hunter Lumber Company sawmill at Penton, Mississippi, on the Illinois Central Railroad near the Desoto-Tunica county line. In 1902 they bought a circle mill and veneer mill at Ebony, Arkansas, six miles northwest of West Memphis. They soon decided that bandmills with resaws were necessary for efficient lumber production and built their first Memphis bandmill in 1904 on their original lot.

Since they accumulated surplus lumber of the higher grades not needed for box production, Anderson-Tully Company entered the hardwood lumber market. The original Memphis bandmill was replaced in 1916 by a new mill built on the former Bennett Hardwood Lumber Company site, which joined company land on the north. In 1926 this mill was replaced by one built on the spur rail line which crossed the Hall Avenue trestle over the Wolf River. Anderson-Tully

Christopher J. Tully (top left) and Seneca B. Anderson (bottom left), founders of Anderson-Tully Company, in a 1903 photograph.

TOP RIGHT
The Waltersville plant of Anderson-Tully Company today.

Metropolis of the American Nile

also operated a bandmill and veneer mill at Madison, Arkansas, from 1908 to 1924, and a bandmill at Stewart, Arkansas, from 1924 to 1930.

When Christopher Tully died in 1929, his son Bart C. Tully assumed the presidency of the organization. Under Bart Tully, the firm expanded its timberland base and its river construction and transport subsidiary, Patton-Tully Transportation Company. Bart Tully, Jr., succeeded his father as president of Patton-Tully.

When corrugated paper boxes began to replace wood containers in the 1920s, Anderson-Tully increased lumber production and closed box and barrel plants, but egg cases remained a significant part of the business until World War II. Immediately following the war they were large producers of hardwood plywood and automobile and furniture parts. Thus as consumer demands changed, company production changed accordingly.

Beginning in 1900, Anderson-Tully built several bandmills, a veneer mill, flooring mill, box plant, and dimension plant at Vicksburg, Mississippi. Vicksburg is downstream from its timberlands, which lie along the lower Mississippi River and its tributaries. They closed the Memphis sawmill and dimension plant in 1975 and expanded Vicksburg operations for more economic production. Today the firm has three sawmills at Vicksburg with a total of five bandsaw headrigs and four resaws. They also have a planing mill, dry kilns, and a laminated truck flooring plant. A similar flooring plant is located at Memphis. Anderson-Tully Company, with its main office at Memphis, has been known for quality hardwood lumber production since 1900, and since then has produced more than 3.3 billion board feet. Annual production is now 70 million board feet.

John M. Tully became president of the organization when his father, Bart Tully, died in 1967. Under his management mill facilities have been modernized and production of lumber and laminated flooring increased. The forestry department installed a continuous forest inventory system under Charles A. Heavrin, timberland manager. Today sawmill production is geared to sustained-yield timber production while ecological conditions on timberlands under company stewardship are monitored by a wildlife manager.

TOP
The Memphis sawmill and box plant about 1922. The veneer plant is to the right and the box plant to the left.

BOTTOM
An early lumber carrier at the Memphis mill in the 1930s. Before these straddle buggies were used, lumber was moved on the yards with mules and wagons.

Chapter Eight: Partners in Progress

BAPTIST MEMORIAL HOSPITAL

Frank S. Groner, administrator of Southern Baptist Hospital in New Orleans, accepted the position as administrator of Baptist Hospital, and with his coming a new era began.

In 1949 a long-range plan for the hospital was developed to meet the growing needs of Memphis and the Mid-South for health care services. The first phase called for the addition of a 450-bed, 13-story addition which was completed in 1955. The second phase projected a companion unit of 450 beds with the addition of six shelled floors on top of the phase one and phase two additions.

Standing in the heart of the Memphis Medical Center is Baptist Memorial Hospital, the largest nongovernmental hospital in the world. The facility far exceeds the expectations of a group of visionary Baptist leaders who first met in 1906 to organize an effort that led to the construction of a 150-bed hospital. Funds were raised in the tri-state area from people of all faiths to finance the original seven-story structure that cost approximately $235,000.

On July 20, 1912, the new hospital was formally opened to the public; it was hailed by the local press as "equal to any in the nation—the last word in hospitals."

Within three years young Baptist Hospital found itself facing serious financial problems; there were but 10 paying patients and 20 charity cases. Worried board members discussed selling the hospital but there were no prospective buyers at any price.

Then Dr. W.T. Lowry, president of the hospital's board of trustees since its founding, spoke from the pulpit of Bellevue Baptist Church, pointing out the great need for this new house of healing in words that deeply impressed A.E. Jennings, a planter from Greenwood, Mississippi, and the largest contributor to the building fund. Jennings offered to underwrite the large indebtedness of the hospital and to become responsible for its operation, assisted by an executive committee.

It was the beginning of a new course for the hospital; the indebtedness was soon paid off and during a 20-year period between 1918 and 1937, five additions were made to the hospital, bringing its bed capacity to 525. Included in the additions were a student nurse dormitory and the first hospital-owned physicians' office building in the nation.

A.E. Jennings served the hospital, supervising its operation from 1915 until his retirement in 1946. Upon his retirement,

The phase two addition, known as the Union East Unit, was opened in 1967.

Between the phase one and phase two hospital additions, two new office buildings for physicians were constructed. The hospital also purchased a 10-acre, 6-story former V.A. hospital which was developed as a comprehensive medical rehabilitation facility. Known as the Regional Rehabilitation Center, this facility includes units for spinal cord injuries, stroke and neurological disorders, rheumatoid arthritis, geriatrics, pulmonary rehabilitation, a pain center, and one of the largest hospital-based renal dialysis units in the country. The unit was

TOP LEFT
Baptist Memorial Hospital Medical Center.

TOP RIGHT
Regional Rehabilitation Center.

ABOVE
Baptist Memorial Hospital East.

Metropolis of the American Nile

designated by the regional planning agency as the regional rehabilitation center for this area.

Between 1967 and 1975 the six shelled floors on top of the phase one and phase two additions were opened, bringing the hospital's bed capacity to 2,068. In 1975 a fourth medical office building was completed.

In the early 1970s it became apparent that it would be necessary to replace the

original hospital facilities constructed between 1912 and 1937. A decision was made to build a 400-bed community satellite hospital in the growing East Memphis suburbs, phasing the older beds out of service as the new hospital was opened. The new hospital was opened for service in March 1979 and was named Baptist Memorial Hospital East.

Frank S. Groner retired as chief executive officer of Baptist Memorial Hospital on April 30, 1980. He was retained as director of development for the hospital and given the title of president emeritus. During the period of his administration the hospital grew to be the largest nongovernmental hospital in the United States. He has been recognized as a national leader in the health care field, serving as president of many prestigious health care organizations.

Baptist Memorial Hospital is recognized as a center for diagnosing and treating patients with cardiovascular disorders, and the neurosurgical and orthopedic services rank among the largest in any general hospital. While developing these extensive services, the hospital has experienced the lowest cost per patient day of any U.S. health care facility operating more than 1,000 beds.

The board of trustees appointed Joseph H. Powell president of the hospital effective May 1, 1980. He had been a member of the administrative staff since 1955. Emphasis was given to developing the extensive ancillary facilities of the hospital. Among the services added were an oncology unit, a cardiac rehabilitation program, a geriatric evaluation unit, a 125-bed critical care center, and a sleep disorders lab.

A major emphasis at this time was to develop a multihospital system in this region of the country with Baptist Memorial Hospital serving as the hub. The governing body of the hospital expressed its belief that Baptist had the size, experience, resources, and expertise to serve as the nucleus for a regional hospital system. The main emphasis of this effort was to maintain the voluntary nonprofit characteristic of the health care delivery system.

Every specialty of medicine is represented among the members of the hospital's medical staff. The staff, recognized as one of the country's finest, is devoted to upholding the high standards of the hospital.

The hospital is owned by the three state Baptist conventions of Arkansas, Mississippi, and Tennessee. Management and control

of Baptist Memorial Hospital is vested in a 27-member board of trustees. The influence and philosophy of the Baptist denomination has guided the hospital's program since its inception, fulfilling the threefold Christian mission: healing, teaching, and preaching. The hospital is dedicated to a program that will continue the tradition of excellence which has been such an important part of its history.

TOP LEFT
A.E. Jennings, administrator, 1915-1946.

BOTTOM LEFT
Baptist Memorial Hospital's original structure, July 1912.

TOP RIGHT
Frank S. Groner, administrator, 1946-1980.

BOTTOM RIGHT
Hospital nurses, circa 1918.

Chapter Eight: Partners in Progress

A.S. BARBORO, INC.

Anthony Sebastian Barboro came to America from Genoa, Italy, in July 1861 at the age of seven. He accompanied an uncle who took him to Chicago. When his uncle died the young man moved to Memphis and then to Arkansas City where he worked in general merchandising for nine years. His parents in Italy tried to persuade him to return to his native country, but his love for America was strong and he would not leave. In 1877 he returned to Memphis and established a wholesale and retail fruit and produce company on South Main Street. The A.S. Barboro Company grew and prospered for 43 years at this location.

World War I brought economic changes and adjustments. To his wholesale fruit and produce business, A.S. Barboro added the distribution of beer to the operation, which proved to be a profitable decision from the start.

Barboro had a zest for living that expressed itself in everything he did—including wild game hunting, promoting the sale of Liberty bonds for the war effort, financing an ambulance that was sent from Memphis to Italy during World War I, and providing excellent products and service to his customers.

In January 1920 A.S. Barboro abandoned the retail branch of his business, moved his entire operation to a new building at the foot of Pontotoc Avenue, and became a wholesaler only.

A.S. Barboro died in 1922 and his only son, Malcolm Goodwin Barboro, took over the business and continued the tradition of hard work and good service. Barboro Alley, behind the world-famous Hotel Peabody, is one of the ways that the citizens of Memphis paid tribute to this respected family.

The firm was incorporated May 6, 1953, with Malcolm G. Barboro as president and his wife Lucy D. Barboro as vice-president. The secretary-treasurer was Charles J. Goggio. In 1961 Barboro assumed the position of chairman of the board and Goggio became president.

In 1966 Malcolm G. Barboro moved the business to 1311 Rayburn in the industrial section of southwest Memphis. For 11 years the distributorship worked out of this location. Goggio retired in June 1974 after more than 52 years of service with the company. Richard Karnes, who had been an officer since 1965, assumed the office of president.

Malcolm G. Barboro died in 1977 but the Barboro tradition did not end. The great-grandson of Anthony Sebastian is now the vice-president of the firm. Malcolm Barboro Wood is the fourth generation of the family involved with the organization.

The company has a beautiful and functional new 50,400-square-foot office-warehouse facility at 4116 B.F. Goodrich Boulevard in the Airport Industrial Park—located in the southeast Memphis suburbs.

The dreams of A.S. Barboro took him from Genoa, Italy, to Memphis, Tennessee. His hard work and plans took his company from apples, pears, grapes, lettuce, and tomatoes, to some of the finest names in quality beers.

TOP
Anthony Sebastian Barboro, founder of A.S. Barboro, Inc.

ABOVE
Early morning is a busy time at A.S. Barboro headquarters as trucks line up for deliveries.

BELZ ENTERPRISES

The cornerstone of downtown Memphis' revitalization is the Peabody, the Grand Old Lady at Union and Second. Belz Enterprises, Tennessee's largest developer of commercial and industrial properties and owner of the famous hotel, has invested over $20 million into her restoration—a tremendous commitment to the city's future. For four generations the Belz family has demonstrated that it ardently believes in Memphis.

Philip Belz, founder and chairman of the board, took over the management of a South Memphis store at the age of 14 when his parents became ill during the great influenza epidemic following World War I. His preparation for a building and real estate career was circuitous; it included becoming an expert butcher, learning accounting and cotton classing, operating a cotton gin, and owning a dry goods business. By the early 1930s, however, he was dabbling in small construction—houses and stores. In 1936 he purchased four acres of land and built

one of Memphis' first suburban shopping centers, at Thomas and Firestone, as well as several nearby duplexes which rented for $15 a month. He thought of himself as a "provider for industry." Within a decade he was building plants for such national concerns as General Motors, Firestone, Bemis Bag, General Electric, Kroger, National Biscuit, and U.S. Rubber.

The Belz organization is still privately owned by members of the family, principally Philip and his son Jack A. Belz, president and chief executive officer. They do not look to overnight profits; rather they invest for the next generation and the one after. Sometimes labeled an "accumulator," Philip has said, "I never did go for a quick profit in anything." Jack, an MIT graduate at age 20, has continued that policy. The third generation of the Belz family—Martin S. Belz, Gary R. Belz, Ronald A. Belz, and Andrew J. Groveman—is actively involved in all aspects of the firm.

Belz Enterprises has been successful in all major developmental projects: regional and community shopping centers, industrial parks, warehousing, corporate office parks, apartment complexes, hotels, recreational facilities, and multipurpose land developments. The Buffalo-based Belz hotel division owns and/or manages 21 hotels, with more planned for the future. With a major concentration of project and land developments in the Memphis area, the Belz holdings include extensive properties and land in all regions of the country.

Belz Enterprises is a multifaceted real estate development and management firm with more than 15 million square feet of building space throughout the United States. The corporation also has extensive land holdings awaiting future uses. Now in its fourth decade, Belz has consistently expanded its interests, fostering innovative technologies in all phases of development and management.

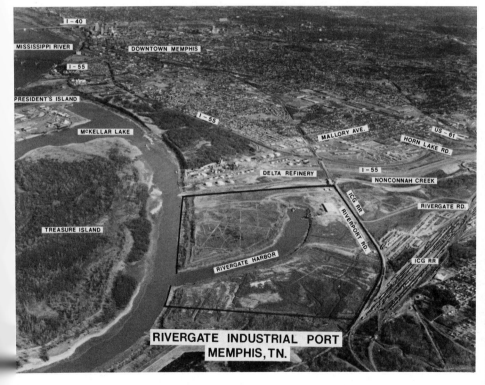

ABOVE LEFT
An aerial view of Rivergate Industrial Port, Memphis.

ABOVE RIGHT
Philip Belz, founder and chairman of the board (left), and Jack A. Belz, president and chief executive officer of Belz Enterprises.

Chapter Eight: Partners in Progress

BLUE CROSS AND BLUE SHIELD OF MEMPHIS

Memphis Hospital Service and Surgical Association, Inc., better known as Blue Cross and Blue Shield of Memphis, evolved from an early prepayment concept which began in Dallas, Texas. In 1929 a group of school teachers at Baylor University, in conjunction with Baylor University Hospital, began to make payments toward their hospital care so that it would be available should the need arise. This later grew to include physician care. The concept spread and eventually Blue Cross and Blue Shield Plans emerged all over the continental United States, Canada, Jamaica, and Puerto Rico.

In 1947 three independent Memphis plans sponsored by St. Joseph, Baptist, and Methodist hospitals, joined to become Memphis Hospital Service and Surgical Association, serving the five West Tennessee counties of Shelby, Tipton, Haywood, Lauderdale, and Fayette. Blue Cross and Blue Shield is a name that has come to mean reliability in health insurance to over 50 percent of the Plan's area population.

The physical face of Memphis Blue Cross and Blue Shield has changed with the years. In 1947 the offices were housed in the Sterick Building and were moved to the Dermon Building in 1950. Another move was made to 2430 Poplar Avenue in 1960, and still another in 1970 to a newly constructed building at 85 North Danny Thomas Boulevard. In 1980 two additional floors were constructed because of its rapid growth.

The operational aspects of the Plan have developed over the years. With changes in environment came changes in competition within the marketplace. Health care costs began and continued to rise rapidly. Services still revolved around the original not-for-profit, prepayment concept of health insurance coverage for individuals and employee groups, but new and more comprehensive programs were added.

Blue Cross and Blue Shield introduced new benefit programs for mental health care, a freestanding dental plan, vision care coverages, as well as multiple major medical programs to help reduce the cost of catastrophic illnesses. It also became an intermediary for the Medicare program.

Cost containment programs have emerged as the costs of medical care continue to increase. Such programs as pre-admission testing, home health care, same-day surgery and second-surgical opinion are administered to help lower medical care costs. Blue Cross and Blue Shield works continually with hospitals, physicians, and other members of the community in cost containment activities because cost containment is a primary concern of the Plan.

Blue Cross and Blue Shield helps promote personal health by emphasizing preventive health care. The WalkerRunn Program of Physical Fitness and On-Site Hypertension Screening Program were developed and are being used in businesses throughout the country. Also, Blue Cross and Blue Shield has initiated an individual Health Risk Appraisal Program which focuses on personal health evaluation and follow-up educational opportunities.

In 1980 the Memphis Individual Practice Association, an alternative to traditional health care coverage, was begun under Blue Cross and Blue Shield sponsorship. The Memphis Individual Practice Association (MIPA) provides comprehensive health care benefits which are overseen by individual member physicians. This new program emphasizes preventive health care.

The image of Blue Cross and Blue Shield of Memphis continues to change. The Plan has moved extensively into administrative services such as sharing of risk with employers in the city, the administration of self-funded group coverages, and electronic data processing support to small area hospitals for their accounting function—Shared Hospital Accounting Service (SHAS).

Growth and change have combined to build a stronger organization. Blue Cross and Blue Shield recognizes the challenges that come with added dimensions and continues to meet those challenges. The primary corporate goal of Blue Cross and Blue Shield of Memphis is to "provide the highest level of benefits to the largest number of subscribers at the least possible cost—while continually seeking to improve the quality of service." While it is committed to maintaining a position of strong leadership in the community, the Plan works always to keep its commitment to each individual subscriber within that community. This is its history—its present commitment—and it will extend into the future.

Blue Cross and Blue Shield of Memphis has serviced West Tennessee since 1947.

BOYLE INVESTMENT COMPANY

Boyle Investment Company has developed some of Memphis' most significant real estate projects over a period of nearly half a century.

The Boyle organization is a group of related companies. Boyle Insurance Agency, one of the Mid-South's largest, provides general insurance for businesses and individuals. Boyle Mortgage Company is one of the foremost residential and commercial lenders in the Mid-South area. At the end of 1980 Boyle Mortgage serviced over $250 million in mortgages for over 30 different investors. Boyle's real estate sales division is a leader in the selling of residences and condominiums.

Boyle also develops, builds, sells, and leases commercial and industrial property. In the residential field Boyle is active as a developer, builder, and realtor. Boyle's property management work involves more than 2,500 apartment units, office buildings, shopping centers, and other types of real estate.

With roots deep in the history of Memphis, the Boyle organization has the vision and the staying power to undertake major development projects that require many years to bring to fruition. An example is Ridgeway Center. The former Ridgeway Country Club was acquired by Boyle approximately 10 years ago and plans were made for a complete development including office buildings in a park setting, the Hyatt Regency, a theater, shopping areas, restaurants, and condominiums. This area has attracted corporate headquarters of many important national companies.

Boyle Investment Company was founded in 1933 by three brothers, Snowden, Bayard, and the late Charles Boyle, direct descendants of John Overton, one of the founders of Memphis. Originally the company's principal activity was the management of business properties. Very few mortgage loans were being made at that time, but New York Life Insurance Company selected Boyle to service its mortgage loans in the Memphis area. Later the firm was chosen to represent National Life and Accident Insurance Company of Nashville and Provident Life and Accident Insurance Company of Chattanooga.

As the '30s drew to a close, a great need for new housing became apparent. Boyle established a real estate sales organization in the early '40s and at the end of World War II

began developing residential subdivisions. One of the most popular was Pleasant Acres, which provided a full acre for each home in contrast to many of the crowded subdivisions of the time.

In 1946 Boyle Insurance Agency was established. From a one-man organization offering limited coverage, it has grown to a major operation licensed in 39 states, representing 17 leading insurance companies, and providing complete coverage for businesses and individuals.

An important development of the 1970s was Farmington, an area of Germantown built around Farmington Country Club. The club, including a championship golf course, was developed, built, and managed by Boyle. Farmington includes single-family residences, apartments, and shopping areas.

The company outgrew its original space at 148 Monroe in the 1950s and moved to the Fargason Building at Second and Monroe. The organization now includes more than 200 people, and with the development of Ridgeway Center, Boyle moved to its present location at 5900 Poplar, the first new structure in Ridgeway.

ABOVE
The Hyatt Regency and office building in Ridgeway Center was developed by Boyle Investment Company.

TOP
The headquarters of Boyle Investment Company is located at 5900 Poplar, Memphis.

Chapter Eight: Partners in Progress

BROWNING-FERRIS INDUSTRIES

Browning-Ferris Industries, now the largest publicly held company in North America engaged in the collection, processing/recovery, and disposal of solid and chemical wastes for commercial, industrial, governmental, and residential customers, combined and merged in 1970 with a small base of operating companies located primarily in Texas, Mississippi, and Tennessee. That base, known as Patterson Services, Inc., was initially organized in 1954 and incorporated two years later.

The Patterson Services "group" was expanded through subsidiaries to Houston, Texas, in 1958; San Juan, Puerto Rico, in 1962; and Biloxi and Jackson, Mississippi, in 1964. The group was combined and merged with Browning-Ferris Industries (formerly known as Browning-Ferris Machinery Company) in 1970. At that time Harry J. Phillips, a lifetime Memphian and founder of Patterson Services, became president of Browning-Ferris Industries.

In 1970 Browning-Ferris (including operations of the Patterson group) had revenues of $15 million and net income of approximately $300,000. Operating locations, including the Patterson group of five companies, totaled 15.

During the '70s, BFI expanded to include operations in approximately 160 cities throughout the United States and Canada. In addition, the company has developed an expanding base of international operations with interests in Spain, Kuwait, Venezuela, and West Germany. From its beginning, Browning-Ferris Industries' revenues have grown to $660 million for fiscal 1981 and net income to $48 million for that same period.

Browning-Ferris Industries has expanded its base of expertise to include the operation of over 70 sanitary landfill disposal sites; several processing, transfer, and recovery facilities; numerous bulk chemical sales facilities; industrial cleaning crews; oil field services; and municipal street-sweeping services.

The company's mentor, Harry J. Phillips, serves presently as chairman of the board, chief executive officer, and president. Phillips, who resides in Memphis, maintains offices in Memphis and at the corporate headquarters in Houston, Texas. In 1979 he was recognized by the National Solid Waste Management Association as "Man of the Year" for his contribution to the industry. Of Phillips' five sons, three (Harry Jr., Julian, and Howard), serve in management positions with the organization.

The original Patterson Services operation in Memphis is now one of the larger operations within the Browning-Ferris network. The firm operates over 66 trucks in commercial and industrial collection services and residential contracts with the cities of Germantown, Bartlett, and the Raleigh section of Memphis. The company also operates the primary sanitary landfills used for disposal of residential, commercial, and industrial waste in the Memphis and Shelby County area.

Developing new waste systems to meet tomorrow's needs, BFI is, in a very real sense, a company building an industry.

TOP
One of the earliest waste-removal vehicles used by the company formerly known as Patterson Services, which today forms an important link in the Browning-Ferris Industries chain.

ABOVE
Entering the new BFI Holmes Road Sanitary Land Fill are three representative modern vehicles designed to serve (from left) residential, commercial, and industrial wastes.

BUCKMAN LABORATORIES, INC.

In the basement of a small house on North McLean Boulevard, Dr. Stanley J. Buckman, a microbiologist, started with an idea and a 50-gallon chemical reactor. This small beginning became the foundation of Buckman Laboratories, Inc., an international industrial chemical company.

Dr. Buckman's idea was that, through basic research, new and unique chemicals could be developed to solve the problems of industry. This idea, which the company continues to pursue, has resulted in the Buckman product line expanding from one product in 1945 to approximately 200. Today most are proprietary products, covered by patents in over 35 countries.

These chemicals are used by industry for the control of microorganisms, scale, corrosion, deposits, foam, and for the preservation of various types of material. The basic industries served by Buckman include agriculture, leather, paint, plastics, pulp and paper, sugar, and textiles. Water treatment in many other industries has been vastly improved with Buckman products. The research program continues to seek new answers to many industrial problems, such as the preservation of wood.

The original 50-gallon reactor was replaced by a considerably larger manufacturing facility at Memphis. In January 1949 a gasket failure on a reactor caused an explosion and fire, severely damaging the fledgling enterprise's manufacturing facilities. Around-the-clock construction proceeded on the new plant under a protective tent. Manufacturing resumed prior to depletion of inventories so that product availability was never interrupted.

Expansion then began in many directions. Enlargement of the Memphis plant was the first priority. Between 1963 and 1974 companies were established in Australia, Belgium, Brazil, Canada, Mexico, and South Africa, as well as a branch in Japan. Concurrent with the worldwide expansion, another U.S. plant was built in Cadet, Missouri. This ensured product availability at strategic locations on an international basis.

Marketing is done by highly educated staff representatives at the various Buckman companies, most of whom hold chemical or science-related degrees. A network of distributors and formulators is used to market the products in 67 additional countries.

Recognition for the international company came with the awarding in 1966 of the Presidential "E" Award. This was followed in 1970 by the Presidential "E Star" Award for superior performance in foreign marketing activities.

Of the 500 employees worldwide, 250 are located at the company headquarters at Memphis. Recognizing Memphis as its home, the corporation and its employees are involved in many local church, civic, and charitable organizations.

One very unique benefit enjoyed by Buckman employees is job security. At no time in the firm's history have there been any layoffs. Should production be slowed temporarily, employees are kept on the payroll while doing maintenance. Another benefit is an established program for educational opportunities for employees and their children.

"Creativity for our customers" has been and will continue to be the motto of the Buckman organization under the present leadership of chairman of the board Robert H. Buckman, son of Dr. and Mrs. Stanley Buckman. The Buckman family of employees will continue to play an important role in the Memphis community.

ABOVE LEFT
Dr. Stanley J. Buckman, founder and chairman of the board of Buckman Laboratories from 1908 until his death in 1978. (Photo courtesy of Gittings.)

TOP
Original headquarters of Buckman Laboratories, March 1945.

ABOVE RIGHT
The modern international headquarters of Buckman Laboratories was completed in 1972.

Chapter Eight: Partners in Progress

CLEO WRAP

Cleo Wrap has grown in the past 25 years to become the largest Christmas gift wrap company in the world. Being number one means printing close to 1.5 billion feet of gift wrap annually—enough to circle the earth a dozen times or to reach the moon and then some. In addition to printed gift wrap, Cleo produces 150 million bows, 300 million feet of ribbon, 425 million enclosure gift cards, 110 million Christmas cards, 150 million gift boxes, and 250 million valentines in a year's time.

Cleo is a company of about 1,400 employees and almost two million square feet of manufacturing, office, and warehouse space. It is not an exaggeration to say that Christmas is Cleo Wrap's reason for being. The firm is busy all year preparing for Christmas. Although shipments are seasonal, work is not. Cleo goes from designing to printing to manufacturing to storing to shipping to collecting over an 18-month to two-year period. Cleo's products are sold in all 50 states and in many foreign countries. Licensees manufacture Cleo's products in Canada, Great Britain, and Australia. Such well-known national retail chains as Kmart, Sears, Roebuck & Co., Montgomery Ward, F.W. Woolworth, Jack Eckerd Drugs, Super D Drugs, and many others handle Cleo's products.

There are reasons for Cleo being number one in its industry. First, it was in the right place at the right time, having entered a growth industry close to its beginning. Twenty-five years ago large department stores and other retailers began to charge for gift wrapping as their operating expenses grew. At about the same time came the beginning of the tremendous growth of the self-service discount outlet—which, due to its low-profit margin, offered no personalized gift wrapping services. Out of these two trends arose the need and demand by customers for do-it-yourself gift wrap materials. Also, in the large self-service department, drug, variety, and supermarket chains, a pattern for mass-marketing of these products needed development. Cleo capitalized on this situation and quickly captured the market.

Cleo Wrap was organized in 1953 as Memphis Converting Company by Leo C. Wurtzburger and his son, Charles L. Wurtzburger. The elder Wurtzburger died in 1959. Charles succeeded him, serving as president until he retired in 1974 and became a consultant to the company. At that time L.R. Jalenak, Jr., took over as general manager and chief operating officer. In September 1977 he was elected president of the company. Other corporate officers are Duane J. Tabor, vice-president, merchandising and corporate planning; William J. Cochran, vice-president, marketing and sales; Roy L. Barton, vice-president, administration; Morris Patterson, vice-president, manufacturing; and Walter M. Langford, vice-president, operations. All are active in community services.

In 1964 Cleo Wrap was brought into the Gibson Greeting Card group of companies, when it was acquired by CIT Financial Corporation. On February 1, 1980, CIT Financial Corporation was acquired by RCA. Cleo Wrap is a division of Gibson Greeting Cards, which is a wholly owned subsidiary of RCA. In 1982 Cleo Wrap was purchased by a private investment group composed of Wesray Corporation of Morristown, New Jersey, and the management of Gibson and Cleo. William E. Simonson, former Secretary of the Treasury, assumed the position of chairman of the board of Gibson and Cleo at that time.

TOP
Cleo Wrap officers (from left): Roy L. Barton, vice-president, administration; William J. Cochran, vice-president, marketing and sales; Duane J. Tabor, vice-president, merchandising and corpo-rate planning; L.R. Jalenak, Jr., president; Charles L. Wurtzburger, former president and consultant; Walter M. Langford, vice-president, operations; and Morris Patterson, vice-president, manufacturing.

BOTTOM
An aerial view of Cleo Wrap headquarters.

COCA-COLA BOTTLING COMPANY

The Coca-Cola Bottling Company of Memphis was formed in 1902. The present family of ownership, the Pidgeons, took over the business in 1909. The first president was J.C. Pidgeon, followed by his son J. Everett Pidgeon, and since 1962 George R. Pidgeon. The first location was at Fourth and Washington.

In 1957 the company acquired an additional location at 499 South Hollywood. For several years it operated both facilities, with the new location servicing the eastern area of Memphis. In 1962 it was decided to move the entire operation to South Hollywood Street. Facilities and acreage have been expanded several times. Today the Coca-Cola Bottling Company encompasses the plant area, service building, accounting and data processing office building, and paint and body shop service building.

The only time the firm has ever closed for any length of time was during World War II. All industries were under restrictions and many necessary items were rationed. Because Coke had used up its allotment of sugar, it distributed everything it had to local dealers by Christmas Day, 1942, then closed up until January 2, 1943.

A big spurt of growth came July 28, 1947, when rationing was eliminated. The next couple of years brought a tremendous increase in the number of Coke employees, many of whom are still working for the company more than 30 years later.

Coca-Cola has adjusted to the needs of the times. Between 1902 and 1955 the 6.5-ounce bottle was the only size available. The year 1955 brought the 10-ounce; 1966, the 16-ounce. Then came the 32-ounce non-returnable, 32-ounce returnable, and 2-liter nonreturnable plastic. In 1977 Coke went from the 32-ounce to a one-liter bottle, the first in the Mid-South area to offer this more convenient size to the customer. The 38-millimeter crown-neck bottle was designed by Coke to retain carbonation during pouring. In the late '60s Coke introduced canned beverages, creating its own canning line in West Memphis, Arkansas, in 1971.

Coca-Cola Bottling Company of Memphis handles the complete line of Coca-Cola products, Dr Pepper products, Barq Root Beer, Rondo, Sunrise line of flavors, and Schweppe's Mixes. Packaging sizes range from 6.5-ounce to 2-liter, returnable and nonreturnable. Taking all the various combinations into account, there are 93 different types of packages offered by Coca-Cola.

The variety of packages is adaptable to all kinds of equipment. A pre-mix (prepared in a tank arrangement with syrup, water, and carbonic gas intact) is offered. A post-mix (pure syrup in a tank) is also available. At the outlet, water and carbonation are added—so that the restaurant, bar, or quick food outlet manufactures its own drinks.

Coke's record of community service equals or surpasses that of any other Memphis firm. For example, in the summer of 1980 Coca-Cola gave a recycling center to Memphis State University to operate—with all profits accruing to MSU. It can separate steel and aluminum.

Coke is the largest local advertiser in the electronic media. The award-winning advertising is youth-oriented, emphasizing a healthy, all-round image. The concern for youth is evident in other areas, such as a promotion of sports, placement of score-boards, and active support of LeBonheur Hospital.

The franchise area of Coca-Cola Bottling Company of Memphis includes Shelby County, Tennessee, and Crittenden County, Arkansas. It also has interests in other plants within a 150- to 200-mile radius, owning percentages of plants in Clarksdale, Greenville, Sardis, and Holly Springs, Mississippi; Brownsville, Tennessee; and Marianna, Arkansas.

TOP
A 1910 audit report depreciated mules and wagons as fixed assets. Pictured here are buildings on Main Street which faced the old Coca-Cola plant, including the Baron Hirsch Synagogue (left), now the location of the West Precinct Police Headquarters.

BOTTOM
An early Coca-Cola Bottling Company motorized delivery truck, circa 1912.

Chapter Eight: Partners in Progress

COMMERCIAL AND INDUSTRIAL BANK

In January 1913 a group of Memphians applied for a charter to open a banking institution in Memphis. The charter was granted to the Mutual Loan Investment Company, and on January 13, 1913, the bank opened for business on Second Street at Court across from Court Square. It operated under a franchise of the Morris Planning Corporation and was capitalized at $100,000.

The founder of the bank was Richard Oliver Johnston, originally from Rosemark, Mississippi. Associated with Johnston in the venture was a close-knit group of men from some of the oldest and most respected families in Memphis. They included F.N. Fisher, John P. Bullington, S.M. Neely, F.D. Smythe, J. Goldsmith, H.H. Litty, C.J. Farris, George C. Love, E.W. Ford, Thomas B. Crenshaw, J.N. Cornatazer, F.H. Heiskell, I. Samelson, Thomas B. King, and C.P. Cooper.

On July 7, 1913, the board of directors voted to change the name of the bank to Industrial Bank and Trust Company. The request was granted by the state of Tennessee only five days later, on July 12. A second name change was effected on September 8, 1927, when the institution became the Commercial and Industrial Bank.

Early in 1940, after Johnston's death, his family became interested in selling its ma-

jority stock to the General Bancshares Corporation of St. Louis, Missouri. In June 1941 Commercial and Industrial Bank became a wholly owned subsidary of General Bancshares. At the time the bank was located at 70 Madison Avenue, but in December 1941 it was moved to the ground floor of the Sterick Building.

In July 1961 the name was changed once again to Commercial and Industrial Bank of Memphis. Today the bank still operates under that name, although it has become familiar as C&I Bank. In 1972, C&I moved

to its new building at 200 Madison Avenue.

Making business a pleasure, the six-story bank provides a lush, green oasis in the middle of downtown Memphis. From the outside, the high, steeply sloping glass roof of the wedge-shaped structure mirrors the sky and surrounding office buildings.

Inside, about half of the main level is devoted to a garden plaza filled with plants. Walkways allow the visitor to wander among the various plants and, for a few moments, escape the pressures of urban life. Because of its controlled climate and rich green vegetation even in the winter, this indoor garden has become not only a functional office building but also an attractive park in the heart of downtown Memphis.

Many magazines have had featured articles on C&I Bank's headquarters, including *Batir* (Italy), October 1973; *L'Architecture d' Aujourd'hui* (France), December 1972; *Domus* (Italy), September 1973; *Fortune*, February 1973; *Architectural Record*, May 1972; and *Progressive Architecture*, March 1974. C&I Bank was selected for the Museum of Modern Art (New York) 1979 exhibition "Transformations in Modern Architecture." It has received such architectural honors as the 1973 Tennessee Society of Architects Design Competition Honor Award; and the 1974 American Institute of Architects, Gulf States Region, Honor Award (for the C&I Bank Kirby Woods Branch). James M. Evans, AIA, vice-president of Gassner Nathan & Partners, architects for C&I Bank, has noted, "This was a passive solar building designed before the energy crises."

TOP
Commercial and Industrial Bank has identity and prominence among buildings of varying size and design. It is a striking triangular structure produced by using a sloping skylight to enclose a garden plaza. Architects: Gassner Nathan & Partners, Architects, Planners, Inc.

BOTTOM
C&I's sloping greenhouse roof encloses a dramatic indoor space that maintains its outdoor flavor year-round.

CONWOOD CORPORATION

Two hundred years ago, in 1782, John Garrett II began manufacturing snuff. This was the beginning of Conwood Corporation. Garrett, a veteran Revolutionary War officer, built a snuff mill at Red Clay Creek near Wilmington, Delaware. He began manufacturing one of the oldest continually produced items in American history—Garrett Scotch Snuff. Today several million pounds of Garrett snuff are still sold annually.

Various members of the Garrett family continued in the snuff business for over 100 years. After a series of mergers, the Garrett brands of snuff were acquired by a new firm, the American Snuff Company. Founded in 1900, the enterprise was part of the vast tobacco empire created by James "Buck" Duke. Duke's tobacco trust was one of Teddy Roosevelt's earliest trust-busting targets. In May 1911 the Supreme Court broke up this monopoly.

The original American Snuff Company was divided into three separate firms. One of these, the surviving but smaller American Snuff Company, was assigned plants in Tennessee and Delaware. Among the brands designated to American Snuff were Levi Garrett, W.E. Garrett, Dental Scotch, and Honest Scotch.

In 1910 a Scotch snuff plant had been established in Memphis in the area of Front and Keel streets. In 1912, after the Supreme Court decision, the American Snuff Company was moved from New York to

Memphis. Offices were located in the Exchange Building at the corner of Second and Madison. The American Snuff Company is the oldest Memphis-based corporation to be listed on the New York Stock Exchange, and the plant at Front and Keel was expanded to the point where it was termed "The Largest Scotch Snuff Plant in the World."

Through four decades, from 1912 to 1952, the firm's business was producing and selling snuff. After that the organization began to diversify. In 1952 American Snuff Company acquired Taylor Brothers, Inc., of Winston-Salem, a large independent producer of chewing tobacco. At that time Bull of the Woods was the company's most famous brand of plug chewing tobacco.

American Snuff entered an entirely new consumer market in 1957—Hot Shot, a line of household insecticides. Hot Shot was to become one of the largest-selling insecticides in the southern United States. The program of diversification continued, and in 1961 the Blevins Popcorn Company of Nashville was acquired. Blevins products are marketed nationally under the labels Popsrite, Presto Pop, and Beehive, a brand especially packed for institutional and concession sales.

In 1967 the firm strengthened its position in the tobacco industry with the acquisition of the Scott Tobacco Company in Bowling Green, Kentucky. Scott manufactures a form of tobacco known as twist. Hand-rolled twists are one of the oldest forms of tobacco, and still enjoy popularity in certain sections of the country. In 1975 Conwood further expanded its household products with the acquisition of Manhattan Products, Inc., of Carlstadt, New Jersey. This company manufactures private-label ammonia, bleach, and fabric softeners.

As the American Snuff Company continued to diversify, its officers felt the need to adopt a corporate identification more compatible with this broadening range of interest. On July 1, 1966, the name of the company was changed to Conwood Corporation. The name Conwood is a contraction of the names of two men whose families have played important roles in the company's early history: Martin J. Condon III, who was president at that time, and James E. Harwood, Jr., who was executive vice-president. In 1975 the corporate offices were moved to 813 Ridge Lake Boulevard.

William M. Rosson is president and chief executive officer of Conwood Corporation.

TOP
A turn-of-the-century scene of tobacco being brought to one of the leaf processing plants of the American Snuff Company.

BOTTOM
Conwood Corporation headquarters is located at 813 Ridge Lake Boulevard in Memphis.

Chapter Eight: Partners in Progress

DOBBS HOUSES, INC.

The original Toddle House Restaurant began in 1931 and was the beginning of what is today one of the premier companies in the food service industry. Dobbs Houses, Inc., founded by James K. Dobbs, has been Memphis-based since its beginnings.

Ten years later Dobbs and his partner, Horace H. Hull, entered the airline catering business and soon achieved outstanding success. Dobbs first proved that high-quality food could be provided for airlines when he took over the restaurant at the Airport Terminal Building in Memphis and used its kitchen to cater the flights of several airlines. Dobbs was an energetic "recipe collector" as well as devoted airline traveler, who loved to visit airports all over the nation, get behind the counters, and whip up meals. Even after the catering services became well-established, his penchant for surprise visits continued. Dobbs was also a pioneer in food, beverage, and gift concessions in airports, a natural outgrowth of his close association with airports throughout the country.

Today Dobbs Houses, Inc., is the nation's second largest airline caterer with airport catering kitchens, airport terminal concessions, and 245 specialty restaurants, known as Steak 'n Egg Kitchens, throughout the nation. The company operates 48 flight kitchens in the United States and six kitchens abroad, servicing 60 airlines. It also has more than 225 concession facilities in 24 airports.

In 1980 Dobbs Houses, Inc., became a subsidiary of Carson Pirie Scott & Co., a diversified Chicago-based conglomerate.

Dobbs maintains extensive support systems to guarantee quality and efficiency. These include a centralized purchasing department; construction services to implement engineering concepts through local contractors; quality assurance programs to set standards for food preparation and service; training; data-processing; marketing; industrial engineering; corporate sanitation; safety programs; and energy, environmental, personnel, real estate, and financial services.

Dobbs Houses, Inc., is planning the construction of new Toddle Houses throughout the nation. Although the new structures will incorporate the latest architectural and culinary advances, they will retain many of the old ideas that made the concept initially successful, including the "dollhouse" appearance with two chimneys, and the original color scheme. Dobbs' president and chief executive officer, Robert P. Bryant, explains, "It will be a modular building ...

welded together on location. We wanted building with positive recognition so you' immediately recognize it as Toddle House.

Dobbs has also entered the contract in stitutional food service business with th purchase of Bowie Foods, a Memphis com pany. It provides food services for privat schools, businesses, and vending distribu tors on the premises of clients. Typica clients include banks, insurance companie major corporate headquarters, and light-in dustry plants.

A system of supportive services, similar t those in Dobbs' other departments, will be in stituted with emphasis upon quality assur ance and testing and energy conservation.

Dobbs' most recent expansion has bee into contract management services. At th present time it operates employee cafete rias for large corporations in Texas an Tennessee.

Today Dobbs ranks as one of America' largest food service companies. Every da more than 300,000 people dine with Dobb Houses, Inc., aboard aircraft, in airline ter minals, and restaurants. The firm employ more than 11,000 people in 450 location worldwide.

Grenada Cotton Compress Company, an

TOP
Dobbs prepares a wide variety of meals and snacks to meet the needs of each individual airline customer.

BOTTOM LEFT
A typical Steak 'n Egg Kitchen, open 24 hours a day.

BOTTOM RIGHT
The Plantation Restaurant at the Memphis International Airport.

FEDERAL COMPRESS & WAREHOUSE COMPANY

Grenada Cotton Compress Company, antecedent of Federal Compress, began operations in 1886 with one plant in the small town of Grenada, Mississippi. The compressing of cotton greatly facilitated storage and shipment of the commodity, providing a tremendous saving of both space and money. The firm, under the leadership of R.L. "Red" Taylor, grew rapidly through the construction and purchase of additional properties, and by 1925 Grenada owned 28 corporations (including the parent company), with a total of 48 cotton compresses and a storage capacity of 1.2 million bales.

In that year these 28 corporations were merged into Federal Compress & Warehouse Company, with its general offices in Memphis. By this time controlling interest had been acquired by R.L. Taylor. The new company continued to expand until it had 100 plants. At one point, on January 6, 1956, it had 4,537,134 bales of cotton on hand in its various plants. W.L. Taylor succeeded his father as head of the world's largest cotton warehouse system.

Roger D. Malkin formed an investment group to purchase the assets of the original Federal Compress & Warehouse Company. From this purchase came the formation of Southwide, Inc., in 1968.

Since 1968 there has been a long-range plan to diversify into other activities with the full knowledge that there was an excess of cotton warehousing space. During the past 12 crops this trend has been accelerated due to a shift in cotton from the Mid-

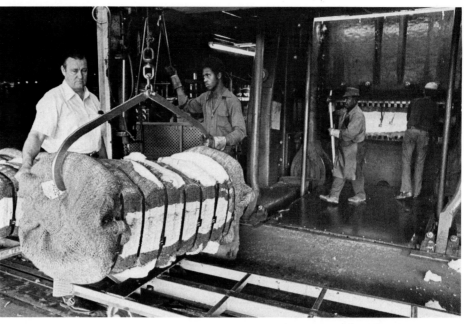

South to Texas, Arizona, and California. The Mid-South farmer has alternate crops, such as soybeans, rice, and wheat, and the prices of these commodities have risen in recent years, hastening the shift in acreage from cotton. So the firm began an aggressive program of redeveloping those plants into alternate uses.

Federal Compress now has a substantial amount of square footage devoted to commercial warehousing, light industry, and many other commercial functions. This new concentration has fostered the creation of

Southwide Development Company, Inc., and the development of new commercial properties. Federal Compress and Southwide Development now have a very active real estate department, developing industrial and commercial real estate throughout the Mid-South region and in Arizona and California.

In addition to these activities, in 1978 Southwide bought Delta and Pine Land Company, located in Scott, Mississippi, 15 miles north of Greenville. It is the world's largest cottonseed breeder and enjoys one of the best reputations in the world for cotton varieties. Delta and Pine Land Company has also introduced several soybean varieties and the long-range plan is to expand its product line into all crops that are grown in the Cotton Belt.

L.P. Brown Company, Inc., one of the largest distributors of bale wrapping and ties, was purchased in 1976. This operation continues to serve the cotton industry.

In summary, Southwide, Inc., through its subsidiaries, Federal Compress & Warehouse Company, Delta and Pine Land Company, L.P. Brown Company, Inc., and Southwide Development Company, Inc., continues to serve agriculture and industry.

Samuel B. Hollis is president and chief executive officer of Federal Compress & Warehouse Company and Southwide, Inc.; Roger D. Malkin is chairman of the board.

TOP
Compress machine at Grenada, Mississippi, site of the plant that later became Federal Compress and Warehouse.

ABOVE
Composite of Southwide and its affiliate companies, with the exception of L.P. Brown.

Chapter Eight: Partners in Progress

DUNAVANT ENTERPRISES, INC.

William Buchanan "Buck" Dunavant went into the cotton business at the age of 20. His father, Colonel William P. Dunavant, and General Nathan Bedford Forrest, Civil War Confederate hero, had started the Memphis and Selmer Railroad, a major cotton carrier, which grew into the southern leg of the Frisco Railroad. In 1929 Buck Dunavant entered a partnership with T.J. White, Sr., located at 112 South Front Street. The firm struggled through the Depression like hundreds of other small cotton companies on Front Street—from the Custom House on the north to Beale Street on the south. It bought most of its cotton on the street, checking out each bale, sample by sample.

After World War II, T.J. White and Company was known as a very reputable and dependable "small cotton shipper," handling about 75,000 to 80,000 bales annually with 10 to 15 percent of this going to foreign customers. The company experienced a somewhat lean period from the early 1950s to 1968. The government was heavily involved in the cotton business, supporting the price of cotton at above-market levels. The Commodity Credit Corporation had tremendous surpluses of cotton that it had taken over from the producers; the loan level was the market and it was so high that the law of supply and demand could not operate. The United States, during these years, became a residual supplier of cotton to the world markets. In the late '60s the government changed its farm programs, reducing the level of supports to a market-oriented philosophy.

In 1952 William Buchanan "Billy" Dunavant, Jr., came into the firm as a junior partner; he became a full partner four years later. He had started out as a squidge in his father's classing room, "pulling cotton," running the fiber over the index finger, measuring the length of each strand with the eye, gauging the quality. A worn knuckle is a proud reminder of these years.

When T.J. White retired in 1960, the name of the firm was changed to W.B. Dunavant and Company with Dunavants Sr. and Jr. in charge. With the death of his father in January 1961, 29-year-old Billy took control of the company. It became a more aggressive and innovative operation. For instance, the company was one of the first to go into "forward crop contracting," whereby a farmer agrees to a price before he plants. It was considered a risky venture but Dunavant prospered while others floundered and failed.

During the lean period from the 1950s to 1968 Dunavant managed to grow in volume and profits by increasing volume and handling it at a lower margin of profit. The main source of supply was the Memphis territory—the states that border the Mississippi River. With the passing years the production of U.S. cotton has moved westward, although the largest merchandisers of cotton in the world are still in Memphis.

When Billy Dunavant took over in 1961, yearly volume was 150,000 to 175,000 bales. By the middle of the '60s it had reached 250,000-300,000; by the early '70s it attained the one-million mark. The next decade volume increased up to three million bales—worth $2.7 billion. The 1980 drought prevented a repeat of this high. But in recent years Dunavant has been either the largest merchandiser of cotton in the world or the second largest.

In 1971 all businesses in which Billy Dunavant had ownerships came into the fold of the newly organized Dunavant Enterprises, Inc. Within 10 years offices were opened in Fresno, California; Phoenix, Arizona; Gastonia, North Carolina; Greenville, South Carolina; Greenwood, Mississippi; Columbus, Georgia; and Lubbock, Texas. Some are buying offices only;

ABOVE LEFT
This portrait of W. B. "Buck" Dunavant, founder of the firm known today as Dunavant Enterprises, Inc., is the focal point in Billy Dunavant's office. (Courtesy James Shearin, *The Commercial Appeal.*)

ABOVE RIGHT
Dunavant Enterprises has moved its location from Front Street. Today the company employs more than 1,000 people in the United States and throughout the world.

others buy and sell. Overseas offices are located in Osaka, Japan; Hong Kong, China; Geneva, Switzerland; Guatemala City; and Obregon, Mexico.

Increased American cotton purchases were supplemented with purchases in every producing area of the world, including Russia, Guatemala, Turkey, Tanzania, Argentina, Pakistan, Egypt, and Israel. Billy Dunavant explains why the company has become active in foreign markets: "We handle foreign growths of cotton to keep abreast and posted of what world prices are doing in each market. Because sooner or later they're going to have some effect on U.S. prices or U.S. prices are going to affect them. You've got to be covered in all areas to know what the demand and supply availability is." Dunavant Enterprises was also the first cotton company to do business with The People's Republic of China.

Dunavant Enterprises is more than a cotton company. It includes oil ventures, trucking, real estate, cotton warehousing, and commodity brokerage. Every division is financially separate. Dunavant trucks and warehouses much of the cotton it buys and sells. Dunavant Exports Corporation makes a commission on export sales. Dunavant Enterprises, Inc., also encompasses Central State Trucking, Memphis Aero Corporation, The Racquet Club Land Company, and Dunavant Commodity Corporation.

Among the major tennis events sponsored by the Racquet Club in the past few years have been the U.S. National Indoor Tennis Championships, Davis Cup, Southern Ladies, Veterans, and National Clay Court 18 Girls. It is the site of the oldest indoor championship tournament in the world. It is number one in junior tennis development.

In 1971 Dunavant Enterprises, Inc., moved from Front Street to a modern complex on New Getwell Road in East Memphis. This new setting offered ample room for expansion and an atmosphere freed from the daily rumors which plague cotton row.

Cotton has always been a changing business and one involving moment-to-moment decisions. Dunavant Enterprises has thrived in the unpredictable world of cotton because of Billy Dunavant's uncanny "knack for timing." As he has succinctly stated: "We try to determine long-range programs that will be best for our firm. We can't tell what will happen on a day-to-day basis."

ABOVE LEFT
The Racquet Club of Memphis, a subsidiary of Dunavant Enterprises, is considered one of the finest indoor facilities in the world.

ABOVE RIGHT
A cotton "snake" is moved across Dunavant Enterprises' cotton room.

Chapter Eight: Partners in Progress

FEDERAL EXPRESS

Memphis-based Federal Express has grown from a handful of packages and aircraft on its first day of operation in April 1973 to more than 100,000 shipments daily and an operating fleet of some 60 aircraft.

At the age of 27, Frederick W. Smith established Federal Express as an all-cargo carrier. The company in 1972 was certified as an air taxi service by the Civil Aeronautics Board, enabling it to operate aircraft with a capacity of not more than 7,500 pounds anywhere in the United States.

Smith received start-up assistance from New Court Securities, a New York investment firm. A total of $72 million in investments was secured, the largest venture capital amount ever raised by a fledgling corporation.

Due to increasing fuel prices, the company was losing more than one million dollars a month by mid-1974, forcing it to return to its original investors for an additional $11 million.

Monthly operations first showed a profit in February 1975. By early 1976, demand for FEC's services was larger than the capacity of its fleet of 48 Falcons. Federal Express petitioned the CAB for permission to use larger aircraft but the agency refused to make an exception. Fred Smith took his case to Washington where he testified before the Senate Commerce Committee. After winning support from such powerful figures as Senators Howard Baker and Ted Kennedy, a bill giving the company the right to fly bigger planes passed both houses of Congress in November 1977. It was signed into law by President Jimmy Carter.

Within a few weeks of deregulation, Federal Express bought seven Boeing 727s with an option for six more. Each aircraft was able to carry five times what a Falcon would carry.

On April 12, 1978, the corporation went public. The stock split two-for-one in September. On December 28, FEC was listed on the New York Stock Exchange.

Today Federal Express is a multimillion-dollar company with about 11,000 employees nationwide and 154 stations providing door-to-door service to more than 240 major markets and 14,500 communities.

FEC has put into service four DC-10s it has purchased. The firm also has twenty-nine 727s and 32 Falcons. Over the next three years, it will be purchasing fifteen 727s. Federal Express also operates more than 2,500 radio-equipped vans, which pick up and deliver shipments.

Packages sent via Federal Express never leave the company's hands because only company employees pick up, sort, transport, and deliver the shipments. This closed-loop system, unique in the industry, has reduced the chances of a shipment's being lost, stolen, or damaged to 4,500 to 1.

FEC carries more than 22 million domestic shipments annually—more than Emery Air Freight, world's largest freight forwarder, and more than the next four largest freight forwarders combined.

Revenues for fiscal 1981, which ended May 31, 1981, were $589.5 million, generating $100.4 million in pretax income.

ABOVE LEFT
A container of packages is loaded onto a Federal Express aircraft. Each package—regardless of its origin or destination—is flown at night to Memphis for processing through FEC's "Super Hub" before being delivered the next morning to the consignee.

ABOVE RIGHT
To make good its promise of "absolutely, positively overnight" delivery of small packages, Federal Express maintains a fleet of approximately 60 airplanes and 2,500 radio-equipped vans.

D.A. FISHER, INC.

The D.A. Fisher Insurance Agency was started by Phillip Alston Fisher in 1864. He had two sons, Drury Alexander and Phillip Allan. There was an 18-year gap in age between the brothers. Since the father died when Phillip Allan was still an infant, his brother D.A. raised him as a son. D.A. was educated as a pharmacist at Vanderbilt and operated a drugstore in Memphis on Main Street. On January 12, 1894, he took over his father's insurance agency.

The firm was incorporated in 1913. The original charter actually grants such broad and sweeping power to the firm that it is technically empowered to issue insurance of its own, which it has never done. When D.A. Fisher died in 1920, his brother Phillip Allan Fisher took over the presidency. He in turn was succeeded after his death in 1949 alternately by his sons, Phillip Allan Fisher, Jr., and D.A. Fisher II. In March 1981 D.A. Fisher III became president. Thus, the firm has been headed by a member of the Fisher family for 118 years—five generations by lifeline, four generations by bloodline.

The original location of the company was 4 Madison Avenue in downtown Memphis. Its present location, since 1971, is 3940 Park.

D.A. Fisher, Inc., originally specialized in fire insurance; later it carried a full line of coverage.

An area of traditional specialization has been hardwood lumber—mills and yard and everything connected with the business. The company historically pioneered new forms of coverage, having copyrighted false arrest and malicious prosecution coverage (now a standard coverage) in 1929. Another area of specialization that dates back to 1948 is aviation insurance. It was the pioneer in aviation insurance in the Mid-South market. The thrust has been in the general and industrial aviation market, such as private passenger-type aircraft used as industrial aids.

Yet another pioneering D.A. Fisher field has been liability arising out of application of chemicals, used so extensively in Mid-South farming. It has even insured experimental chemicals that no other firm would handle.

Fisher has many business associations of extraordinary longevity. Since 1898, the year the Maryland Casualty Company was founded, it has represented that firm. It has represented St. Paul since 1912, I.N.A. since 1915, and Hartford since 1932.

For many years D.A. Fisher was the claims servicing office for the Mid-South area for both the Hartford and the St. Paul, handling all claims regardless of who the agent was. As a result, it has long-standing relationships with a host of agencies throughout the region. Friendly associations with other agencies throughout west Tennessee, north Mississippi, and east Arkansas date from this period.

D.A. Fisher places extensive coverages with Lloyd's of London and many other international companies. Many manufactured products shipped worldwide are automatically insured by Fisher. This "open-cargo" policy permits the company to fill out coverage amounts as the goods are shipped to such places as Germany, Australia, and India. In the '80s Fisher will operate increasingly on an international scale.

ABOVE LEFT
Phillip Alston Fisher, founder of the Fisher Agency in 1864.

ABOVE RIGHT
The D.A. Fisher office building at 3940 Park. The clock (the only Seth-Thomas street clock still operating in the tri-state area) is a Memphis landmark, having stood at four different locations of the firm.

Chapter Eight: Partners in Progress

FOGELMAN PROPERTIES

Fogelman Properties, the South's largest apartment owners and managers, was started in 1940 by Morris S. Fogelman as a real estate and insurance brokerage firm. During the '50s he moved into home building and was a major subdivision developer in Memphis. When sons Robert and Avron returned to Memphis from college in 1958 and 1962, Fogelman Properties entered the commercial construction business and began to phase out real estate sales and insurance brokerage; they focused on apartment building and management.

Both the young Fogelmans majored in business, Robert at the Wharton School at the University of Pennsylvania and Avron at Tulane University. Gradually, as their business grew, Robert concentrated his efforts in development, construction, and finance, while Avron's direction was toward management and sales. By 1967 the brothers were well established and their father retired. Fogelman Properties is now a family-owned partnership managed and directed by Avron Fogelman.

Today Fogelman Properties owns and/or manages over 13,000 apartments. The latest and largest Fogelman apartment complex exceeds 1,000 units. Since 1962 the family's business interests have been devoted to building, acquiring, and managing income-producing apartment properties. Approximately one out of every three people who rents an apartment in Memphis rents from the company.

Fogelman Properties is the corporate name of several affiliate companies and subsidiaries, including Fogelman Investment Company, Fogelman Management Corporation, and Fogelman and Company. When the firm started in 1962 the modern apartment industry did not exist. The Fogelmans were leaders in developing the apartment concept in Memphis, fulfilling a need and filling a void in the marketplace. In the early '60s, the brothers built the first garden-type apartments; later they constructed high-rise apartments. At first they built family-type complexes; now they are building for all markets in all areas of the city. There are apartments for single renters as well as for families. The Fogelmans have built and brought the market to their developments by the innovative use of total amenity packages for their tenants.

In November 1980 Avron and Robert Fogelman were uniquely honored when Memphis State University dedicated their business college, The Fogelman College of Business and Economics, in their honor. This was done because "Avron and Robert Fogelman, who are native Memphians, have provided outstanding leadership for many years in furthering the interests of the city of Memphis and Memphis State University. They have contributed significantly to the enrichment of the MSU academic community, as evidenced by their establishment of the Morris S. Fogelman Chair in Real Estate in 1972. ... [They] have effectively maintained and expanded the family business since their father's retirement in 1967 while providing unselfish service to Memphis State's College of Business Administration."

The Fogelmans have contributed energetically and creatively to Memphis in many other ways. Ownership of the Memphis Chicks baseball team is an example of the vital role they have played in Memphis' development and advancement. The brothers' unselfish civic contribution and outstanding leadership is widely heralded and they serve as president or chairman of the board of numerous business and civic boards and also as chairman or president of educational institutions in Memphis.

ABOVE LEFT
Avron Fogelman (left), Morris S. Fogelman, and Robert Fogelman, creators of Fogelman Properties. (Photo courtesy of Gittings.)

ABOVE RIGHT
Fogelman Properties office building.

HOLIDAY INNS INC.

In recent years the Holiday Inn hotel system has changed from its original roadside inn concept to a multi-market chain with hotels in metropolitan centers, resorts, airports, small towns, suburbs, and interstate sites.

The chain has continued to set the pace for the industry with innovations such as a computerized reservations system, in-room television, full-scale indoor recreational centers, and most recently, video teleconferences via the hotel industry's largest satellite receiving network.

Though Holiday Inns Inc. diversified extensively in the late '60s and early '70s, the firm today is focused on the hospitality industry. Hotels continue to be the core business, though the organization has additional interest in gaming casinos, restaurants, and transportation. With the acquisition of Harrah's casino/hotel firm, Holiday Inns became the largest U.S. gaming company. Holiday Inns also owns The Perkins Inc. restaurant chain and Delta Steamship Lines Inc.

The company is headed by pioneer franchisee Roy E. Winegardner, who is chairman of the board, a position he assumed in 1979 following Kemmons Wilson's retirement, and by Michael D. Rose, president and chief executive officer.

Although the Holiday Inn hotel system reached an expansion plateau in the mid-1970s, the company entered the '80s by resuming system expansion in a steady, orderly fashion, opening an average of one hotel a week somewhere in the world.

With a spectacular 30 years behind it, Memphis-based Holiday Inns Inc. is well-prepared for a bright future.

In the automobile boom that followed World War II, Holiday Inns Inc. founder Kemmons Wilson saw the untapped market potential for a chain of comfortable, moderately priced roadside motels offering standardized conveniences.

This need was impressed upon Wilson during a family vacation in 1951. "It was the most miserable vacation I ever had," he said afterward, as he told of cramped quarters and extra charges for his five children.

Quick to spot a business opportunity, the young Memphis home builder opened the first Holiday Inn hotel a year later on the outskirts of Memphis. The inn had 120 rooms, each with a private bath, free ice, free parking, free dog kennels, and children under 12 could stay free in their parents' room—an unheard-of accommodation.

The inn was such a solid success that Wilson quickly opened three more Memphis inns. Then, in partnership with another home builder, Wallace E. Johnson, he revolutionized the lodging industry by introducing the franchising concept as a means of expanding on a national, and eventually international, basis.

Holiday Inns of America, was incorporated in 1954 and became a publicly held company in 1957. The growth of its ever-widening network of hotels, more than three-fourths of which today are franchised, has dominated Holiday Inns' strategy since. The company name was changed to Holiday Inns Inc. in 1969, to reflect its growing international status.

Through the years the worldwide Holiday Inn hotel system has grown into the largest hotel chain in the world, with nearly 1,800 hotels in 58 countries providing more than 310,000 guest rooms.

ABOVE RIGHT
Michael D. Rose (left), president and chief executive officer, and Roy E. Winegardner, chairman of the board of Holiday Inns Inc.

ABOVE LEFT
Corporate headquarters of Holiday Inns Inc. is located in Memphis, Tennessee.

GUARDSMARK, INC.

Guardsmark, Inc., has its roots in an established family business, but its history as a major corporation has been surprisingly brief and remarkably eventful. When the company was founded in 1963 by Ira A. Lipman, it took its place as one of 3,000 firms in the growing private security business. Today Guardsmark is the nation's sixth largest of 10,000 security services companies.

Much of Guardsmark's success is attributed to its founder, who now serves as chairman and president. Ira Lipman was just 22 years old when he brought his company into being, but he had spent most of his life learning about his chosen field. His initial interest stemmed from family involvement. His father, Mark Lipman, had gotten into investigative work during the Depression years while tracing "skippers" for his brothers' finance company in Philadelphia. In 1935 he moved to Little Rock, Arkansas, and opened a private detective firm, the Mark Lipman Service.

Ira Lipman began working for his father in 1949, when he was eight years old. His assignment as an undercover "shopper" was to go into a client's store and make small purchases to test the honesty of the clerks. Then, as now, such internal security checks were valuable; the young agent's reports gave store owners a good indication of how dishonest employees operated.

Young Lipman remained interested in the family business throughout his high school years. After attending college, he went to work as a salesman for his father, who by then had moved his agency to Memphis. He honed his selling skills on the road, traveling to small towns in Tennessee, Arkansas, North Carolina, South Carolina, and Georgia during the week and returning to Memphis on weekends to type his own sales letters. In just three years, the sales he generated tripled the company's annual gross.

During the course of hundreds of investigative sales calls, Ira Lipman realized the growing need for quality uniformed guards at a variety of facilities. In the summer of 1963 he used a $1,000 capital investment to start a guard service. Lipman incorporated his father's name into the name of the new company, and Guardsmark was born. The first office was a small room on the fourth floor of the building at 22 South Second Street in downtown Memphis, which now houses Guardsmark's national headquarters.

When he hit the road selling for his own company, Ira Lipman was intent on offering a special kind of service—the most professional guards available from a single, dependable source. He formulated the systems for selection, training, and supervision that are at the heart of the firm's success today. The emphasis on quality paid off: within 10 months the company had

ABOVE LEFT
Ira A. Lipman, founder and president of
Guardsmark, Inc. (Photo courtesy of Gittings.)

revenues of $50,000. By 1967 Guardsmark had $1.5 million in sales and offices in Memphis, Little Rock, Nashville, and Knoxville.

In the company's early years Lipman's marketing expertise contributed significantly to Guardsmark's growth. By the end of the 1960s, Guardsmark had eight branch offices serving operations in 18 states in the East, South, and Midwest. Memphis headquarters had grown from a single office to several floors of the original downtown building.

The 1970s saw Guardsmark embark upon an aggressive acquisition program, which accelerated its growth rate. In November 1970 the company acquired the former Mark Lipman Service, which became the Mark Lipman Division of Guardsmark, the company's investigative arm. Subsequent acquisitions included firms furnishing uniformed security personnel and polygraph, training, and security consulting services. As a result of that expansion and acquisition program, Guardsmark now has 53 offices and 5,000 employees serving more than 400 cities across the country.

The nine-story building at 22 South Second, purchased by the company in 1976, has become the nerve center for Guardsmark's national operations. From eight key cities, regional managers fly into Memphis monthly for intense analysis of each operation in the nationwide Guardsmark system; someone involved with Guardsmark takes off or lands at Memphis International Airport approximately every three hours.

At the core of Guardsmark's services is the Guard Division, managed by executive

vice-president Alan R. Hawley. Counted among its clients are many Fortune 500 and New York Stock Exchange companies, as well as a broad sampling of regional and local organizations and institutions. Guardsmark security officers are entrusted with the protection of thousands of people and billions of dollars in assets at oil refineries, airports, manufacturing plants, construction sites, corporate offices, department stores, public utilities, hospitals, and hotels. The company's stringent selection and training procedures—recognized as the most comprehensive in the industry—help ensure that service at each location is the best available.

To fill executive positions, Guardsmark also prides itself on attracting the best. Many important offices are held by former employees of the FBI, CIA, Secret Service, Securities and Exchange Commission, Internal Revenue Service, United States Customs Service, and other prestigious agencies.

The Mark Lipman Division provides undercover agents and investigative services to clients across the country, helping companies solve the ever-growing problems of inventory shrinkage and employee theft. Mark Lipman is still with the company, and many of the techniques that made him one of the best investigators in the business are outlined in his book *Stealing* (Harper's Magazine Press, 1973). The Technical Services Division conducts sophisticated security sur-

veys and offers consultation for contingency planning, executive protection, and sensitive white-collar crime investigations.

Guardsmark publishes one of the most authoritative industry newsletters, *The Lipman Report*, which treats security issues and trends of importance to the business and financial community. *Day to Day* is a monthly pocket calendar for Guardsmark security officers which features a monthly lesson on pertinent security subjects, and also enjoys wide use as a subscription item for other companies.

Many of Guardsmark's achievements in the private security industry have gained national exposure in such publications as *The Wall Street Journal, The Washington Post, Reader's Digest, Business Week,* and *People.* Of significant note, in 1982 *The New York Times* editorially praised Ira Lipman and Guardsmark for leading "a sensible counter trend ... abandoning the use of firearms"; now only four-tenths of one percent of Guardsmark's 5,000 guards are armed. *How to Protect Yourself from Crime* by Ira A. Lipman is a complete handbook of crime prevention. First published in 1975, the book was reprinted in 1981 as a government manual by the U.S. Department of Justice. An updated edition of the comprehensive security guide was published in paperback by Avon Books in 1982, and quickly won acclaim by international crime prevention advocates.

Innovative ideas and attention to the details of quality service have played a leading role in Guardsmark's remarkable success. In just two decades, the foundation for continued success has been firmly laid.

OPPOSITE RIGHT AND ABOVE
Guardsmark security officers protect a wide
variety of facilities for clients around the country.

Chapter Eight: Partners in Progress

HOHENBERG BROS. COMPANY

"Hohenberg" and "cotton"—these words are nearly synonymous and have been for more than a century. The association can be traced to one small general store in one county of Alabama; now it is known all over the world.

Adolphe and Morris Hohenberg, young immigrants from Germany, started with a general store in Wetumpka, Alabama, in 1879. In half a generation they were the leading citizens of the area. A general merchandise store at that time would take cotton, or other merchandise, as payment for bills that people ran up. In that way the brothers "backed into" the cotton business. But they were also bankers and insurance agents. In fact, they were "into" anything that anybody in the vicinity needed.

Adolphe's son Elkan saw Memphis as the center of the cotton business; he moved the organization there in 1932. It was always located on Front Street—originally in the Falls Building on North Front, then behind Goldsmith's Department Store, and since 1957 in its present location at 266 South Front Street. The building was extensively remodeled and modernized in 1980.

The venture remained a partnership, known as M. Hohenberg & Company, until 1943, when it was incorporated as Hohen-

berg Bros. Company, named after Elkan and his brother Charles. Elkan expanded the firm's operation nationwide and into Europe. His son Julien advanced expansion on an international level.

Julien Hohenberg received a bachelor of arts degree in international studies and a bachelor of science degree in naval science from Yale in 1946. He was then 19 years old. The following year he entered the firm

at the bottom of the ladder, learning every aspect of the cotton business. Later he took a year's leave of absence and earned a master's degree at the Fletcher School of Law and Diplomacy, concentrating on the Far East in general and China in particular.

In August 1948 Julien traveled to Japan and China on company business. Hohenberg entered Mexico full-scale in 1950, Brazil in 1952, and various Central American countries in 1955. Julien stayed in these countries until business affairs were functioning smoothly and routinely. In the '60s, '70s, and '80s Hohenberg's burgeoning growth continued into new countries and continents.

Hohenberg Bros. has enjoyed healthy expansion throughout its existence. During World War II, however, a large percentage of the company's executives—including Elkan and Charles Hohenberg—joined the armed services. This necessitated the firm's operating under a virtual "caretakership" arrangement during the duration of the war, greatly reducing its activities. For example, the Texas and Alabama branches were closed at that time and were reopened when the war was over.

Hohenberg is one of the few survivors in a highly competitive field. Many larger com-

ABOVE LEFT
Early employees of Hohenberg's general store in Wetumpka, Alabama. Included here are the founders—Morris at the far right and Adolphe, striking a pose, fourth from left.

ABOVE RIGHT
Elkan Hohenberg, who moved the company to Memphis in 1932.

BOTTOM
Adolphe Hohenberg, cofounder of the firm known today as Hohenberg Bros. Company.

panies of the 1930s and 1940s floundered and disappeared while Hohenberg continued to thrive. To do this it has weathered the vicissitudes of international economics and politics—which Julien Hohenberg believes are inseparable. He has explained the company's flexibility and durability. "We go with the production....We've moved west with the crop and to foreign lands....You can't merchandise something that doesn't exist. The history of our company is to go where the opportunities are; the opportunities follow the crop." It is not surprising that the cotton business entails constant travels, contacts, and international communications. Julien, for instance, is on the board of managers of the New York Cotton Exchange. Huge stacks of telexes come in every morning; answers are sent out every afternoon. The pace never slows.

Hohenberg has offices, agents, and representatives in over 50 countries. It has buying offices in most producing areas such as Dallas, Lubbock, Harlingen, and Corpus Christi, Texas; Fresno, California; Selma, Alabama; Greenwood, Mississippi; Phoenix, Arizona; and Rayville, Louisiana. It has subsidiaries in Guatemala, Mexico, and Argentina. Thus Hohenberg has representatives all over the world; it does business with government agencies as well as private. Julien, who first went to The People's Republic of China in 1973, and Rudi Scheidt, his brother-in-law, who has been many times since, have fostered business and cordial relations with people and institutions of that country.

On November 1, 1975, Hohenberg Bros. Company became a subsidiary of Cargill, Inc., a large privately owned international commodity trading and processing corporation headquartered in Minneapolis. Julien Hohenberg and Rudi E. Scheidt have continued the successful management of Hohenberg Bros. In July 1981 Ralli, a large international cotton and commodity trading firm headquartered in England, was added to the group.

Throughout its history, Hohenberg's officers and personnel have played a major role in encouraging charitable, artistic, cultural, religious, and civic endeavors in Memphis. The success of Hohenberg Bros. is due not only to the efforts of present-day management but also to the efforts of many loyal, longtime officers and employees of the firm.

TOP
Hohenberg's enormous sample room contains trays of cotton from all over the world. Rudi Scheidt (left) and Julien Hohenberg check fiber length and quality.

BOTTOM
President Rudi Scheidt (left) and board chairman Julien Hohenberg discuss cotton in the field—at Lee Wilson Plantation in Wilson, Arkansas. In honor of Hohenberg's 100th anniversary in October 1979, a special delegation from the China National Textiles Import and Export Corporation of Peking visited Memphis.

Chapter Eight: Partners in Progress

LAYNE AND BOWLER, INC.

Layne and Bowler's origin can be traced back to 1882, when Mahlon E. Layne drilled his first water well. He revolutionized water supply methods throughout the world by designing a vertical turbine pump in 1902 that could be installed in the Layne well to furnish large amounts of water.

P.D. Bowler joined Layne in 1904 and the company was incorporated in Houston, Texas, three years later. Layne and Bowler, Inc., moved its headquarters and factory to Memphis in 1914 because of its central location, river port, and rail facilities. Branch offices had already opened in several states.

By 1920 Layne and Bowler had a worldwide reputation—with its pumps providing millions of gallons of water for cities, factories, and farms. The availability of plentiful water for human consumption and irrigation caused food production and cities to flourish in areas never before possible. Associate companies had been located in all regions of the United States as well as in Canada, France, Indochina, Argentina, and Mexico to handle sales, well-drilling, and installation work. By the 1930s Layne pumps were also used for a multitude of services in chemical plants, power plants, oil refineries, packing plants, and sugar refineries.

During World War II Layne and Bowler was totally committed to the war effort, from replacing damaged pumps at Pearl Harbor to providing water supply to dozens of arms, munitions, and equipment plants.

By the 1950s Memphis had become identified internationally as the home of Layne and Bowler. The spectrum of users ranged from the elegant Ritz-Carlton Hotel in Atlantic City to a Hollywood studio producing special effects for the movie *The Ten Commandments*. Cities from Las Vegas to Saigon were provided water by Layne pumping equipment. Layne had also become the predominant supplier of vertical turbine pumps to Memphis and the Mid-South area through its associate company and sales outlet, Layne Central Company.

Layne and Bowler was acquired by the Singer Company in 1969. J.I. Seay, president, stepped aside after 60 years of loyal service to Layne and the pump and well-drilling industry.

Layne and Bowler was acquired by the Marley Company in 1975 and now operates as a wholly owned subsidiary. Today the Memphis facility, covering more than .5 million square feet and employing over 400 people, continues to be the administrative and manufacturing headquarters. The Memphis factory houses iron, ni-resist, bronze foundries, machine and fabrication shops, and a modern testing facility. Layne and Bowler owns another manufacturing plant in Lubbock, Texas, and distribution centers in Nebraska, Minnesota, Idaho, and Washington. A new factory has also been constructed recently in Saudi Arabia to meet the ever-increasing demand for pumps in the Middle East.

Today Layne and Bowler's vertical turbine pumps, ranging in capacity to 75,000 gallons per minute, are used in major oil refineries, petrochemical plants, mining operations, oil tankers, electric generating plants, fire-protection systems, municipal water supply, and irrigation, to name only a few general areas of service.

ABOVE LEFT
M.E. Layne

ABOVE RIGHT
P.D. Bowler

BOTTOM
Layne plant facing east from University Street, circa 1920.

LOEB INDUSTRIES

On August 29, 1860, Henry Loeb, Sr., was born in Goat Hill, North Memphis, to parents without a laundry to wash their clothes in. They were up against it, like everyone else, since there wasn't a laundry in town in those days. This got Henry thinking since the wash was bad enough on Momma, but then Momma made him help her with it every Monday morning! He thought so much about it, in fact, that 1,400 Monday mornings later (on his 27th birthday, August 29, 1887), Henry Loeb opened the finest all-steam laundry borrowed money could build—and right downtown at Main and Monroe. It was the bet of his lifetime, but the best one Henry Loeb ever made, and on an extra-long shot like the growth of struggling Memphis.

Washing harder than he ever had for Momma, hustling Henry hit the jackpot, and by 1905 he upped his bet and built a revolutionary plant to house the finest power laundry in all America—again on borrowed money—and promptly called "Loeb's Folly." Now he was way out at 282 Madison Avenue—almost four blocks from Main Street—where any fool could see he was too far from the heart of town. Those who knew it all this time knew "Headless Henry" had really lost his marbles. But Henry Loeb had all his marbles—and by then some

horse-drawn wagons too. With them he pioneered the original white fleet of Memphis, foresaw the future of door-to-door service, and then made these doors the real trading center of town.

Since 1887 millions of gallons of soapy water have gone down the drain, trucks have displaced the wagons, and coin-operated laundries have been built all over to serve the horseless carriage trade.

In 1936 Henry Loeb had to die to stop betting on Memphis, but since then his company has been putting down all it's got on the same old growth of the city. Today, 121 years after the birth of the founder—Loeb's Laundry is Loeb Industries, a land-use company widely diversified in a multitude of service areas. Chains of convenience stores (themselves self-serve gas outlets); fast-food pit barbecue restaurants; coin-operated, fully automatic laundries; and a network of leaseable outdoor display signs cover Memphis and the Mid-South region like magnolias and moonshine. The Memphis landmark company has changed and grown along with Memphis, but it is still 100 percent home-owned and home-operated by the William Loeb family—and still expanding its services to accommodate the growth of the greater Mid-South region.

Copy supplied by Loeb Industries.

TOP LEFT
The original great white fleet of Loeb's Laundry.

TOP RIGHT
"Horseless" delivery trucks represent progress for Loeb's Laundry.

ABOVE
Henry Loeb, Sr., founder of Loeb Industries.

Chapter Eight: Partners in Progress

MALONE & HYDE, INC.

When Malone & Hyde opened for business on July 11, 1907, the first day's receipts amounted to $10.08. Today annual sales are more than two billion dollars and the firm has 8,000 employees, compared to two that first day.

In 1902 Joseph R. Hyde, Sr., had joined the wholesale grocery firm of W.W. James to handle the accounting. Later he and Taylor Malone, the buyer, bought into the firm. And, in 1906, they sold their interests to James and contemplated entering the wholesale grocery business themselves. Many people warned them that they would not last more than six months. For, when it opened that fateful day in 1907, Malone & Hyde was the 24th wholesale grocery operating in Memphis; city business was pretty well locked up.

Distribution was limited to service by railroad, horse and wagon, or riverboat. The only way to obtain new business was to serve the plantation commissaries, which were controlled by Memphis cotton factors. So Malone and Hyde shipped goods down the river to where the opportunities were. The young grocery men were able to gain business from almost every cotton factor—

and this was their entire business for several years.

The growth of supermarket chains in the '30s presented grocers and wholesalers with a life-threatening challenge. The supermarkets changed the way the grocery operated. In some cases independents could buy their grocery products less expensively from their chain competition than from their own wholesalers. The independents desperately needed a source of low-price food and comprehensive support services to combat the aggressive price and merchandising policies of the chains; Hyde thought the company should take up the challenge. As J.R. Hyde III, chairman and president of Malone & Hyde, and Hyde's grandson, notes, "Mr. Malone, a conservative businessman, was not interested in growth." Hyde bought out Malone and brought his son, Joe Hyde, Jr., into the company, where he remained president from 1948 to 1968.

World War II delayed the introduction of Malone & Hyde's voluntary plan until 1945, which may be considered the birthdate of the modern company. Basically the M&H voluntary plan provided the retailer with goods on a cost-plus basis. The standard

markup, 3.5 percent, was introduced in 1945 and remains the same today.

Over the decades Malone & Hyde added product lines, expanding into produce, dairy, meat, housewares, and drugs. In addition, the company gradually introduced a wide variety of services for the retailer. It offered to keep his books, help him with advertising and promotion, consult on store engineering, and even put him into business.

Malone & Hyde went public in 1961 and has continued to expand and diversify dramatically. In the 1970s sales increased at a compound annual rate of 16.7 percent and net income at 16.5 percent. The company is comprised of two different businesses, food distribution and specialty retailing.

Joseph R. Hyde III has attributed Malone & Hyde's success to two major factors: "Our structure—a lean, small staff at headquarters and many profit centers elsewhere ... we motivate our people. More than 60 percent of the cost of business is in people and ours have high incentive to perform. ... Our voluntary cooperative program is unquestionably the underlying source of our stability and growth. It keeps us honest; it keeps us competitive."

ABOVE LEFT
Three generations of Malone & Hyde leadership are shown here: J.R. Hyde III, chairman and president of the company, J.R. Hyde, Jr. (portrait on left); and J.R. Hyde, Sr. (portrait on right).

ABOVE RIGHT
An engraving of the original Malone & Hyde warehouse.

MEMORIAL PARK FUNERAL HOME AND CEMETERY

In August 1924 E. Clovis Hinds purchased the first land for Memphis Memorial Park Cemetery far from the city limits at the corner of Yates Road and Poplar Pike. Engineers and landscape architects were employed immediately to design and build a park-like cemetery. At that time there were no such cemeteries in the entire Mid-South and few in the nation. Clovis Hinds, at the age of 56, had become a pioneer in the cemetery business.

Hinds was a north Mississippi merchant, cotton buyer, and founder of an insurance company, the Cotton States Life Insurance Company, which he moved to Memphis from Tupelo in 1916. Travel and acquaintance with Hubert Eaton of Forest Lawn Cemetery in California prompted his decision to sell his business in 1924 and purchase land for Memorial Park. He devoted the rest of his life to the development of the park, which features rolling terrain and points of interest planned and constructed primarily during the 1930s by Hinds.

His goal was to create "a perpetual garden of promise." To fulfill his dream, he brought to Memphis the remarkable Mexican artist and sculptor, Dionicio Rodriguez, to create replicas of Biblical shrines, natural phenomena, and legendary showplaces out of Arkansas fieldstone, wrought iron, and semiprecious stones.

Today the cemetery covers 150 acres, including 35 acres for future development. Every year over 100,000 visitors come to enjoy the beauties of the Sunken Garden, the Annie Laurie Chair, "God's Garden," the covered bridge (fashioned as if hollowed from a giant oak), the fountain in the Pool of Hebron, the Cave of Machpelah (a replica of the tomb of Abraham), Abraham's Oak, and the Crystal Shrine Grotto (containing scenes depicting the life of Jesus). Thousands of annuals, roses, flowering trees, and shrubs, changing with the seasons, attract local garden clubs and church organizations. Visitors travel on buses furnished by Memorial Park, guided by its horticulturist and other staff members.

The mausoleum, dedicated in 1974, was designed to blend with the surrounding environment. A hillside was scooped out, the building set into it, and the entire roof covered with sod and trees. Renowned weaver and artist Henry Easterwood of Memphis was commissioned to create the tapestries that enhance the mausoleum, carrying out the theme of "Creation."

Beginning in 1977, Memorial Park has been able to offer the public a complete range of services: traditional burial, mausoleum entombment, lawn crypt burial, cremation, inurnment, garden mausoleum, and funeral home. The funeral home, opened in September 1977, was designed to blend with the surrounding environment. Fulfilling its desire to provide total service, Memorial Park opened a flower shop in 1980.

Since Clovis Hinds' death in 1949, his family has dedicated itself to the maintenance and expansion of Memorial Park in accordance with his ideals. For he envisioned a park-like cemetery to attract visitors, not just for burials, but for enjoyment anytime, especially in the spring when the flowers exhibit their most brilliant colors. Katherine Hinds Smythe, granddaughter of the founder, has served as president since 1976.

ABOVE
E. Clovis Hinds and granddaughter Katherine in the Cave of Machpelah area, 1938.

TOP
Memorial Park, Inc., Funeral Home and Cemetery.

ABOVE
Traditional Easter sunrise service at Memorial Park, sponsored by the Knights Templar.

Chapter Eight: Partners in Progress

MEMPHIS COMPRESS & STORAGE CO.

In 1924 B.L. Mallory, Sr., a business and civic leader of Memphis, organized the Memphis Compress & Storage Company at 2350 Florida Street, with 200,000 square feet of space. Upon Mallory's death in 1938, his son, William Neely Mallory, became president and served until he was killed in World War II. At that time, B.L. Mallory, Jr., was elected president of the company and served until 1973, when he became chairman of the board and William Neely Mallory, Jr., now president, was elected president and chief executive officer. B. Lee Mallory III is executive vice-president. Under the leadership of the Mallorys the company owns and/or operates four million square feet of warehouse space from Memphis to Oakland, California, and offers full transportation services—warehousing, trucking, air and ocean freight forwarding, and custom house brokerage business.

The company made its first expansion out of Memphis by building a warehousing facility in Wilson, Arkansas. In 1960 the firm entered the public warehouse business under the name of Chickasaw Warehouse Company. This division handles everything from paper products to toothpaste, from agricultural chemicals to automobile mufflers, and has become a major agricultural distribution center in the Mid-South. Realizing the importance of prompt delivery of the products to the customer, the firm began a local delivery operation in the late 1960s under the name of Shelby Delivery Service.

In the mid-1970s Memphis Compress entered into the contract warehousing field, selling its expertise to others to operate their facilities. In addition, the firm invested in speculative warehouses in Memphis which are leased out to other operators.

Trans-International Warehouse in New Orleans was established in 1977. This facility is located on the Mississippi River and is adjacent to one of the major wharves in New Orleans. It is used for cotton and the storage of general merchandise moving in international trade. In 1979 the company leased 225,000 square feet in Houston, Texas, and is operating a warehouse for cotton and general merchandise also under the name Trans-International Warehouse. The third Trans-International Warehouse was opened in 1981 in Oakland, California, to handle cotton for international trade. Also in 1979 the company purchased a cotton warehousing operation, Planters Compress Warehouse, in West Memphis, Arkansas.

In 1971 Memphis Compress purchased an international foreign freight-forwarding business known as V. Alexander & Company with offices in Memphis and New Orleans. Since that time this operation has expanded with offices in Atlanta and Savannah, Georgia, and Houston, Texas, and has entered into the customs house brokerage business, handling imports. The name has been changed to Alexander International.

Thus the firm, which has handled over 20 million bales of cotton and millions of pounds of general merchandise since 1925, is a major factor in cotton and general warehousing; its large freight-forwarding operation is a natural evolution of its warehousing and transportation-related services.

The officers of Memphis Compress are B.L. Mallory, Jr., chairman of the board; W. Neely Mallory, president; B. Lee Mallory III, executive vice-president; Cecil W. Rutledge, secretary-treasurer; W.L. Wadsworth, Jr., vice-president of Alexander International; Donald Serens, vice-president of the general merchandise operations, and Robin Coffman, vice-president of cotton operations.

TOP
(From left) W. Neely Mallory, president of Memphis Compress & Storage Company; B.L. Mallory, Jr., chairman of the board; and B.L. Mallory III, executive vice-president, surrounded by some of the products handled and forwarded by the firm.

ABOVE
Delivery dock of Memphis Compress & Storage, 1926.

Metropolis of the American Nile

MEMPHIS EYE AND EAR HOSPITAL/SHEA CLINIC

"Memphis is soon to have an eye, ear, and throat infirmary. This is to be the first institution of its kind located here." This announcement in the June 2, 1893, *Evening Appeal* signaled the beginning of the Memphis Eye and Ear Hospital, the dream of Dr. Louis Levy. He sold first, second, and third mortgage bonds to his family and friends and at the cost of approximately $300,000 the hospital, located at 1060 Madison, was completed in July 1926. In 1928 a donation by Abe Plough made possible the opening of the Moses Plough Memorial Hay Fever Clinic.

In less than three years the hospital was recognized for high achievement and placed on the honor role of the American College of Surgeons with one of the highest ratings in the United States. Nevertheless, the hospital was plagued with financial woes, even after control was passed to a group of leading Memphis doctors who formed a corporation which underwrote the deficits. After one year and the loss of considerable money, Dr. Levy resumed its management

ABOVE
Memphis Eye and Ear Hospital (left)/Shea Clinic medical complex. (Photo courtesy of Jim Hilliand.)

and financial responsibility until Methodist Hospital bought it in 1943.

In January 1966 the hospital was closed and patients were moved to Methodist. In April of that year the vacant hospital was purchased by Dr. John J. Shea, Jr., and renamed Memphis Eye and Ear Hospital.

Dr. Shea was destined to be a great physician. His father, John J. Shea, Sr., was a prominent Memphis ear, nose, and throat specialist. He planned his son's career in otology; the younger Shea got his M.D. from Harvard Medical School in 1947 at the age of 22. Later he went to Europe, where he spent two years studying at universities and hospitals throughout the continent: Paris, Zurich, London, Vienna.

In 1956 Dr. Shea developed a revolutionary operation that proved 90 percent effective in dealing with otosclerosis, a form of deafness that attacks the sound-conducting bones of the middle ear. The operation earned Dr. Shea widespread recognition, including a place in the *London Times'* list of "1,000 Makers of the 20th Century." In 1957 Dr. Shea founded the Deafness Foundation to foster otological research.

The hospital again underwent renovation in October 1975. Property located at 1080 Madison was purchased and now houses the Deafness Foundation and the Shea Clinic. A crosswalk connects the buildings.

On April 11, 1981, Humana Inc., an investor-owned hospital corporation, purchased the Memphis Eye and Ear Hospital from Dr. Shea.

ABOVE
Dr. Shea examines the ear of a patient under a microscope before operation. (Photo courtesy of Hal Jaffe.)

Chapter Eight: Partners in Progress

METHODIST HOSPITALS OF MEMPHIS

Methodist Hospital began as a hope—a dream—in the mind of one man, J.H. Sherard, Methodist layman and planter of North Mississippi. He visited Memphis in 1899 and found to his chagrin that his pastor was a patient in the charity ward of a hospital. During the next decade Mr. Sherard, at his own expense, attended district meetings, annual conferences, and women's missionary society gatherings, gaining endorsements and winning people over to his commitment that Methodists build a hospital for themselves and others.

Initially seven Methodist conferences were invited to participate; however, by 1921 ownership of the hospital was reduced to three conferences: Memphis, North Mississippi, and North Arkansas.

The first contribution to a building fund was made in February 1911 by Mr. Sherard; the second came from the Women's Home Mission Society of the North Mississippi Conference. Financial and practical considerations dictated several shifts in locations, but since 1918 there has always been a Methodist Hospital in Memphis.

Dr. Henry Hedden was the hospital's first administrator; Mr. Sherard, president of the hospital board; L.M. Stratton, Sr., secretary; and J.R. Pepper, treasurer. Dr. W. Battle Malone became the first president

of the 42-member medical staff. During the first year of operation a staff, including three trained nurses and 30 student nurses, received 1,712 patients.

A hospital on Lamar, built by Methodist, was sold at a handsome profit to the federal government in 1921 for use as a veteran's care institution. Methodist's patients were moved back to the Lucy Brinkley Hospital at 855 Union. A new hospital was completed in 1924 at 1265 Union, the present address of Methodist Central. Subsequently the Lucy Brinkley was sold and the proceeds

were used to construct a 1927 addition, aptly named the Lucy Brinkley Pavilion.

The next decades witnessed extensive improvements, renovations, and additions in plant and equipment; new wings were added to the Central complex in 1940, 1950, 1958, 1966, 1970, and 1974. Bond issues and church support funded these efforts with individual gifts and bequests priming the campaigns.

Since 1918 Methodist Hospital has operated a school of nursing and has been accredited by the American Medical Association for medical internship programs. A $3.7-million nursing school and dormitory was built in 1969, dedicated to the memory of "Doll" Wilson, mother of Kemmons Wilson, founder of Holiday Inns and member of the hospital board.

In order to meet the expanding demands of quality health care in the area, two satellite hospitals, the John R. Flippin Memorial Hospital/Methodist South and the Jesse Harris Memorial Hospital/Methodist North were opened in 1974 and 1978, respectively. Methodist was the first to in-

troduce this "satellite" concept in the area. Each full-service hospital operates as an integral unit of the Methodist System, linked by many services. Patients can be transported to Central for special procedures, avoiding wasteful duplication of costly equipment and personnel and providing the best in medical technology available. Such services include radiation therapy; total body scan by computerized axiotomography, a non-invasive diagnostic procedure; cardiac catheterization; and care in the highly specialized neuro-trauma unit.

Methodist continues to pioneer quality programs. From the array of services representing all medical specialties and major subspecialties, two programs typify the comprehensive approach to patient care.

An oncology program, the first hospital program in the area designated as A.M.A. Category I approved, provides for total care of patients with cancer. In a special unit patients are cared for by a multidisciplinary team of professionals: doctors, nurses, therapists, pharmacists, and dietitians, incorporating mental health, pastoral care, and social services. Patient and family education is integral to the program. Communication is maintained so that patients

know what is happening and why. Total care, focusing on quality of life, does not end with discharge; home nursing care services are also made available by the hospital. The hospital tumor registry has served as a model for registries across the country with its readily accessible storehouse of data on cancers, treatment modalities and results, and long-term follow-up.

The cardiovascular program is no less comprehensive with complete diagnostic laboratories, surgical facilities where up to five open-heart procedures are performed daily, a CV surgical intensive care unit, step-down units with telemetry monitoring for medical and surgical patients, and a multidisciplinary cardiac rehabilitation program provided by Methodist and cosponsored by the YMCAs of Memphis.

Methodist is pioneering in other ways. In the forefront of utilizing the cost-effective shared services concept, Methodist makes services available to other health care agencies. Laundry, laboratory, nuclear pharmacy, purchasing, and management services are among those being provided.

With a licensed bed complement of 1,354 (1,006 at Central and 174 at both South and North), the Methodist System is the fifth

largest private hospital in the country. Through more than a half century of growth and expanding services, the hospital/church affiliation has unquestionably given an extra dimension to Methodist's health care services—namely, the highest quality of person-centered care and caring.

In 1975 Central's Sherard Wing was completed, adding much-needed ancillary space. A $12-million medical arts center adjacent to Central opened in late 1981 and provides additional physician offices, an outpatient diagnostic center, and a parking garage. By 1985 a $78-million renovation of Methodist Central should be completed. This will include a three-floor base and a six-story nursing tower, replacing older patient areas and allowing easy access to all areas of the hospital complex. These projects represent Methodist Hospitals' continuing commitment to Memphis and the health care of the people of Memphis and the Mid-South.

TOP LEFT
This rear view of Methodist Hospital undergoing construction was taken on April 1, 1924.

TOP RIGHT
Opening day celebrations took place on the front lawn of the hospital on September 15, 1924.

ABOVE
Perfect conformity in hemlines was the order of the day for the graduating nurses, class of 1927.

Chapter Eight: Partners in Progress

MID-SOUTH TITLE INSURANCE CORPORATION

Mid-South Title has several distinct "founding" dates. Commerce Title Guaranty Company, which was merged into Mid-South Title to form the present firm, was founded in 1934. Memphis Abstract Company, now a department of Mid-South, was originally L.B. Eaton Company, dating back to 1866. However, it was on January 10, 1946, five months after the end of World War II, that Mid-South Title Company, Inc., was founded.

The postwar economy of the nation—especially the South—was beginning to surge with renewed activity. The immense volume of real estate transactions caused home buyers to wait months for a closing. The methods and technologies capable of hastening and improving service had not yet caught up with the industry.

J.L. Boren, manager of Bluff City Abstract Company, recognized that now was the time for a new title company to utilize these technologies. George M. Houston, staff attorney for Union Planters Title Guaranty Company, agreed. It was an idea whose time had come.

The organization, from the beginning, avoided the "business as usual" attitude and evidenced its sensitivity to the needs of the real estate industry by recognizing and serving the specific needs of its individual customers.

The extensive use of photography, microfilming, the origination of the "title search," the division of examination and closing functions, and the operation of branch offices soon established Mid-South as the leader.

The firm, continuing its growth, in 1954 entered into an exclusive agency agreement with Commerce Title. This agreement gave Mid-South control of the only complete abstract plant in Shelby County and presented new opportunities in the area.

This relationship proved to be the impetus of tremendous growth. While Commerce was qualifying in Arkansas, Mississippi, Alabama, Louisiana, and Florida, Mid-South was establishing a network of attorneys and issuing agents.

Boren continued to guide the firm through its formative years, until passing the presidency on to Houston in 1962. The company continued to grow. Broadening its scope of service, it acquired title agencies in Sarasota and Bradenton, Florida, and in Forrest City and Mountain Home, Arkansas. In 1973 James L. Boren, Jr., became the corporation's president.

Mid-South took a giant step in 1976 by acquiring the majority ownership of Commerce Title. Out of this merger came Mid-South Title Insurance Corporation, qualified to issue its own policies. This had been an objective of the founders of Mid-South Title.

The year 1979-80 was one of moves. The title plant was moved to the Centrum Building while the national department and the corporate offices were relocated to the 12th floor of Commerce Square.

Continuing its progress, the company recently introduced a new homeowners' title policy which recognizes the effect of inflation. It also has brought automation to the title plant and implemented modern innovative marketing techniques—all dedicated to the courteous, accurate, prompt, and efficient service that always has kept the organization in the forefront of the title industry.

TOP
James L. Boren, Jr., president of Mid-South Title Insurance Corporation, between portraits of cofounders George M. Houston (left) and J.L. Boren.

ABOVE
Chairman of the board George M. Houston (left), pointing out to Mr. Boren a parcel of property under examination.

Metropolis of the American Nile

WILLIAM R. MOORE, INC.

William R. Moore was born in Huntsville, Alabama, on March 28, 1830. His father died when he was only six months old, leaving his mother in strained circumstances. His early youth was spent on a farm and his facilities for formal education were limited. But he took advantage of every opportunity, and at the age of 15 became a clerk in a store in Beech Grove in Coffee County, Tennessee, at a salary of $24 a year, and board and clothes. At the end of a year he had managed to save $12, a record of thrift that few had equaled.

A few years later he went to Nashville as a salesman for a retail dry goods store and later was associated with the old Nashville firm of Eskin and Company, where he learned the basis of his business. In 1856 he went to New York to work for the wholesale house of Crittendon and Company. The metropolitan experience proved invaluable and it sparked his ambition to have a great wholesale house of his own. He promptly severed his New York connection and moved to Memphis.

At the age of 29, with his life savings of $6,000, he began his business, associating himself with Joseph H. Shepard; the house was known as Shepard and Moore. It flourished and was reorganized as William R. Moore and Company with Robert M. McLean and Orrin M. Peck as the other members of the organization.

The store was established in a small building on South Main; each partner had a bedroom on the third floor of the building. All three were bachelors and merchants of the old school—no extra expenses, no regular hours, no 15-minute breaks or hour-long lunches.

Moore was the buyer. After an unusually good business period, he would have to go to New York to replenish the stock. Peck was the traveling salesman, but in those days travel was very limited. All the traveling he did was on horseback with his samples in his saddlebags.

Poor health forced Moore into semiretirement in 1905 and O.C. Armstrong was named president. It is remarkable that in its long history the firm has had only six presidents—all with distinguished tenures. A.M. Heisman succeeded to the presidency in 1913, George R. James in 1915, W.R. King in 1932, and Donald Drinkard, 1954 to the present. King not only served as president of William R. Moore, Inc., but also served as president of the National Bank of Commerce from 1933 to 1940. He is credited with guiding both firms through the dark days of the '30s so that they emerged strong and healthy when so many others failed.

Today William R. Moore, Inc., is a wholly owned subsidiary of Washington Industries, Inc., of Nashville, Tennessee, and does business in a 10-state area. There are also branch offices in Memphis, Indianapolis (floor covering), Louisville, and Little Rock (floor covering), and subsidiary companies involved in retailing and the distribution of hardware and appliances. Headquarters of both of these organizations are located in Nashville, Tennessee. Although the ways and means of doing things have altered, the principles by which the firm lives and does business—honesty and fair dealing—remain the same.

ABOVE LEFT
In 1859 William R. Moore founded the company known today as William R. Moore, Inc.

TOP RIGHT
William R. Moore's first motorized delivery van was purchased around 1918.

ABOVE
Expanding business led to several moves, until 1913 when William R. Moore, Inc., came to occupy its present eight-story home at Third and Monroe.

Chapter Eight: Partners in Progress

MORGAN, KEEGAN & COMPANY

Morgan Keegan was founded in Memphis in the summer of 1969 by Allen Morgan, Jr., and James F. Keegan with a capitalization of $500,000 and a staff of five. It occupied a modest space in the Sterick Building. Today it fills the entire 28th floor of One Commerce Square (as well as part of two other floors); employs over 175 workers; has branch offices in East Memphis, Jackson, Mississippi, New Orleans, Louisiana, Nashville, Tennessee, and Boston, Massachusetts; and has a net worth of over $6 million. In 1980 it traded hundreds of millions of dollars in stocks and bonds for its customers, participated in $12 million in new equity issues and $12 million in corporate debt issues, managed or comanaged $450 million in municipal issues, and participated in another $69 million in 164 municipal issues. Today's inventory of Morgan Keegan products and services includes stocks, bonds, tax-exempt securities, option, tax shelters, the daily cash trust money market fund, underwriting public issues, private placement of debts and securities, arranging mergers and acquisitions, evaluation services, SBA-guaranteed loans, other government-guaranteed loans, industrial revenue bonds, pollution control bonds, raising venture capital, financial counseling, and financial public relations.

Morgan Keegan is the first and only New York Stock Exchange member with headquarters in Memphis. One of its major goals is to know more about large businesses in the Mid-South region than any other comparable firm and to disseminate and market this research locally, nationally, and internationally. The local and regional focus does not preclude national companies.

Morgan Keegan has cultivated an extensive international clientele and 10 percent of its total business in 1980 was overseas. With excellent people in its Mid-South location, Morgan Keegan has a great advantage competing against New York firms.

Because Morgan Keegan was disillusioned with research and ideas coming out of New York—information that was too late, too superficial, and too diffuse—it determined to create its own high-powered on-board research capability, to spend a substantial percentage on research, and still maintain a high return on equity. Thus, today it does as much municipal credit research as any organization in the securities business. The research philosophy of Morgan Keegan resulted in a fourfold concentration: to know companies in its own region better than anyone else anywhere, to know regional municipal credits better, to keep an accurate and timely national and international scan, and to generate money-producing ideas.

About 80 percent of Morgan Keegan's total business is brokerage, divided equally between equities and fixed income instruments. Of the brokerage activity, 70 percent is institutional and 30 percent is individual. When Morgan Keegan opened a money market fund in December 1980, it rose to $65 million in four months.

Each of the 17 principals in Morgan Keegan has a minimum of 10 years' experience in the securities business. As an established firm in Memphis, it is part of the Mid-South's heritage.

TOP
An early morning meeting of the board of directors of Morgan, Keegan & Company.

ABOVE
One of the trading areas at Morgan, Keegan & Company.

Metropolis of the American Nile

ORGILL BROTHERS

Most lifelong Memphians have heard of Orgill Brothers even though it has done no advertising or retail business for almost 60 years. The perception is "the hardware company that's been around so long." This perception is only half true. Founded in 1847, the oldest business in Memphis and still controlled by the same family, Orgill Brothers has survived wars, plagues, and depressions and is indeed one of the nation's largest wholesale hardware firms. At the same time, it has diversified into several other businesses and sells its various products nationally with hardware, though still important, no longer the main line of business.

Orgill Brothers opened on April 1, 1847, on Front Row, under the Henrie House, which was a well-known local hotel at the time. In 1850 the business moved to the corner of Front and Jefferson, where it remained until 1922. The early business consisted of the retailing of general hardware items, especially fine cutlery and guns imported from England. In fact, in November 1847, an editorial in *The Daily Inquirer* states: "A *better* lot of guns have certainly never been offered in the western market. . . ." Incidentally, prices ranged from $100 to $48 per dozen, the latter apparently pistols from Germany.

The fortunes of Orgill Brothers in the second half of the 1800s ebbed and flowed with those of Memphis, but throughout all, the company remained a vital part of Memphis' commerce, and its stature is indicated by this quotation (according to an article in *The Commercial Appeal*) from the 1883 "Commercial and Statistical Review of the City of Memphis": ". . . to say that you do not know this house (Orgill Brothers) is to declare yourself unknown."

Orgill Brothers was incorporated in 1898 and has had an Orgill at its head ever since. Beginning in 1900, the company began to concentrate more on the wholesale business, ceasing retail sales entirely in 1908 and beginning in 1915 to build up a group of salesmen to call on retail merchants throughout the area. The first branch warehouse was set up in Jackson, Mississippi, in 1923, and the branch system now has grown to 10 locations. Hardware sales grew dramatically and other lines, such as floor covering and furniture, were added, further increasing sales. Since 1960 the company has acquired the sales forces of liquidated competition, purchased other distributors, and added new lines, with the result that today Orgill Brothers is among the nation's largest distributors.

In order to diversify further, Orgill Brothers in 1968 started Mid-American Industries in Memphis to manufacture plastic pipe and in 1969 purchased the Jordan Lumber Company, itself an old Memphis firm founded in 1896. Jordan manufactures prefabricated building components and aluminum doors and windows. In 1975 it acquired Kirkpatrick Lumber Company in Nashville to add capacity in components and, in 1980, ASG in Phoenix, Arizona, to provide more door and window production. Jordan and its subsidiaries have achieved national prominence, particularly in the window and related products industry.

Thus the company has changed from a retail hardware store to a large, diversified, national distributor and manufacturer, these operations having been combined under the management of Orgill Brothers Corporation.

TOP
(Left to right) Joseph Orgill, J.M. Crutchfield, Ben Owen, Walter Hippel, Frederick Commander, J.J. Nolan, Mr. Timberlake, unknown, stand in front of Orgill Brothers & Co.

ABOVE
Girls in the Orgill office—1900.

Chapter Eight: Partners in Progress

RICHARDS MANUFACTURING COMPANY, INC.

Richards Manufacturing Company, Inc., is a surgical equipment manufacturer best known for pioneering work in biomedical engineering, the development of permanent replacement implants for the human body, and for the engineering of internal fixation devices that promote healing by holding broken bones together under pressure. The impants include replacements for the hearing mechanism in the middle ear, and for the hip, knee, ankle, shoulder, and finger joints. The fixation devices include a compression hip screw that returns patients, particularly older patients, to an active life, usually in a matter of days, thus relieving the complications that often result from prolonged inactivity.

In addition, Richards manufactures a variety of surgical instruments and other surgery-related products, primarily for orthopedic and microsurgery specialties. Surgical supplies for the veterinary profession are also developed and manufactured at Richards.

Founded during the Depression in June 1934 by the late J. Don Richards, the company, then located at 756 Madison, produced splints and rib belts for Memphis hospitals. As the product line and the market area expanded, so did the need for more space. In 1963 the firm bought a 20-acre farm bordering Brooks Road, then outside the city limits, and moved to a newly constructed plant.

After two major expansions to increase production space, the company in 1978 built a 65,000-square-foot manufacturing facility on the north end of the property. The original plant was then renovated to serve as the headquarters office.

Two manufacturing subsidiaries began operation in the early 1970s: Comfort Care Products, Inc., in Pontotoc, Mississippi, which produces soft goods; and Richards Surgical Manufacturing Company, Inc., in Santa Monica, California, which produces joint replacement implants.

Richards markets its products in 50 countries as well as the United States. Subsidiaries are located in Germany, Switzerland, Brazil, France, Italy, and the Scandinavian countries. A headquarters-based subsidiary, Richards International, Inc., administers international sales.

Richards remained president of the company until his death in 1964. Harry T. Treace, formerly vice-president, succeeded him and continued as president until 1979 when he was named chairman of the board. Executive vice-president L.D. Beard then assumed the president's post, where he remained until appointed chairman upon Treace's retirement. Jack Blair, Richards International president, succeeded Beard as president on March 1, 1982.

Working with progressive surgeons in this country and abroad, Richards has contributed significantly to the advancement of health care, primarily in the microsurgery and orthopedic areas. In the field of otology, the first successful replacement implant for the stapes (stirrup) bone in the hearing mechanism of the middle ear was hand-carved by Harry T. Treace and used by Dr. John Shea, Jr., in his history-making operation to restore hearing, performed in Memphis in 1956. Today Richards is the leading manufacturer of surgical products designed for otological use.

Long established as an innovator in the medical products field, Richards will continue to work with leading surgeons to develop the new products and new product lines that assure a vigorous and ever-growing company.

In 1968 Richards became a wholly owned subsidiary of Rorer Group, Inc., one of the nation's major pharmaceutical firms.

ROBBINS AND MYERS, INC.

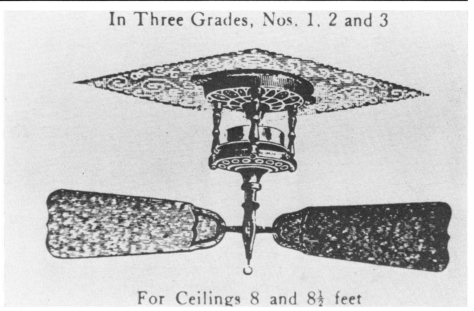

In Three Grades, Nos. 1, 2 and 3

For Ceilings 8 and 8½ feet

The first Hunter Ceiling Fan was not as simple in design as today's Olde Tyme Ceiling Fan. James C. Hunter and his friend, Samuel Tuerk, designed the first ceiling fan with dragons, spirals, and curlicues. It came with two blades and was operated by a system of belts and pulleys powered by a water-pressure motor.

The Hunter family, Irish immigrants, started in business in 1886 in Syracuse, New York, building water-pressure motors. In 1889 they moved to Fulton, New York, and opened the Hunter Arms Company, producing a high-quality shotgun, the L.C. Smith. They also made bicycles and continued making water motors. It wasn't long after this move that James and Samuel built the first fan. The fan sold well and soon that division took over two floors of the Arms factory. In the early 1900s, with the invention of electricity, the fan was redesigned to the simple four-blade concept still popular today.

The fan business continued to thrive. Over the years the company added several other circulating and ventilation products. These included the desktop oscillator, commercial and industrial air-spread circulating fans, whole-house attic fans, portable box fans, window fans, portable floor fans, and a line of heating products. Hunter fans were found in African jungles, Moroccan deserts, and Southern plantation homes.

The popularity of fans in the South led to the firm's relocation to 400 South Front Street in Memphis, Tennessee, in 1946. The company, though still called Hunter Fan, was no longer owned by the Hunter family, but rather by Gould Electric Company.

Three years later, in 1949, Hunter Fan was purchased by a respected competitor, Robbins and Myers, Inc., of Springfield, Ohio. In 1953 a new plant was built at the present location at 2500 Frisco Avenue. Although from 1964 through 1981 the facility housed a small portion of the Motor Division of Robbins and Myers, it is once again a single-division location.

Today Hunter is the Comfort Conditioning Division of Robbins and Myers, Inc. The division has grown from an operation where one man built the 25 fans needed each day to an operation employing over 1,300 workers to produce thousands of fans daily. Under the direction of its current president, Terence Tannehill, the divisional headquarters oversees the operation of the Memphis plant as well as a new plant in Foley, Alabama. With the Olde Tyme Ceiling Fan as its mainstay, the division continues to research and develop new high-quality products to meet the energy-related needs of today's consumer.

TOP LEFT
Modern or antique decor, a variety of present-day Hunter Ceiling Fans add personality to any setting.

TOP RIGHT
Ornate designs, brass dragons, curlicues, and only two blades were typical features of the original Olde Tyme Ceiling Fan.

ABOVE
The Comfort Conditioning Division Headquarters has been located at 2500 Frisco Avenue since 1953.

Chapter Eight: Partners in Progress

Ronco Foods

John S. Robilio, Sr., came to the United States in 1900 from Bassignana, Italy, at the age of 18. He and his Memphis-born wife (the former Jennie Gaia) owned a grocery store at Lane and Manassas and their residence was behind the store. Robilio made spaghetti for personal consumption, sale in his store, and sale to several other small retail grocers.

In 1920 Thomas A. Cuneo joined Robilio in the food-importing business, which included foodstuffs, cheese, anchovies, sardines, and specialty items. Both Cuneo and his wife (*nee* Zadie Scruggs) were native Memphians. By 1929 the sale of pasta had risen to the point that larger manufacturing equipment was necessary and a partnership was officially started. The original partners were Mr. and Mrs. John S. Robilio, Sr., and Mr. and Mrs. Thomas A. Cuneo. The name Ronco was derived from the letters "R O" (first and last letters in Robilio); "N" (from the word "and"); and "C O" (first and last letters in Cuneo).

Ironically, John Robilio, Sr., died the same year the partnership was formed. His son, Albert F. Robilio, followed in the footsteps of his father. By 1933 the plant was semiautomated and the company's daily production was up to 6,000-7,000 pounds a day. It took as many people to make those 6,000 to 7,000 pounds as it takes to make 170,000 pounds today.

The original plant was located in a four-story building at 124 North Front Street. From this modest beginning, the firm expanded to two additional buildings on Front Street and a new office and warehouse addition on Adams, at the site of the present Memphis City Hall.

When the company started, product distribution was limited to the Memphis area and only bulk merchandise was packed. It was packed by hand in 10-pound and 20-

TOP
In the 1930s importing was the livelihood of Ronco Foods; pasta manufacturing was secondary.

ABOVE
John S. Robilio, Sr., and his four sons, all of whom worked for the business at one time or another. From left, Victor, Albert, John Jr., and Eugene.

800 South Barksdale Street, where full automation was introduced in manufacturing as well as in packing.

Today Ronco is a privately held company, in the form of a partnership—still owned by the Robilio and Cuneo heirs. Some of the family members are active in the current operation of the organization. It is one of the largest remaining independent pasta manufacturers. (Sixty to 65 percent of the total pasta industry is controlled by conglomerates.)

From 1959 until his death in 1971, Albert F. Robilio supervised the day-to-day activities of Ronco. The present general manager is L.M. Anderson, who has been with the company for 32 years. L.P.A. Giannini is assistant general manager and John S. Robilio III is general sales manager.

The firm does business with wholesalers and chain headquarters in a 28-state area throughout the South and Southeast. Ronco's success from the early days of producing 6,000-7,000 pounds a day to today's 170,000 pounds a day is attributed by its management to quality products, quality packaging, and quality service.

pound boxes. Grocery stores would lay it out, weigh it, wrap it in brown paper, and tie it with string. As sales increased so did the product line. Packaging machinery was added and consumer pack products were introduced. By 1933, for instance, Ronco products were distributed (store-door delivery) by trucks. Six assorted packages were placed in a wire stand for consumer purchase.

Ronco flourished during World War II, as did many other businesses. Although the importing and distributing business was limited to a 150-mile radius, the sale of pasta products expanded throughout a 20-state area.

When Cuneo died in 1959, the business had grown to such a size that a major decision had to be made. Should the firm stay in the importing business with a secondary interest in pasta manufacturing, or should it abandon the distribution business and concentrate solely on the manufacturing and sale of pasta? The decision was to go with the latter course, because of the potential of the pasta industry. In 1962 Ronco Foods moved into its new, and present, location at

TOP
Tom Cuneo stands by a display of noodle products. Thirty years ago Ronco meant quality products, quality packaging, and quality service, as it does today.

ABOVE
L.M. Anderson, general manager of Ronco Foods (left), and L.P.A. Giannini, assistant general manager, in the company's packaging department.

Chapter Eight: Partners in Progress

SHONEY'S SOUTH, INC.

Although a late arrival on the Memphis business scene, Shoney's South, Inc., has wasted no time in becoming one of the largest and most important sectors of the food industry in Memphis, the Mid-South, and the nation.

James H. Prentiss III, president of the newly formed Shoney's Southwest, Inc., opened his first Memphis restaurant at 3320 Summer Avenue on April 17, 1963. Another at 3422 Elvis Presley Boulevard (then South Bellevue) opened a year later, followed quickly by another at Avalon and Poplar, another at Eastgate Shopping Center, and still another in Frayser. Shoney's original offices were located at 3835 Lamar Avenue (prior to June 1980).

Meanwhile the company was growing outside the Memphis area also—into Alabama, Arkansas, and Louisiana. In 1970 a merger was formed between Erwin D. Latimer's Shoney's of Chattanooga, W. Terry Young's Shoney's of Charlotte, and Prentiss' Shoney's Southwest, bringing the three groups together under the Shoney's South, Inc., banner. At that time there were 37 Shoney's restaurants. In just 10 short years the company has swelled to a total of 182 outlets in 9 states.

Shoney's South, Inc., owns and operates Shoney's Big Boy, Captain D's, The Hungry Fisherman, Danver's, J.P. Seafield's, and Hodie's restaurants in North Carolina, South Carolina, Georgia, Alabama, Tennessee, Arkansas, Mississippi, Kentucky, and Texas. The firm also owns and operates Insurex, a general insurance agency; Mid-South Engineering and Equipment Company, the construction division; Mid-South Restaurant Distributors, Inc.; and Spy Advertising Agency, an in-house group that handles marketing for all restaurant concepts.

Stores are serviced weekly by over-the-road trucks leaving the Shoney's South Commissary, a 50,000-square-foot facility located at 3264 Democrat Road in Memphis. This division handles over five million pounds of merchandise per month. At this writing, Shoney's South annual sales exceed $100 million. With over 6,400 employees, millions of dollars in payrolls, and other millions in purchases, the Shoney's South firm is now a major asset in scores of southern communities.

The firm's corporate offices are located in its own building at 2158 Union Avenue. James Prentiss, now chairman of the board and chief executive officer, is active in local, state, and national affairs.

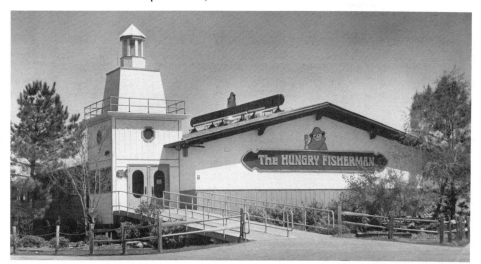

Shoney's South, Inc., owns and operates Shoney's Big Boy (top left), Danver's Restaurant (top right), The Hungry Fisherman (center), and Captain D's (bottom).

WILLIAM B. TANNER COMPANY, INC.

William B. Tanner Company, Inc., is the world's largest media placement service and supplier of broadcast services. There is no facet of advertising that cannot benefit from Tanner services. These include animation; broadcast media planning and placement; trade products for advertising and services; custom musical commercials; feature film distribution; group and incentive travel; music for movies; sales films; outdoor, transit, and magazine advertising; sales and production musical libraries; sports programming; station IDs; station promotions and contests; syndicated advertising campaigns; syndicated radio programming; TV commercial production; and vehicle leasing.

The origin of the Tanner firm dates back to 1957, when Bill Tanner became advertising and sales manager of Berjon, a drug company. At that time local radio stations were given a percentage of sales in exchange for free advertising.

In 1959 Berjon bought out the Ever-Dry Corporation. John Pepper, an owner, also owned Pepper Records, which was losing $6,600 a month selling station IDs. Bill sold the station ID package to radio stations, trading it for advertising time. That time was used to advertise Ever-Dry. During the first year Bill Tanner sold 400 stations nationally, trading the ID package for spots on each station.

In 1962 the firm entered the commercial concept business and Bill Tanner became president. The first year sales reached one million dollars.

The second year Tanner added the library services. IDs were produced to fit all station formats. Tanner offered the first ID packages for all-black stations, country and western stations, the first all-talk package, the first all-news package, and the first stereo library for both AM and FM stations.

As Apollo II lifted off the moon, the world heard the Tanner singers tell that the craft was on its way home. The astronauts' weather forecast began with another Tanner jingle. Tanner produced the first jingle for the BBC and is the exclusive producer for the New Zealand Broadcasting Corporation.

The year 1967 saw two new divisions: automotive leasing, which furnishes cars, trucks, news cruisers, mobile units, boats, airplanes, and helicopters; and Airplay International, which provides contest promotions and background music. In 1969 Tanner developed a travel agency division.

The firm became the William B. Tanner Company, Inc., on January 1, 1973. Today the firm has 475 employees, branch offices in six major cities, and is the undisputed industry leader.

William B. Tanner's energetic business activities have been matched by his community service endeavors. The American Cancer Society, the Memphis Arts Council, Memphis State University, Christian Brothers College, Tulane University, the University of Tennessee, the International Racquetball Association, National Foundation March of Dimes, Cystic Fibrosis Foundation, St. Jude's Children's Research Hospital, Boys Club of America, and the Arthritis Foundation are just a few of the organizations in which he has played a prominent leadership role and which have benefited from his generosity.

ABOVE LEFT
William B. Tanner, founder and president of the organization that bears his name.

ABOVE RIGHT
The Tanner Building houses the international headquarters of William B. Tanner Company, Inc.

Chapter Eight: Partners in Progress

TREADWELL & HARRY

Treadwell & Harry, insurance brokers in Memphis, is a respected name in the business world. Very few people realize that the original Treadwell & Harry were women.

Mrs. Timmons Treadwell was widowed in 1909 with two sons to support, 11-year-old Tim and 9-year-old George. At that time insurance was a very limited business, insuring businesses, houses, and property. Most people who had automobiles did not have any insurance. Someone suggested this new field as a possible means of livelihood for Mrs. Treadwell. She immediately called her sister, Mrs. Georgia Harry, who, after a brief marriage, had resumed her maiden name. "Miss Georgia" (as she was known) joined her younger sister in Memphis and they started an insurance business of their own in 1910.

Neither one had any business experience whatsoever. Mrs. Treadwell did not even know how to write a check. Nevertheless they had certain advantages. They were young (30 and 32), attractive, charming, known among the families of the leading businessmen of Memphis—and they were

the daughters of a famous steamboat man, Captain Milton Harry of Augusta, Arkansas.

From the beginning Mrs. Treadwell and Mrs. Harry were producers, combining ladylike elegance with persistence, courage, and drive. They were a huge success, so much so that they branched out into other lines of insurance and soon auto coverage was just a part of the whole package.

In one case Mrs. Treadwell rode all the way to the end of the streetcar line on North Second Street to visit the office of the lumber firm of Anderson-Tully (then considered "out in the country"). Tully was so taken by her boldness and businesslike manner that he changed his insurance to the Treadwell & Harry agency. Another example involved a cool reception by J.T. Harahan, retired executive of the I.C. Railroad and president of a company formed for building the second Memphis bridge. He avoided talking business by naming a man in New York empowered to place the insurance. "Miss Georgia" took the next train to New York and obtained the insurance coverage for the bridge.

In 1926 the sons of Mrs. Treadwell persuaded their mother and aunt to retire. They were starting families of their own and wanted to be the breadwinners. George Treadwell, who started with the company in 1919 and is still very active and serves as honorary chairman of the board, recalls, "They retired with great reluctance because they enjoyed associating with people and rendering service. We were able to expand the business because of the foundation and reputation they had made. They made it very easy for us."

Insurance had opportunities for expansion in the 1920s. As other agencies were reluctant to change with the times, Treadwell & Harry purchased some of these agencies and increased its own personnel. Because Memphis was the cotton center and the cotton industry was focused on South Front Street, Treadwell & Harry moved its office from the Exchange Building down to Union and Front—where it could be near the cotton business. It became one of the largest brokers of cotton insurance in the area. As the value of cotton went from 5 cents a pound to 40 cents, the necessity for good insurance increased accordingly; it benefited directly from the increases.

Treadwell & Harry concentrated on the cotton and lumber industries but gained

clients from all areas of business, such as Goldsmith's Department Store, William R. Moore, and Abe Plough.

The late 1920s witnessed extensive road-building programs in the states of Tennessee, Arkansas, and Mississippi and the state highway departments made large appropriations for the first asphalt roads. Treadwell & Harry was one of the few agencies whose producers would follow their contractors wherever they went. They furnished contractors with their contract bonds, liability, and workers' compensation insurance.

By the mid-'30s Treadwell & Harry was the second or third largest insurance agency in the Mid-South. It grew and prospered through the next decades and in 1971 was merged into Cook Industries, the well-known Memphis-based conglomerate, and became known as Cook-Treadwell & Harry. The firm founded by Captain Harry's girls, based upon the watchwords integrity, industry, stability, and enthusiasm, remains one of the most prominent insurance brokerage firms in the entire South.

ABOVE LEFT
Mary Harry Treadwell

ABOVE RIGHT
Georgia Harry

UNION PLANTERS NATIONAL BANK

Union Planters National Bank of Memphis traces its origins back to the DeSoto Insurance and Banking Company, chartered by the state of Tennessee in 1857, which did insurance and banking business. In 1869 its affairs were assumed by the newly formed Union and Planters Bank. At that same time the Tennessee State Legislature allowed the company "to discontinue the business of Insurance and adopt the Banking business whenever so decided by a vote of the stockholders." The president of the insurance company, William M. Farrington, called a stockholders' meeting and they decided to concentrate solely on banking. The name was picked to honor the Union Bank and Planters Bank, branches of Nashville banks that had served Memphis 20 years prior to 1862—when Federal occupation prompted the decision to move. Farrington remained president and the bank at 73 Madison Avenue prospered.

When survival was threatened by a yellow fever epidemic and the financial Panic of 1873, S.P. Read, the bank's cashier (who would later be president in 1897) "threw open his doors and piled the money high, assuring the people that the money they had entrusted to his bank was subject to their demand and that all depositors would be paid dollar for dollar 'in coin of the realm' for every demand they had against the bank."

Even when Memphis lost its charter in 1878 and was reduced to a tax district of Shelby County, and yellow fever gutted the city, the bank retained its reputation of "having been open every business day since 1869."

The next century witnessed a series of dramatic mergers and growth spurts for Union Planters. In 1917 it became the first bank in Tennessee to join the Federal Reserve System. Two years later it was the largest bank in Memphis and one of the largest in the South.

The healthy growth continued in the next half century and during the late 1950s and early 1960s Union Planters was considered "*The* Bank in the Mid-South." The 1961 annual report to the stockholders was typical: "... largest bank in the entire Mid-South as well as a high place among the major banks of the nation ... national ranking of 44th among the 'largest Banker's Banks' ... We take pride again, as in the past, in telling you that More Memphians Bank at Union Planters Than Any Other Bank. ..."

Incredibly, in November 1974 UP was on the brink of insolvency and failure due to a series of miscalculated strategies, employee infidelity, and inadequate internal controls. Ultimately some other banks in better financial condition closed while UP continued to operate and dramatically reverse its financial prospects.

Due to the new leadership of chairman and chief executive officer William M. Matthews, Jr., new policies were instituted; operating expenses were cut; automation of many areas was initiated; assets were reduced; proper tax planning created a loss carryforward that allowed the bank to recoup federal taxes paid in prior years; innovative and effective strategies dealing with public relations and marketing were promptly introduced; wages were made commensurate with responsibilities; and problems were honestly discussed with the media, investors, employees, and stockholders. A July 18, 1980, *Commercial Appeal* headline accurately described the turnaround: "UP Tops State Banks in Profitability." Union Planters today enjoys the reputation of being one of the country's most technologically advanced financial services institutions.

ABOVE LEFT
William M. Farrington was the first president of Union Planters Bank.

ABOVE RIGHT
This rendering of Union Planters Bank, located at 73 Madison Avenue, Memphis, was done in the mid-1920s.

Chapter Eight: Partners in Progress

UNITED INNS, INC.

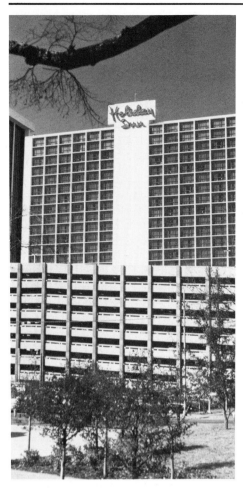

United Inns, Inc., one of the nation's largest licensees of Holiday Inns and now listed on the New York Stock Exchange, was originally chartered to do business as United Enterprises in 1956.

United Enterprises was the vision of Dr. William B. Cockroft, then a practicing dentist and entrepreneur who strongly believed in the future of the motel business.

In 1956 Holiday Inns of America Inc. (later Holiday Inns Inc.) was in its infancy, also. The recently organized company was busily developing the Holiday Inn motel concept and selling franchises to rapidly expand the Holiday Inn name. It was a propitious time for entry into a field just beginning to emerge as the travel-hungry American family's alternative to shabby tourist courts and second-rate hotels.

The nation's modern superhighway system was just around the corner and with it would come an astonishing increase in family and business travel. Dr. Cockroft was one of the first to foresee this opportunity and his alliance of United Enterprises with Holiday Inns was the beginning of a long and profitable relationship for both young organizations.

United Enterprises, with Cockroft as sole owner, obtained an exclusive franchise to build Holiday Inns in Jackson, Mississippi. The first inn, Holiday Inn Jackson North, opened in January 1957. The first inn-keeper was J. Tom Kizer, a patient of Cockroft's, who is today vice-chairman and treasurer of United Inns. Soon other franchises were obtained, including those for dynamic cities like Atlanta and Houston.

By 1961 the business was demanding so much attention from the still-practicing dentist that he reluctantly turned from his chosen profession to devote full time to his Holiday Inn activities.

Later that year, looking ahead to further expansion, the company's name was changed to United Inns, Inc., and in 1962 a public offering of stock was made to enable more rapid growth of the firm. In 1971 another milestone in the stock market life of United was passed when the company's stock was listed on the New York Stock Exchange.

United's growth is reflected from its early beginning of one 56-room motel to today's 37 properties comprising over 9,000 rooms in 10 cities. These Holiday Inns are located as follows: 11 in Atlanta; 2 in Colorado Springs; 5 in Dallas; 9 in Houston; 4 in Jackson, Mississippi; 2 in Jacksonville, Florida; and one each in San Jose and Santa Barbara, California; and Flagstaff and Scottsdale, Arizona.

Additionally, United is developing a Hilton Inn that will open in Richardson, Texas, a Dallas suburb, in 1982, and another Holiday Inn in Dallas scheduled for a 1983 opening. Several other Holiday Inn licenses have recently been granted and United expects to build and open more Holiday Inns in the near future.

Over the years United has also diversified into other areas of operations. In September 1968 the company entered the car wash business and has developed a chain of 20 "Mr. Pride Car Washes" in the Memphis, Atlanta, and Houston metropolitan areas. Gaines Furniture Company, a wholly owned subsidiary, purchased in February 1968, manufactures and sells upholstered furniture from its plant in McKenzie, Tennessee.

Senior officers of United are: Dr. William B. Cockroft, chairman of the board; Don William Cockroft, president; J. Howard Lammons, executive vice-president; and J. Tom Kizer, vice-chairman and treasurer.

ABOVE LEFT
Holiday Inn Jackson Downtown, one of the 37 inns that make United one of the nation's largest licensees of Holiday Inns.

ABOVE RIGHT
Dr. William B. Cockroft, Don William Cockroft, and trading specialist John Kennedy as the first trade of United Inns stock is registered on the New York Stock Exchange ticker tape December 9, 1971.

PATRONS

The following individuals, companies, and organizations have made a valuable commitment to the quality of this publication. Windsor Publications and The West Tennessee Historical Society gratefully acknowledge their participation in *Metropolis of the American Nile: An Illustrated History of Memphis and Shelby County.*

Allen & O'Hara, Inc.
Anderson-Tully Company*
Baptist Memorial Hospital*
A.S. Barboro, Inc.*
Belz Enterprises*
Blue Cross and Blue Shield of Memphis*
Boyle Investment Company*
Brandon Underwriting Specialists, Inc.
Browning-Ferris Industries*
Buckman Laboratories, Inc.*
Cleo Wrap*
Coca-Cola Bottling Company*
Commercial and Industrial Bank*
Conwood Corporation*
Dobbs Houses, Inc.*
Dunavant Enterprises, Inc.*
Federal Compress & Warehouse Company*
Federal Express*
D.A. Fisher, Inc.*
Fogelman Properties*
Gary Gothard
Guardsmark, Inc.*
Haverty Furniture Company

Helena Chemical Company
Hank Hill Investment Co. Inc.
Hohenberg Bros. Company*
Holiday Inns Inc.*
Huber Farm Service
Labor Source, Inc.
Layne and Bowler, Inc.*
Loeb Industries*
Malone & Hyde, Inc.*
Marx & Bensdorf Real Estate and Investment Company
Memorial Park Funeral Home and Cemetery*
Memphis Compress & Storage Co.*
Memphis Eye and Ear Hospital/Shea Clinic*
Memphis Stone & Gravel Co.
Methodist Hospitals of Memphis*
Metropolitan Inter-Faith Association
Mid-South Title Insurance Corporation*
William R. Moore, Inc.*
Morgan, Keegan & Company*
Olsten Temporary Service
Orgill Brothers*
Richards Manufacturing

Company, Inc.*
River Oil Company
Robbins and Myers, Inc.*
Ronco Foods*
The Sherwin-Williams Co.
Shoney's South, Inc.*
Slumber Products Corporation
T.M. Wallcovering Co., Inc.
Wiliam B. Tanner Company, Inc.*
Thomason, Crawford & Hendrix
Treadwell & Harry*
Union Planters National Bank*
Union Service Industries, Inc.
United Inns, Inc.*
The West Tennessee Historical Society*

*Partners in Progress of *Metropolis of the American Nile: An Illustrated History of Memphis and Shelby County.* The histories of these companies and organizations appear in Chapter 8, beginning on page 168.

BIBLIOGRAPHY

For Further Reading

Books:

Capers, Gerald. *Biography of a River Town: Memphis, Its Heroic Age*. New Orleans: by the author, 1966.

Chapman, Mary Winslow. *I Remember Raleigh*. Memphis: Riverside Press, 1977.

Church, Annette E. and Church, Roberta. *The Robert R. Churches of Memphis*. Ann Arbor: Edwards Brothers, 1974.

Coppock, Paul R. *Memphis Memoirs*. Memphis: Memphis State University Press, 1980.

_____. *Memphis Sketches*. Memphis: Friends of Memphis and Shelby County Libraries, 1976.

Crawford, Charles W. *Yesterday's Memphis*. Miami: E.A. Seemann, 1976.

Davis, James D. *The History of the City of Memphis*. Memphis: Hite, Crumpton & Kelley, 1873. Reprint facsimile edition, Ed. James E. Roper. Memphis: West Tennessee Historical Society, 1972.

Durham, Walter T. *James Winchester, Tennessee Pioneer*. Gallatin, Tennessee: Sumner County Library Board, 1979.

Embree, Edwin R. *13 Against the Odds*. Port Washington, N.Y.: Viking Press, 1944; Reprint ed. Kennikat Press, 1968.

Goodspeed's History of Hamilton, Knox and Shelby Counties. Nashville: C. and R. Elder Booksellers, 1974. A reprint of portions of the 1887 edition published by Goodspeed Brothers, Nashville.

Hamilton, Green P. *The Bright Side of Memphis*. Memphis: n.p., 1908.

Horn, Stanley F., Compiler & Ed. *Tennessee's War, 1861-1865: Described by Participants*. Nashville: Tennessee Civil War Centennial Commission, 1965.

Hutchins, Fred L. *What Happened in Memphis*. Kingsport, Tenn.: n.p., 1965.

Keating, John M. *History of the City of Memphis and Shelby County*. 2 vols. Vol. 2 by O.F. Vedder. Syracuse: D. Mason & Co., 1888.

Lanier, Robert A. *Memphis in the Twenties*. Memphis: Zenda Press, 1979.

Lee, George W. *Beale Street: Where the Blues Began*. New York: R.O. Ballou, 1934.

McIlwaine, Shields. *Memphis, Down in Dixie*. New York: E.P. Dutton and Company, Inc., 1948.

Malone, James H. *The Chickasaw Nation: A Short Sketch of a Noble People . . .* Louisville: J.P. Morton & Co., 1922.

Mathes, J. Harvey. *The Old Guard in Gray*. Memphis: Press of S.C. Toof & Co., 1897.

Meeman, Edward J. *The Editorial We: A Posthumous Autobiography*. Ed. by Edwin Howard. Memphis, Memphis State University Press, 1976.

Miller, William D. *Memphis During the Progressive Era, 1900-1917*. Memphis: Memphis State University Press, 1957.

Miller, William D. *Mr. Crump of Memphis*. Baton Rouge: Louisiana State University Press, 1964.

Pattan, James Welch. *Unionism and Reconstruction in Tennessee, 1860-1869*. Chapel Hill: University of North Carolina Press, 1934, reprinted Gloucester, Mass.: Peter Smith, 1966.

Plunkett, Kitty. *Memphis: A Pictorial History*. Norfolk: Donning Co., 1976.

Roper, James. *The Founding of Memphis, 1818-1820*. Memphis: The Memphis Sesquicentennial, Inc., 1970.

Sigafoos, Robert A. *Cotton Row to Beale Street: A Business History of Memphis*. Memphis: Memphis State University Press, 1979.

Tucker, David M. *Black Pastors and Leaders: The Memphis Clergy, 1819-1972*. Memphis: Memphis State University Press, 1975.

_____. *Lieutenant Lee of Beale Street*. Nashville: Vanderbilt University Press, 1971.

_____. *Memphis Since Crump: Bossism, Blacks, and Civic Reformers, 1948-1968*. Knoxville: University of Tennessee Press, 1980.

Williams, Edward F. III. *Confederate Victories at Fort Pillow*. Memphis: Nathan Bedford Forrest Trail Committee, 1973.

_____ *Early Memphis and Its River Rivals*. Memphis: Historical Hiking Trails Inc., 1968.

Williams, Samuel Cole. *Beginnings of West Tennessee, In the Land of the Chickasaws: 1541-1841*. Johnson City, Tennessee: The Watauga Press, 1930.

Young, J.P., ed. *Standard History of Memphis, Tennessee*. Knoxville: H.W. Crew, 1912.

Articles:

The overwhelming majority of articles on Memphis and Shelby County history are in the *West Tennessee Historical Society Papers*. They address a multitude of subjects and are the best single source for revision of standard or general histories of the city.

Bailey, Robert. "The 'Bogus' Memphis *Union Appeal*: A Union Newspaper in Occupied Confederate Territory." *WTHS Papers* 32 (1978) 32-47.

Baker, Thomas H. "The Early Newspapers of Memphis, Tennessee, 1827-1860." *WTHS Papers* 17 (1963) 20-46.

Bejach, Lois D. "The Seven Cities Absorbed by Memphis." *WTHS Papers* 8 (1954) 95-104.

_____."The Taxing District of Shelby County." *WTHS Papers* 4 (1950) 5-27.

Blankinship, Gary R. "The *Commercial Appeal's* Attack on the Ku Klux Klan." *WTHS Papers* 31 (1977) 44-58.

Bobbitt, Charles A. "The Memphis Gold Cup." *WTHS Papers* 30 (1976) 67-82.

_____. "The North Memphis Driving Park, 1901-1905; The Passing of an Era." *WTHS Papers* 26 (1972) 40-55.

Boom, Aaron M. "Early Fairs in Shelby County." *WTHS Papers* 10 (1956) 38-52.

Born, Kate. "Memphis Negro Workmen and the NAACP." *WTHS Papers* 28 (1974) 90-107.

_____. "Organized Labor in Memphis, Tennessee 1826-1901." *WTHS Papers* 21 (1967) 60-79.

Bridges, Lamar Whitlow. "Editor Mooney Versus Boss Crump." *WTHS Papers* 20 (1966) 61-76.

Bruesch, S.R. "Early Medical History of Memphis." *WTHS Papers* 2 (1948) 33-94.

Clotfelter, Charles. "Memphis Business Leadership and the Politics of Fiscal Crisis." *WTHS Papers* 27 (1973) 33-49.

Coleman, Leslie H. "The Baptists in Shelby County to 1900." *WTHS Papers* 15 (1961) 8-39.

Cooper, W. Raymond. "Four Fateful Years— Memphis, 1858-1861." *WTHS Papers* 11 (1957) 36-75.

Coppock, Paul R. "History in Memphis Street Names." *WTHS Papers* 11 (1957) 93-111.

_____. "Huntington's Pacific-to-Atlantic Rails Through Memphis." *WTHS Papers* 9 (1955) 5-28.

_____. "Parks of Memphis." *WTHS Papers* 12 (1958) 120-133.

Daniel, Larry. "The Quimby and Robinson Cannon Foundry at Memphis." *WTHS Papers* 27 (1973) 18-32.

Edson, Andrew S. "How Nineteenth Century Travelers Viewed Memphis Before the Civil War." *WTHS Papers* 24 (1970) 30-40.

Ellis, John H. "Business Leadership in Memphis Public Health Reform, 1880-1900." *WTHS Papers* 19 (1965) 94-104.

_____. "Disease and the Destiny of a City: The 1878 Yellow Fever Epidemic in Memphis." *WTHS Papers* 28 (1974) 75-89.

Fakes, Turner J. "Memphis and the Mexican War." *WTHS Papers* 2 (1948) 119-144.

Findlay, Stephen M. "The Allegheny: A Revisionist Note on a Memphis Myth." *WTHS Papers* 32 (1978) 70-83.

Fox, Mrs. Jesse W. "Beale Street and the Blues." *WTHS Papers* 13 (1959) 128-147.

Fraser, Walter J., Jr. "Lucien Bonaparte Eaton: Politics and the Memphis *Post*, 1867-1869." *WTHS Papers* 20 (1966) 20-45.

Halle, A. Arthur. "History of the Memphis Cotton Carnival." *WTHS Papers* 6 (1952) 34-63.

Hill, Raymond S. "Memphis Theatre—First Decade." *WTHS Papers* 9 (1955) 48-58.

Holmes, Jack D.L. "The Effects of the Memphis Race Riot of 1866." *WTHS Papers* 12 (1958) 58-79.

_____. "The First Laws of Memphis: Instructions for the Commandant of San Fernando de las Barrancas, 1795." *WTHS Papers* 15 (1961) 95-104.

_____. "Fort Ferdinand of the Bluffs: Life on the Spanish-American Frontier, 1795-1797." *WTHS Papers* 13 (1959) 38-54.

_____. "Three Early Memphis Commandants: Beauregard, Deville Degoatin, and Folch." *WTHS Papers* 18 (1964) 5-38.

House, Boyce. "Memphis Memories of Fifty Years Ago." *WTHS Papers* 14 (1960) 103-112.

Hutchins, Fred L. "Beale Street As It Was." *WTHS Papers* 26 (1972) 56-65.

Kalin, Berkley. "Isaac L. Myers: A Man Who Brought the Best in the Arts to Memphis." *WTHS Papers* 26 (1972) 74-93.

_____. "Rabbi William H. Fineshriber: The Memphis Years." *WTHS Papers* 25 (1971) 47-62.

_____. "Young Abe Fortas." *WTHS Papers* 34 (1980) 96-100.

Kinnaird, Lawrence and Lucia B. "San Fernando de las Barrancas: Spain's Last Outpost of Empire." *WTHS Papers* 35 (1981) 25-39.

Kitchens, Allen H. "Ouster of Mayor Edward H. Crump." *WTHS Papers* 19 (1965) 105-120.

_____. "Political Upheavals in Tennessee: Boss Crump and the Senatorial Election of 1948." *WTHS Papers* 16 (1962) 104-126.

Lanier, Robert A., Jr. "Memphis Greets War With Spain." *WTHS Papers* 18 (1964) 39-58.

Laws, Forrest. "The Railroad Comes to Tennessee: The Building of the La Grange and Memphis." *WTHS Papers* 30 (1976) 24-42.

Lovett, Bobby L. "The West Tennessee Colored Troops in Civil War Combat." *WTHS Papers* 34 (1980) 53-70.

Majors, William R. "A Reexamination of V.O. Key's Southern Politics in State and Nation: The Case of Tennessee." *ETHS Papers* 49 (1977) 117-136.

Mallory, Laula G. "The Three Lives of Raleigh." *WTHS Papers* 13 (1959) 78-94.

Matthews, James S. "Sequent Occupance in Memphis, Tennessee." *WTHS Papers* 11 (1957) 112-134.

Mehrling, John C. "The Memphis and Charleston Railroad." *WTHS Papers* 19 (1965) 21-35.

_____. "The Memphis and Ohio Railroad." *WTHS Papers* 22 (1968) 52-61.

Miller, William D. "J.J. Williams and the Greater Memphis Movement." *WTHS Papers* 5 (1951) 14-30.

_____. "Rural Ideals in Memphis Life at the Turn of the Century." *WTHS Papers* 4 (1950) 41-49.

Mitchell, Enoch L. "The Role of General George Washington Gordon in the Ku Klux Klan." *WTHS Papers* 1 (1947) 73-80.

Nash, Charles H. "The Human Continuum of Shelby County, Tennessee." *WTHS Papers* 14 (1960) 5-31.

Newcomer, Lee N. "The Battle of Memphis." *WTHS Papers* 12 (1958) 41-57.

Nickolds, Mary Costillo. "Reminiscences of My Childhood and Youth." *WTHS Papers* 12 (1958) 80-108.

Norris, John. "Park Field—World War I Pilot Training School." *WTHS Papers* 31 (1977) 56-76.

Phillips, Mrs. Virginia. "Rowlett Paine, Mayor of Memphis, 1920-1924." *WTHS Papers* 13 (1959) 95-116.

Pierce, Gerald S. "The Great Wolf Hunt: Tennessee Volunteers in Texas, 1842." *WTHS Papers* 19 (1965) 5-20.

Pittman, Carolyn. "Memphis in the Mid-1840s." *WTHS Papers* 23 (1969) 30-44.

Pool, Charles; Shankman, Sam; and Fitzpatrick, Annie Mayhew. "Three Views of Old Higbee School." *WTHS Papers* 20 (1966) 46-60.

Prescott, Grace Elizabeth. "The Woman's Suffrage Movement in Memphis: Its Place in the State, Sectional, and National Movements." *WTHS Papers* 18 (1964) 87-106.

Rauchle, Robert. "Biographical Sketches of Prominent Germans in Memphis Tennessee in the Nineteenth Century." *WTHS Papers* 22 (1968) 73-85.

Rayner, Juan. "An Eye-Witness Account of Forrest's Raid on Memphis." *WTHS Papers* 12 (1958) 134-137.

Ritter, Charles C. "'The Drama in Our Midst'— The Early History of the Theater in Memphis." *WTHS Papers* 11 (1957) 5-35.

Robinson, James Troy. "Fort Assumption: The First Recorded History of White Man's Activity on the Present Site of Memphis." *WTHS Papers* 5 (1951) 62-78.

Roper, James E. "Fort Adams and Fort Pickering." *WTHS Papers* 24 (1970) 5-29.

_____. "Fort San Fernando de las Barrancas: Where Was It, Exactly?" *WTHS Papers* 34 (1980) 5-27.

_____. "Paddy Meagher, Tom Huling, and the Bell Tavern." *WTHS Papers* 31 (1977) 5-32.

_____. "The Earliest Pictures of Memphis: Charles Le Seur's Drawings, 1828-1830." *WTHS Papers* 25 (1971) 5-25.

_____. "Marcus B. Winchester, First Mayor of Memphis: His Later Years." *WTHS Papers* 13 (1959) 5-37.

_____. "Marcus Winchester and the Earliest Years of Memphis." *Tennessee Historical Quarterly* 21 (1962) 326-351.

_____. "The Revolutionary War on the Fourth Chickasaw Bluff." *WTHS Papers* 29 (1975) 5-24.

Stanton, William M. "The Irish of Memphis." *WTHS Papers* 6 (1952) 87-118.

Stathis, John C. "The Establishment of the West Tennessee State Normal School, 1909-1914." *WTHS Papers* 10 (1956) 78-99.

Tilly, Bette B. "The Spirit of Improvement: Reformism and Slavery in West Tennessee." *WTHS Papers* 28 (1974) 25-42.

Tollison, Grady. "Andrew J. Kellar, Memphis Republican." *WTHS Papers* 16 (1962) 29-55.

Tracy, Sterling. "The Immigrant Population of Memphis." *WTHS Papers* 4 (1950) 72-82.

Tucker, David M. "Black Politics in Memphis, 1865-1875." *WTHS Papers* 26 (1972) 13-19.

Walker, Randolph Meade. "The Role of the Black Clergy in Memphis During the Crump Era." *WTHS Papers* 33 (1979) 29-47.

Watson, Robert M., Jr. "The Memphis Sound, 1913-1925, As Played by the Egyptians: Leadership Profiles and Attitudes in a Southern City." *WTHS Papers* 25 (1971) 63-89.

Wax, Rabbi James A. "The Jews of Memphis: 1860-1865." *WTHS Papers* 3 (1949) 39-89.

Wax, Jonathan I. "Program of Progress: The Recent Change in the Form of Government of Memphis." *WTHS Papers* 23 (1969) 81-109. 24 (1970) 74-96).

Williams, Bobby Joe. "Let There Be Light: Tennessee Valley Authority Comes to Memphis." *WTHS Papers* 30 (1976) 43-66.

Wingfield, Marie Gregson. "Memphis as Seen Through *Meriwether's Weekly*." *WTHS Papers* 5 (1951) 31-60.

_____. "The Memphis Interracial Commission." *WTHS Papers* 21 (1967) 93-107.

The procession of the Memphi down Main Street. From *Harper's Weekly*, Memphis/Shelby County Room (M/SCPLIC)

Bibliography

INDEX

ABOUT THE AUTHORS

John E. Harkins, long a resident of Memphis, is the Archivist of the Memphis/Shelby County Archives. After two years as a library assistant in the Memphis/Shelby County library system, he assumed his present position, providing a variety of research services to the historical records of city and county governments and working in the Main Library's history department. He is currently secretary of the West Tennessee Historical Society.

Having served for seven years in the U.S. Navy, Harkins attended Memphis State University, receiving a B.S. in history in 1967. He then earned an M.A. from Louisiana State University in 1971 and a Ph.D. from MSU in 1976, both in history. Dr. Harkins was a history instructor and later department chairperson at Memphis University School. He has also taught at MSU and LeMoyne-Owen College.

Berkley Kalin holds a B.A. from Washington University and an M.A. and Ph.D. from the University of St. Louis. He teaches history at Memphis State University. Actively involved with the West Tennessee Historical Society, Dr. Kalin regularly contributes to its journal as well as to other scholarly publications.

THIS BOOK WAS SET IN
SOVRAN AND KORINNA TYPES,
PRINTED ON
70 LB. WARRENFLO
AND BOUND BY
WALSWORTH PUBLISHING COMPANY
HALFTONE REPRODUCTION BY ROBERTSON GRAPHICS

Published Books in Windsor Local History Series

St. Paul: Saga of an American City, by Virginia Brainard Kunz (1977)

The Heritage of Lancaster, by John Ward Willson Loose (1978)

A Panoramic History of Rochester and Monroe County, New York, by Blake McKelvey (1979)

Syracuse: From Salt to Satellite, by Henry W. Schramm and William F. Roseboom (1979)

Columbia, South Carolina, History of a City, by John A. Montgomery (1979)

Kitchener: Yesterday Revisited, by Bill Moyer (1979)

Erie: Chronicle of a Great Lakes City, by Edward Wellejus (1980)

Montgomery: An Illustrated History, by Wayne Flynt (1980)

Omaha and Douglas County: A Panoramic History, by Dorothy Devereux Dustin (1980)

Charleston: Crossroads of History, by Isabella Leland (1980)

Baltimore: An Illustrated History, by Suzanne Ellery Greene (1980)

The Fort Wayne Story: A Pictorial History, by John Ankenbruck (1980)

City at the Pass: An Illustrated History of El Paso, by Leon Metz (1980)

Tucson: Portrait of a Desert Pueblo, by John Bret Harte (1980)

Salt Lake City: The Gathering Place, by John S. McCormick (1980)

Saginaw: A History of the Land and the City, by Stuart D. Gross (1980)

Cedar Rapids: Tall Corn and High Technology, by Ernie Danek (1980)

Los Angeles: A City Apart, by David L. Clark (1981)

Heart of the Commonwealth: Worcester, by Margaret A. Erskine (1981)

Out of a Wilderness: An Illustrated History of Greater Lansing, by Justin L. Kestenbaum (1981)

The Valley and the Hills: An Illustrated

History of Birmingham and Jefferson County, by Leah Rawls Atkins (1981)

River Capital: An Illustrated History of Baton Rouge, by Mark T. Carleton (1981)

Chattanooga: An Illustrated History, by James W. Livingood (1981)

New Haven: An Illustrated History, edited by Floyd Shumway and Richard Hegel (1981)

Albany: Capital City on the Hudson, by John J. McEneny (1981)

Kalamazoo: The Place Behind the Products, by Larry B. Massie and Peter J. Schmitt (1981)

Mobile: The Life and Times of a Great Southern City, by Melton McLaurin and Michael Thomason (1981)

New Orleans: An Illustrated History, by John R. Kemp (1981)

Regina: From Pile O' Bones to Queen City of the Plains, by William A. Riddell (1981)

King County and Its Queen City: Seattle, by James R. Warren (1981)

To the Setting of the Sun: The Story of York, by Georg R. Sheets (1981)

Buffalo: Lake City in Niagara Land, by Richard C. Brown and Bob Watson (1981)

Springfield of the Ozarks, by Harris and Phyllis Dark (1981)

Charleston and the Kanawha Valley, by Otis K. Rice (1981)

Dallas: Portrait in Pride, by Darwin Payne (1982)

Heart of the Promised Land: An Illustrated History of Oklahoma County, by Bob L. Blackburn (1982)

Winnipeg: Where the New West Begins, by Eric Wells (1982)

City of Lakes: An Illustrated History of Minneapolis, by Joseph Stipanovich (1982)

Rhode Island: The Independent State, by George H. Kellner and J. Stanley Lemons (1982)

Calgary: Canada's Frontier Metropolis, by Max Foran and Heather MacEwan Foran (1982)

Greensboro: A Chosen Center, by Gayle Hicks Fripp (1982)

Norfolk's Waters: An Illustrated Maritime History of Hampton Roads, by William L. Tazewell (1982)

At the River's Bend: An Illustrated History of Jackson County, by Richard D. McKinzie and Sherry Lamb Schirmer (1982)

Beaumont: A Chronicle of Promise, by Judith W. Linsley and Ellen W. Rienstra (1982)

Boise: An Illustrated History, by Merle Wells (1982)

Broome County Heritage: An Illustrated History, by Ross McGuire and Lawrence Bothwell (1982)

Hartford: An Illustrated History of Connecticut's Capital, by Glenn Weaver (1982)

Raleigh: City of Oaks, by James Vickers (1982)

At the Bend in the River: The Story of Evansville, by Kenneth P. McCutchan (1982)

Duluth: An Illustrated History of the Zenith City, by Glenn N. Sandvik (1982)

The Valley and Its Peoples: An Illustrated History of the Lower Merrimack River, by Paul Hudon (1982)

The Upper Mohawk Country: An Illustrated History of Greater Utica, by David M. Ellis (1982)

Chicago: Commercial Center of the Continent, by Kenan Heise and Michael Edgerton (1982)

Corpus Christi: The History of a Texas Seaport, by Bill Walraven (1982)

Cape Fear Adventure: An Illustrated History of Wilmington, by Diane Cobb Cashman (1982)

The Lehigh Valley: An Illustrated History, by Karyl Lee Hall and Peter Hall (1982)

Windsor Publications, Inc.
History Book Division
Editorial Offices:
21220 Erwin Street
Woodland Hills, California 91365
(213) 884-4050